The Flight from

The Flight from
Ambiguity

Essays in Social and Cultural Theory

Donald N. Levine

The University of Chicago Press

Chicago and London

The University of Chicago Press, Chicago 60637
The University of Chicago Press, Ltd., London

Library of Congress Cataloging in Publication Data

Levine, Donald Nathan, 1931–
  The flight from ambiguity.

  Bibliography: p.
  Includes index.
  1. Sociology—Methodology.   2. Ambiguity.   I. Title.
HM24.L456   1985   301′.01′8   85-8762
ISBN 0-226-47555-7 (cloth)
ISBN 0-226-47556-5 (paper)

To Robert K. Merton

Literary economists . . . are to this day dilly-dallying
with speculations such as "What is *value*?" "What is
capital?" They cannot get it into their heads that things
are everything and words nothing, and that they may
apply the terms "value" and "capital" to any blessed
thing they please, so only they be kind enough—they
never are—to tell one precisely what those things are.

Vilfredo Pareto

We proceed as if we were faced with a choice between
the univocal and the ambiguous, and we come to the
discovery . . . that the univocal has its foundations and
consequences in ambiguities.

Richard McKeon

Contents

Preface

The recent ascendancy of computerized thoughtways constitutes a profound alteration in the system of world culture. This development grows out of a long process of formal rationalization rooted in Hellenic geometry which has advanced with increasing momentum since the seventeenth century. Among other outcomes it has energized a recurrent modern wish to produce a wholly logical, univocal system of language.

Some devotees of this process have sought to map human "natural" language onto a computer program. This goal, however, has recently been pronounced futile by even its most dedicated proponents, who have come to conclude that, for all the phonological, morphological, grammatical, syntactical, and semantic rules that govern them, natural languages remain incorrigibly ambiguous.

Although this conclusion seems maddening to computer scientists, is it really so unfortunate? Partly yes, partly no—just as the wish to reduce all human problems of thought and discourse to the manipulation of formulable bytes is partly admirable, partly dreadful.

This book expresses my deep conviction that the proper stance of moderns toward ambiguous language and thought is one of pronounced ambivalence. That conviction stems from intermittent reflection about this problem over three decades. My love for ambiguity has two main sources. As a graduate student at the University of Chicago in the mid-1950s I listened with mounting fascination to Richard McKeon's studied skepticism toward the then dominant commitment of American philosophers to exclusively univocal formulations. In the late 1950s I spent three years among the Amhara of Ethiopia, where I encountered a culture whose devious imprecision was necessarily vexing to an American of my age and time, but a culture that finally attracted me deeply with its flair for artistically ambiguous utterance.

On the other hand, a long personal struggle to overcome inhibitions that made it difficult for me to express myself in a direct and straightforward manner made me wary about being drawn in too deeply by the lures of ambiguity. And rarely do I feel so much impatience as I do for colleagues in the social sciences who proceed in utter oblivion of the ambiguities of the notions they set forth under the banner of scientific rigor—not least when they deal with the texts I know best, the classics of modern social theory.

Indeed, this book may be taken as a set of meditations on how to read the classics of social theory no less than as a statement about the uses and abuses of ambiguity. After more than three decades of studying and teaching those classics I find myself scandalized by the way they have been appropriated by contemporary social science. So these essays also serve to express my conviction that the classics of social theory remain works of perennial value; that they contain untapped riches; and that they are commonly read at an embarrassingly low level of sophistication.

Creative readers will find more in these pages than the themes of the mixed blessings of ambiguity and the mixed reception of the blessed classics. They may discern recurrent glosses on the question of promoting mature encounters with otherhood, on the character of intellectual progress in a pluralistic science, on the nature of modernity, and perhaps other matters. Surely it is appropriate for a book on ambiguity to harbor a multiplicity of meanings.

1

The Flight from Ambiguity

Among the peculiarities of the modern epoch must be reckoned an intermittently voiced and sometimes potent urge to fashion the language of moral and political discourse in strictly unambiguous terms. This disposition takes two forms. A disposition toward theoretic rigor would create clean primitive concepts and construct relations among those concepts in systematically deductive form. A disposition toward metric precision would scrap all but clearly defined observational categories and corresponding procedures for measurement. A belief in the possibility of attaining metric precision and theoretical rigor informs the contemporary sense that scholars can produce scientifically valid propositions about human conduct and social forces.

From the perspective of world history such a belief must seem eccentric if not preposterous. Surely no one in the West before 1600 intended to cast the discussion of human affairs in the language of precise propositions. The best knowledge of human conduct, to be garnered through experience, travel, conversation, and reflection, was thought to be a kind of worldly wisdom about the varieties of character and regimes and the vicissitudes of social life. What was knowable about the human condition seemed pitched between Aristotle's dictum that the subject matter of human action admits of only rough generalities and the reflection of the author of Ecclesiastes that to everything there is a season, and a time to every purpose under heaven.

Congruent with that outlook, the language used to represent human affairs was valued for being vivid and evocative more than for its denotational precision. Metaphor, irony, and analogies of all sorts were the stock in trade of those who trafficked in social knowledge. At certain junctures, to be sure, some made determined efforts to find precise language in which to depict human relations—most notably, perhaps, the Roman jurisconsults who developed the private civil law that reached its zenith during the Principate period. Yet it is questionable whether their effort produced a mentality that permeated an entire culture, and in any case it fell into decline and near oblivion in the West for several centuries after Justinian's codification.

The Modern Assault on Ambiguity

Several developments from the seventeenth century onwards began to change all that. Administrative needs of centralizing monarchies revived the impetus for legalistic language and led to the compilation of precise codes. Technical developments in warfare and production and the increased use of money in commerce diffused a disposition toward more precise calculation in human transactions. Ascetic Puritanism tended to promote an aseptic use of language, as in the famous "plain style" sermons of the New England divines. The ideal of sincerity came to replace a courtly ideal of grace and charm with a call for plain and direct speaking.

Above all, however, it was the impressive advances in mathematics and the physical sciences that quickened an impulse toward symbolic precision. Those advances inspired many seventeenth-century philosophers to extol the benefits to be gained from recasting all language and thought into a "mathematicalized" mode. Descartes sought to reconstruct all knowledge through the agency of ruthlessly clear and distinct ideas, finding certainty only by imitating the deductive method of mathematics. Leibniz envisioned a universal technical language, based on the decomposition of all notions into distinct elementary terms comparable to the prime factors of arithmetic, and a calculus adequate to handle all questions. Hobbes eulogized the geometricians for having made possible the advantages which men of his day enjoyed over the rude simplicity of antiquity, and thought that "were the nature of human actions as distinctly known as the nature of *quantity* in geometrical figures, the strength of *avarice* and *ambition,* which is sustained by the erroneous opinions of the vulgar as touching the nature of *right* and *wrong,* would presently faint and languish; and mankind should enjoy such an immortal peace, that . . . there would hardly be left any pretence for war" ([1651] 1978, 91; italics in original).

The heightened prestige of mathematical expression encouraged philosophers to assault types of utterance that fed on ambiguity. John Locke, in a celebrated diatribe "On the Abuse of Words," lampooned the ways men communicate by rendering signs less clear and distinct in their signification than they need to be, as, for example, "When Men have names in their Mouths without any determined *Ideas* in their Minds, whereof they are the signs"; or "When they apply [names] very unsteadily, making them stand now for one, and by and by for another *Idea*." In a concluding snipe at the masters of rhetoric, Locke asserts that "all the artificial and figurative application of Words Eloquence hath invented, are for nothing else but to insinuate wrong *Ideas*, move the Passions, and thereby mislead the Judgment; and so indeed are perfect cheats"; and goes on to suggest that "those, *who* pretend *seriously* to *search after*, or maintain *Truth*, should think themselves obliged to study, how they might deliver themselves without Obscurity, Doubtfulness, or Equivocation, to which Men's Words are naturally liable" ([1690] 1975, 504–9; italics in original).

The wish to strip language of its allusions, figures, and ambiguities—in short, its poetic character—became a passion that transformed British letters in the eighteenth century. Following Locke's sentiment that if a child has poetic leanings the parents should labor to stifle them, Hume attacked poetry as the work of professional liars who seek to entertain by fictions, and Bentham portrayed poetry as a silly enterprise, full of sentimentalism and vague generalities, proving nothing. For Bentham, in fact, the ideal language would resemble algebra: ideas would be represented by symbols as numbers are represented by letters, thus eliminating ambiguous words and misleading metaphors.

The poets of the age responded to such assaults by identifying with the aggressor. As that distinguished anatomist of ambiguity, William Empson, has written, even the poets in eighteenth-century England "were trying to be honest, straightforward, sensible, grammatical, and plain" (1947, 68). In the wake of John Dryden's dictum that a man required a mathematical head to be a complete and excellent poet, Addison and Pope constructed a poetic code that extolled the rational elements in style and likened the principles of form in poetry to the axioms of mathematics.

Perhaps the most influential expression of this move to sanitize language was Samuel Johnson's effort to standardize the usage of English words. Johnson's dictionary set forth clear and precise definitions with the aim of fixing univocal meanings in perpetuity, much like the univocal meanings of standard arithmetic terms.

Beyond this standardization of vocabulary, the movement to depoeticize language use extended to the reformation of prose style. In a masterly chapter on the Newtonian influence on literature, Morris Kline argues:

> It was well recognized in the Newtonian age that statements in a mathematical discussion or demonstration are concise, unambiguous, clear, and exact. Many writers believed that the success enjoyed by mathematics could be credited almost entirely to this naked and pristine style, and therefore resolved to imitate it. (1953, 274)

The theme that valid knowledge depended on the cultivation of univocal language was pursued with unparalleled energy in eighteenth-century France. Bernard de Fontenelle, permanent secretary of the Royal Academy of Sciences in Paris from 1697 to 1741, wrote an agenda for the century when he credited *l'esprit géométrique* for inspiring new levels of precision in contemporary writing, and urged the extension of that geometric spirit to the fields of ethics and politics. Condillac advanced the cause by developing a theory of signs which reduced the art of reasoning to the employment of properly constructed linguistic symbols and led him to conclude: "The creation of a science is nothing else than the establishment of a language, and to study a science is to do nothing else than to learn a well-made language" (Baker 1975, 112). Turgot linked the project to a philosophy of history. For Turgot, the progressive development of language use was the record of the progress of humanity, a record of movement from primitive stages of fixation on concrete expressions to the highest levels of abstraction. Along the way men had resorted to images and poetic metaphors, but "in the future language was destined to become an even superior instrument; it would be stripped of its rhetoric, cleansed of its ambiguities, so that the only means of communication for true knowledge would be the mathematical symbols, verifiable, unchanging, eternal" (Manuel 1965, 29).

Such were the ideas in vogue when the term "social science" was first given wide currency through the literary efforts of the marquis de Condorcet. This prodigious philosophe devoted the last decade of his life to laying the foundations of social science by applying the methods that had proved so successful in the physical sciences. This meant, above all, introducing the certainty of mathematical calculations to the analyses of morals and politics. The moral sciences had been obscure and ineffective, Condorcet argued, because they relied on a vague and ambiguous terminology drawn from everyday parlance. The first step in reconstructing them had to be the creation of a precise, unambiguous language. The value of mathematics for physics lay not in the self-evidence of its propositions but in the precision it afforded for representing phenomena. This was the order of certainty Condorcet claimed for his nascent social mathematics, and he spent his last years on three projects designed to disseminate it.

In a series of memoirs on public education, Condorcet outlined curricular proposals that would inculcate this new mode of thinking. Primary education would include, beyond reading, writing, arithmetic, and elementary natural science, a course of instruction in social science aimed at enhancing the student's capacities for the clarifying analysis of common moral and political notions. Secondary and higher education would concentrate on the physical and moral sciences, conspicuously avoiding the traditional classical curriculum. Condorcet would abandon the classics, Keith Baker has written, "to preserve the reason of citizens against the wiles of eloquence, hastening the transition towards a rational political science that would replace the passionate force of will with the peaceful authority of reason" (1975, 298).

A second project was the publication, together with Abbé Sièyes and others, of a *Journal d'instruction sociale*. The journal quite avowedly aimed to help the populace combat political despotism by equipping them to reason soundly on their own about social questions. Of this project, Baker writes:

> On the grounds that one of the principal obstacles to such an enterprise was the imperfection of everyday language in these matters, the prospectus promised an analysis of political vocabulary. Precisely because this vocabulary was made up of words used in everyday language in vague and uncertain senses, Condorcet maintained, it was difficult to bring men to give these words the clarity of meaning necessary for rational political conduct. (1975, 330)

In his final and best-known project, the testamentary *Esquisse d'un tableau historique des progrès de l'esprit humaine,* Condorcet extended Turgot's effort to provide an evolutionary framework in which this perfection of univocal social language found historic justification. Facing the future, Condorcet envisaged a final epoch of human progress marked by a new universal language of the sciences.[1] "We shall show," Condorcet exclaimed,

> that the formation of such a language, if confined to the
> expression of those simple, precise propositions which form the
> system of a science or the practice of an art, is no chimerical
> scheme . . . and that, indeed, the chief obstacle that would
> prevent its extension to others would be the humiliation of
> having to admit how very few precise ideas and accurate,
> unambiguous notions we actually possess. We shall show that
> this language, ever improving and broadening its scope all the
> while, would be the means of giving to every subject embraced
> by the human intelligence, a precision and a rigour that would
> make knowledge of the truth easy and error almost impossible.
> ([1795] 1955, 198–99)

Condorcet's vision, less apocalyptically limned, reappears in the writing of that Frenchman who did so much to inspire the modern disciplines of sociology and social anthropology. Emile Durkheim was quick to affirm the need for scientific sociology to divest itself of those casual modes of interpreting human behavior that inform common usage. This was necessary no less for the sociologists' use of language than for their methods of observation. "The words of everyday language, like the concepts they express, are always susceptible of more than one meaning, and the scholar employing them in their accepted use without further definition would risk serious misunderstanding," he warned at the opening of his first empirical monograph. "If we follow common use, we risk distinguishing what should be combined, or combining what should be distinguished, thus mistaking the real affinities of things, and accordingly misapprehending their nature" ([1897] 1951, 41). However impatient Durkheim was with the unwholesome effects of "Cartesian thinking" in the French educational system, he expressed a quasi-Cartesian profession of faith when noting that science "is the highest grade of knowledge and there is nothing beyond it. It is distinguished from the humbler forms of knowledge only by greater clarity and distinctness" (1895, 146). He advised social scientists

1. Condorcet's vision of a purified language entailed as well the perfection of a mathematicalized social science and its appropriation by the public. Informed by social mathematics, the decisions of rational actors would rest on a properly estimated sense of consequences, and would avoid the antisocial conduct that generally springs from the erroneous calculation of interests. By applying the calculus of probabilities to such areas as life insurance and pension plans, moreover, rational social provisions would alleviate the common miseries of working-class life.

always to begin their inquiries by resolutely abandoning all concepts that derive from common usage, and then proceed to forge precise unambiguous concepts that capture the true nature of the things to be studied.

The ideal of securing a univocal language to represent the facts of human experience has not been restricted to articulate spokesmen like Condorcet and Durkheim. Classical mechanics has long been a lodestar for social scientists, and the record of our disciplines is dappled with the claims of those purporting to be the Newton of the moral sciences. Although the appeal of the Newtonian exemplar has generally been thought to lie in the prospect of producing tersely formulated universal laws, it has also provided scholars with an alluring model for fashioning a social-scientific language in the univocal terms of mathematical discourse.

Not many social scientists have managed to practice what Condorcet and Durkheim preached about language, yet a few have tried. Vilfredo Pareto found in physics a model social science should employ to counteract the inexactness of everyday language and its use by sentimentalists to mask defects of logic and carry conviction. In his treatise on general sociology Pareto swore "to exert every endeavour to use only words that are as far as possible precise and strictly defined, and which correspond to things unequivocally and without ambiguities" (1963, 57). Indeed, Pareto confessed, he would gladly have replaced word-labels with objectively defined letters of the alphabet or with ordinal numbers but for the fear that such a practice would have exhausted the energies of his readers. Even some who held quite different epistemic assumptions and emphases have shared this concern; so Max Weber, ever mindful of the problem of terminological ambiguity, proposed that a distinctive advantage of sociology over history—offsetting the relative vacuity of sociological notions—derived from "the heightened *univocality* of its concepts," and it was for the sake of attaining "something *univocal*" (*etwas* Eindeutiges) that he urged sociologists to construct pure ideal-typical constructs ([1921] 1976, 10; emphases in original).

Even more common than fastidious terminological practice among social scientists has been a disposition to *believe* that to be scientific means to be unambiguous, that what they do is "scientific," and therefore that what they do is properly unambiguous. Some of the consequences of this belief and its intermittent practical realization have been beneficial. These consequences include the clarification of murky subjects; the detached analysis of topics charged with passions; the improved communication of findings among fellow scholars; the cumulative advancement of research traditions.

However, the disposition to flee from the ambiguities of human life and utterance has produced three characteristic failings in modern social science. These failings reflect (1) a trained incapacity to observe and represent ambiguity as an empirical phenomenon; (2) insufficient awareness of the multiple meanings of commonly used terms in the social sciences; and (3) where such awareness exists, an inability to realize the *constructive* possibilities of ambiguity in theory and analysis.

The Obscuring of Experiential Ambiguities

The ambiguities of life or experience must be distinguished from the ambiguities of language and thought that I have considered thus far. In designating the former as ambiguities we take the liberty of extending the literary notion of ambiguity to nonliterary facts, much as the literary notion of irony has been extended in such phrases as "the ironies of history" or "the ironies of existence." Literary ambiguity signifies the property of words or sentences of admitting more than one interpretation; experiential ambiguity signifies a property possessed by any stimuli of having two or more meanings or even simply of being unclear as to meaning. (In discussions of linguistic ambiguity, the latter sense is sometimes distinguished as 'vagueness' from ambiguity proper.) Now I wish to posit a connection between the two modalities of ambiguity by asserting that the ambiguities of life are systematically underrepresented, when they are not ignored altogether, by methodologies oriented to constructing facts through strictly univocal modes of representation.

In their quest for precision, social scientists have produced instruments that represent the facts of human life in one-dimensional terms. They have defined concepts with rigor in order to represent dominant traits and tendencies univocally. They have constructed scales in order to measure the strength of specified variables on one-dimensional continua. Investigations that rely on such instruments produce representations of attitudes and relations that strike us time and again as gratuitously unrealistic. For the truth of the matter is that people have mixed feelings and confused opinions, and are subject to contradictory expectations and outcomes, in every sphere of experience.[2]

Three lines of work can be adduced to counter the ill effects of such univalent methodologies. The first addresses that pervasive form of empirical ambiguity represented by the notion of ambivalence. Among the founding figures of modern sociology, Georg Simmel—Durkheim's exact contemporary—stands out as one who adumbrated a methodology oriented to capturing the ambivalences of human action. Simmel repeatedly expressed the view, for example, that a condition for the existence of any aspect of life is the coexistence of a diametrically opposed element. Simmel treated conformity and individuation, antagonism and solidarity, compliance and rebelliousness, freedom and constraint, publicity and privacy, as so many sociological dualisms compresent in social interactions and constitutive of various social relationships. These dualisms, he held, are inherent in social forms both because of man's ambivalent instinctual dispositions and because society needs to have some ratio of discordant to harmonious tendencies in order to attain a determinate shape.

Although Simmel influenced the development of American sociology, his work was appropriated only in fragments and never with full appreciation of the scope of his research program or of the assumptions that inform it (Levine et al. 1976). Of sociologists of the last generation, Robert Merton is one of few to have possessed a working grasp of Simmel's sociology, and Merton stands out as one of the few social scientists of our time to have shown real concern for the problem of univocal methodologies. As early as 1940 Merton faulted instruments like the Thurstone attitude scale for assuming

2. Robert Coles made this point in a recent interview. "We love to make categorizations. We've learned from social scientists to say, 'This person is this or that.' But people are many things. The mind has many rooms." Commenting on an interview with a boy in which the boy laughingly told his friends that he had convinced Coles that the world was coming to an end, Coles observed: "That boy was bored with his parents and his sister, who were active in the nuclear-freeze movement. But he was also scared. We have the right to expect of children the same kind of complexity and ambiguity that we ourselves presumably have" (*Chronicle of Higher Education*, July 18, 1984: 7).
Even methodologies that rely on less formalized procedures experience this difficulty. Noting that ethnographers frequently seem unprepared to acknowledge that "in human cultural repertoires there may actually be more domains which derive their salient semantic order from ambiguity and variation than there are domains whose orderliness reflects consensus and uniformity," Marvin Harris has pointed out a number of research strategies that are "inherently incapable of accommodating ambiguity" (1968, 582–89).

that the judgments that make up an opinion inventory represent a linear continuum and that the scale values of endorsed opinions may be algebraically summed and averaged. He noted that these assumptions contain the "suppressed premise . . . that subjects do not 'really' subscribe to 'logically' contradictory judgments," which is "to fly in the face of a store of clinical observations" and the awareness of "John Doe himself" (1976, 259–60). Some two decades later, Merton offered a similar critique of survey instruments used to measure the prestige of occupations in industrial societies. Noting that occupational prestige studies have uniformly attested the high status of the professions and failed to tap widespread hostility directed against professionals over the years, he suggests that this failure may be an artifact of the research tools used in the social rating of occupations, since those inquiries typically call for net ratings and often do not expressly include statements of negative as well as positive bases of evaluation (1976, 20).

The ideas needed to deal with ambivalent realities may be difficult to implement, but they are not difficult to describe. In dealing with psychological ambivalence, one needs to set up instruments that deal simultaneously with divergent orientations to the same object. Bradburn and Caplovitz, in a study of happiness (1965), showed one way of doing this, by measuring respondents' reports both of happiness and of unhappiness rather than by considering happiness as a single variable along a univalent continuum. In dealing with sociological ambivalence, Merton has charted a perfectly plausible agenda: to look at socially structured alternatives not as coherent sets of normative expectations but as clusters of norms and counternorms which codetermine action. Rose Laub Coser has now produced a study in this vein which describes the contradictory expectations directed toward psychiatric residents and patients in a mental hospital, in a work titled *Training in Ambiguity*.

Besides a focus on phenomena in which opposed dispositions and norms are compresent, a related line of work has drawn attention to situations where social realities are largely *indeterminate*. Some of this work can be said to follow Durkheim's seminal analysis of the vagueness of normative regulations in modern societies. Other work, mainly by economists and psychologists, proceeds by assuming that individuals make judgments and take risks in situations describable as inherently ambiguous—situations where information is scanty, conflicting, unreliable, or otherwise of a high order of uncertainty. In the last decade, still another research tradition has opened up the analysis of a whole class of organizations that are characterized by ambiguities of this sort. Cohen and March (1974) define this class of organizations as "organized anarchies," settings that are characterized by *problematic goals,* such that the organization appears to operate on a variety of inconsistent and ill-defined preferences; *unclear technology,* such that the organization does not understand its own processes, and operates through a motley assortment of procedures; and *fluid participation,* such that the extent to which participants contribute to the organization varies among members and in their individual participation over time.

Concluding their analysis of one type of organized anarchy, the American college, Cohen and March write that the ambiguities they have identified in the role of the college president are fundamental because

> they strike at the heart of the usual interpretations of
> leadership. Where purpose is ambiguous, ordinary theories of
> decision making and intelligence become problematic. When
> power is ambiguous, ordinary theories of social order and
> control become problematic. When experience is ambiguous,
> ordinary theories of learning and adaptation become
> problematic. When success is ambiguous, ordinary theories of
> motivation and personal pleasure become problematic. (1974,
> 195)

In chapter 3 I argue that our prevailing images of premodern societies have typically suffered from a tendency to view them as embodiments of monolithic patterns and show that the kinds of empirical ambiguities systematically exposed by approaches to modern societies like those of Merton or Cohen and March need to be identified in traditional societies as well.

A third corrective to the impaired vision for empirical ambiguities stems from work that affirms the psychological value or the social utility of apprehending ambiguity. Psychological aspects of the matter were broached early in this century by two research traditions: psychoanalysis, which documented the permeation of normal psychic life by mixed emotions and semantically complex, "overdetermined" symbols; and Gestalt psychology, which demonstrated the oscillating meanings commonly attached to visual objects. It was probably the Nazi psychologist Erik Jaensch, however, who first isolated the predilection for ambiguity as a diagnostically significant psychological variable.

In *Der Gegentypus* (1938) Jaensch differentiated two basic personality types according to whether or not individuals maintain a stable coordination between univocally determined points in space and corresponding points of the retina. The normal type, for Jaensch, evinced such stable coordination and, beyond that, traits of firmness, consistency, and regularity. In contrast, Jaensch delineated the "antitype," one whose spatial perceptions are labile and unstable and whose style of perceptual "liberalism" has parallels in cognitive and social liberalism as well—all manifestations of what Jaensch considered a morbid psychic disposition (and a political element that threatened to pollute German culture and public life). Accordingly, Jaensch accused Gestalt psychology of morbidity in its emphasis on the ambiguous character of perceptual processes.

In related work Else Frenkel-Brunswik confirmed the utility of treating "tolerance of ambiguity" as a generalized personality variable of some diagnostic interest. In her analysis, however, Jaensch was faulted for glorifying "the precise, machine-like, unswervingly unambiguous perceptual reaction" (1949, 135). Frenkel-Brunswik's psychoanalytically oriented studies found that low tolerance for ambiguity was dynamically related to a denial of emotional ambivalence and was associated with crude stereotyping, rigid defenses, and general lack of insight. For Frenkel-Brunswik, then, it is *intolerance* of ambiguity that constitutes the morbid type of disposition, a judgment supported by the research for *The Authoritarian Personality* (Adorno et al. 1950) with its discovery of a significant correlation between high scores on ethnocentrism and authoritarianism scales and an intolerance of ambiguity. Although independent investigations later failed to replicate the finding of a high correlation between authoritarianism and intolerance of ambiguity, Frenkel-Brunswik's dynamic formulation remained plausible: excessive "emotional ambiguity" (ambivalence) is counteracted by denial of that ambivalence and consequent intolerance of "cognitive ambiguity," a condition which results in a simplistic view of the environment and hence, finally, is maladaptive. This notion found wide acceptance among developmental psychologists; in their influential *Measuring Ego Development* (1970), Loevinger and Wessler placed toleration for ambiguity at the highest, "autonomous," stage of cognitive development.

Anthony Davids made the inevitable move beyond a simple association of ambiguity tolerance with psychological health or morbidity. In "Psychodynamic and Sociocultural Factors Related to Intolerance of Ambiguity" (1966), Davids advanced the problem in two respects. After administering tests that measure whether or not persons have a liking for ambiguity to diverse groups of subjects—

navy personnel, college students, and hospitalized mental patients—
Davids determined that "ambiguity tolerance is not necessarily a
sign of healthy emotional adjustment" (1966, 170), since it was the
schizophrenics in his study who evinced the highest predilection for
ambiguity. Neither is it a clear sign of pathology, however, since
quite competent, creative thinkers also reveal a high degree of liking
for ambiguity. Rather, he concluded, creative individuals and the
emotionally incapacitated both experience similar inconsistencies
and disturbing complexities during the earliest stages of psycho-
sexual development. Consequently, although as children the two
types cope with such complexities in radically different ways, as
adults they both manifest a high tolerance of ambiguity.

From the work of psychologists like Frenkel-Brunswik and
Davids, then, it could be argued that enhanced tolerance of ambiguity would be adaptive at least for certain kinds of personalities. A
whole new dimension was then opened up by Davids' observations
about the *sociological* implications of ambiguity tolerance. Commenting on his findings for the navy men, who showed a somewhat
lower frequency of liking for ambiguity than did his college students,
Davids observed:

> It seems apparent that in the subculture of a Navy base no
> great premium is placed on the tolerance of ambiguity. . . .
> Orderly, competent, effective functioning in that social system
> requires clarity and consistency, and there is little room for
> tolerance of ambiguity either in ideas or in interpersonal
> relations. . . .
> In the college setting, on the other hand, students
> undoubtedly listen to and are accustomed to dealing with
> controversy, conflict, and contradiction of ideas. In such a
> social setting, it is probably a desirable and rewarded
> personality characteristic to be tolerant of ambiguity. Moreover,
> in general, ambiguity does not seem to be particularly
> disrupting in the usual college setting. Rather, ambiguity of
> ideas and lack of certainty may well be necessary ingredients
> for maintenance of an intellectually stimulating atmosphere.
> (1966, 170–71)

What these lines suggest is that a pronounced openness for
experiential ambiguities may be functional for and reinforced in
specific kinds of social contexts. I examine that suggestion systematically in the following chapter, which considers the widespread
appreciation of ambiguous utterance in traditional cultures and
focuses on one case, that of the Amhara of northern Ethiopia, where

ambiguity is extravagantly prized. The contrast between this pattern
and that of modern American culture becomes the occasion for
reflection about the forms and functions of ambiguity more generally, and finally about the proper role of ambiguity in any modern
society.

Indifference to Conceptual Ambiguity

If human realities are intrinsically ambiguous, so is the language
that social scientists use in attempting to represent them. The
conceit of many social scientists that willy-nilly they are doing
univocal work frequently blinds them to the persisting confusions
introduced by vague or multivocal categories. Richard Dewey made
the point for sociology a few years back: "The pervasive indifference which sociologists have demonstrated toward the absence of
semantic consensus in the terms they use is nearly as shocking as
their ambiguity-ridden vocabulary itself" (1979, 190). This blindness
produces errors of three sorts: inconsistent applications of apparently clearcut categories in empirical studies; unwitting use of the
same concept with different meanings in differing discursive contexts; and failure to appropriate adequately the different senses of
polysemous terms even when their ambiguities have already been
pointed out.

The first of these errors has been duly exposed by William
Kruskal. Kruskal points to the widespread existence of statistics
that are misleading because they employ classifications that initially
seem very clearcut but on closer inspection reveal unexpected
depths of ambiguity. He cites as one illustration a study by the
Bureau of the Census which compared occupational classifications
in the 1970 census (obtained by clerical coders from responses to
census questions) with classifications in a 1972 postcensal man-
power survey in which respondents themselves reported their 1970
occupations. The study reveals, for example, that of the 663
mathematical scientists classified as "statisticians" in the 1970
census, only 340 called themselves statisticians in the postcensal
survey. Conversely, of the 471 self-styled statisticians in the
postcensal survey, only 340 were designated statisticians in the 1970
census!

Reflecting on the numerous problems of this sort in contemporary
statistical surveys, Kruskal observes:

It would be lovely if there were a truth that one might hope to approach asymptotically and treat deviations from as simple measurement errors. Alas, no; there is essential ambiguity most or all of the time, yet an ambiguity that needs to be understood as well as possible if society is sensibly to use statistical results based on ineluctable fuzziness. (1981, 511)

If census makers and survey takers suffer from the ambiguities involved in applying clearcut categories when constructing sets of facts, social theorists suffer no less from the ambiguities of the basic terms they use in forming propositions. The work of probably every major figure in the social sciences reveals shifts in the meaning attached to certain terms. In chapter 4 an egregious example of this tendency is examined. Despite Durkheim's clarion call for clear and univocal definitions, his oeuvre shows a scandalously high number of instances where his central analytic concepts are used in differing ways as though they always meant the same thing. To this day that fault has frustrated efforts to appropriate his work. Even Merton's famous attempt to build on Durkheim, his series of papers on social structure and anomie, has exacerbated rather than relieved the problem. Yet Durkheim's failing becomes illuminating if we examine it carefully enough to find the ways in which his ambiguities are overdetermined, both by intellectual traditions he inherited and by epistemological positions that he pioneered.

In contrast with Durkheim, Max Weber can be taken as one who struggled more successfully to disentangle the multiple meanings of some of his central polysemous concepts. This is particularly true for the concept that arguably forms the core of Weber's substantive work, rationality. In chapter 7 I shall show that subsequent scholars failed to appropriate Weber's subtly differentiated treatment of rationality, to the detriment of the current state of understanding both Weber's work and the general phenomenon of rationality.

The Pathos of Ambiguity

If some social scientists remain indifferent to conceptual ambiguities much of the time, many appear keenly aware of the problem some of the time. This awareness frequently finds expression as the pathos of ambiguity, a sense that the concept in question is hopelessly multivocal and so one had better fix, once and for all, a univocal meaning for it or else stop using the concept altogether. Such drastic remedies are proposed because the condition of protracted conceptual ambiguity is diagnosed as pathological, for it is said to constitute an insuperable obstacle to clear communication and genuinely cumulative inquiry in the field in question.

Heinz Eulau offers a characteristic expression of the pathos of ambiguity when he writes that "'elite,' like so many other concepts in the lexicon of the social sciences, has become an all-purpose term with so many cognitive and affective meanings and uses that one might well wish to banish it from serious social-scientific discourse" (1977, 394). Reviewing a book that sets forth no fewer than 108 distinct interpretations of the concept of equality, Brian Barry observes: "The whole idea of equality is a mess—probably the term should be scrapped" (1982, 37). Similarly, Richard Schacht concludes a book-length examination of ambiguities linked with 'alienation' by suggesting that scholars might do well to stop using the term, Aubrey Lewis cites a number of psychoanalysts who want their colleagues to get rid of the ambiguous word 'anxiety,' and David Martin argues that sociologists of religion should simply abandon the concept of 'secularization.'

The difficulty with that remedy is that not many are willing to abide by a plea to stop using concepts so deeply embedded in their thinking and the literatures they work with. Even proponents of such an aseptic strategy have a hard time following it. Thus, Eulau goes on to write about 'elites'; Barry qualifies his advice to scrap 'equality' by adding "except in highly specified contexts"; Lewis wryly observes that "the prospect of killing the term [anxiety] is slender" (1970, 79); Martin published two books with 'secularization' in the title; and Schacht suggests a face-saving alternative: scholars might legitimately continue to use 'alienation,' but only so long as they seriously restrict the way in which they use it.[3]

This brings us to the other response to the pathos of ambiguity: fixing a univocal definition for terms that have been notoriously multivocal. The work of Talcott Parsons attempts this solution. Parsons responds, for example, to the notable lack of agreement concerning the definition of 'power' by attempting to identify its "core complex of meaning" and to legitimate the univocal definition he proposed by placing it in the context of a general conceptual scheme. One difficulty with this sort of solution is that other authors may not be willing to accept the proposed definition, especially if they do not find the associated conceptual context congenial. A

---

3. Martin Albrow has made a similar point: "In spite of prefacing their work with remarks such as: 'bureaucracy eludes definition,' or 'the term bureaucracy is devoid of any established meaning,' writers have gone on to discuss bureaucracy, whatever it may be" (1970, 14).

more serious difficulty, I believe, is that with regard to a number of basic concepts in social science, the very attempt to formulate a universally applicable univocal definition seems ill-advised.

The problem with that aspiration is that important insights often are linked with a particular way of construing a concept. To take an example from authors to be considered below, Simmel, Weber, and Park—unlike Durkheim—have a clear and distinct notion, consistently employed, of what each of them means by 'society,' and much of what is valuable in their work is tied to their particular definitions. Yet the three meanings are radically different from one another, and to resolve those differences by espousing just one of them—or a fourth—is to cut ourselves off from many of their valuable contributions. This represents a case of what W. B. Gallie (1964) has described as "essentially contested concepts"—concepts whose meaning must be permanently a matter of dispute. Gallie argues that such a condition of permanent irresolution must be the fate of concepts that are internally complex, linked with changing historical circumstances, productive of disputes that cannot be easily resolved, and used in an aggressive and defensive manner by their proponents. This would certainly include, in social science, concepts like 'elite,' 'equality,' 'alienation,' 'anxiety,' 'secularization,' 'anomie,' 'stranger,' 'form,' 'rationality,' 'freedom,' and hundreds of others.

If this is acknowledged, then it appears that to become aware of the multivocality of certain central concepts is not necessarily to identify a need to eliminate their ambiguities. When census facts are reconstructed, surely, it is important to reduce ambiguities of classification as much as possible. But elsewhere, other types of response may be preferable.

The toleration of ambiguity can be productive if it is taken not as a warrant for sloppy thinking but as an invitation to deal responsibly with issues of great complexity. I see two general strategies to deal with conceptual ambiguities in a productive way. The first strategy is to clarify the unrecognized ambiguities surrounding the use of a term and to analyze them, together with whatever prevailing contenders for its definition may exist, and then to determine, at some higher level of abstraction, what those diverse usages have in common (so far as possible). One can then locate, through some classificatory scheme, the diverse current meanings and how they may be said to relate to one another. This was the strategy adopted in the two-volume work by Mortimer Adler et al. (1958–61) on the concept of freedom, and to a large extent followed by Schacht in

Alienation (1970). In the present volume this strategy is exemplified
by chapter 5, which first sorts out some of the confusions produced
by literature on the sociology of strangers, and then develops a
paradigm for articulating the diverse meanings of 'stranger' and how
they are related.

The second type of strategy entails an even greater degree of
toleration of ambiguity. It is one that begins by acknowledging the
incommensurability of the diverse meanings associated with essentially contested concepts, and attempts to clarify those semantic
differences and the larger intellectual contexts and agendas they
imply. The inability of two or more authors to agree on definitions of
major terms does not require wholesale rejection of one another's
work, nor that third parties be obliged to pick sides. If different
authors have radically disparate notions of 'society,' for example,
they can nonetheless agree with one another on a number of
substantive points and be stimulated to enlarge their domain of
understanding without abandoning their deepest assumptions. In the
language of Richard McKeon, the exercise of historical semantics—
grasping the array of diverse meanings associated with our commonplace concepts—is an appropriate prolegomenon to any elaboration of one's own interpretive schema and conclusions, and the
exploration of the series of questions which grow from the plural
treatment of common issues is quite preferable to "the abrupt
termination which closes controversies in univocal statements of a
single truth" (n.d.; 1964, 245).

Two chapters of this volume present cases of enormous intellectual achievement which are marred by the failure to adopt this
kind of approach. Chapter 6 provides an extended case study of the
phenomenon of compulsive negation. It documents the inability of a
number of originative social scientists to sustain the degree of
ambiguity and tension needed to accommodate themselves produc-
tively to someone with whom they discovered certain essential
disagreements. The figure of Georg Simmel is doubly instructive in
that story, both as the object of a series of disavowals described
there and as the progenitor of a pluralistic conception of the
intellectual enterprise that justifies this more capacious mode of
dealing with ambiguities.

If this type of accommodation may be fruitful within the theoretic
sciences, it is relevant a fortiori to dealing with ambiguities oc-
casioned by the intersection of theoretic and practical interests.
Perhaps there is no more tragic consequence of the compulsive
avoidance of ambiguity in our times than the belief in the reducibility

of practical to theoretical modes of analysis—that is, the notion that the practical merely involves an "application" of the theoretical, that it is simply a different way of treating the same terms and subjects. Such a belief has led grown men to suppose that the only finally compelling rhetoric is one structured by the norms and values of scientific inquiry. Chapter 8 examines this problem in the case of Freud and Weber, the two towering analysts of human conduct in this century, men who struggled intensely with these issues and reached denouements that are illuminating in many ways.

Concluding in a more constructive vein, chapter 9 presents an exercise in which the analysis of chapter 7 is confronted with the "lesson" of chapter 6. Returning to the theme of the multiple meanings of rationality, I seek there to bring together resources for that problem provided by Simmel and Parsons as well as Weber. Chapter 9, then, exhibits a mode of analysis that both respects the diverse contexts in which these authors employ essentially ambiguous notions and seeks ways to relate complementary treatments of those concepts in a productive manner—with results, I suggest, that no one of them could have achieved by himself.

2

Ambiguity and Modernity

Ambiguous modes of expression are rooted in the very nature of language and thought. Although linguists disagree about whether some natural languages harbor more ambiguity than others, no linguist disputes the point that ambiguity is an inherent property of all natural languages.

Language generates ambiguity, first, because lexical elements tend to be imprecise. A single word or phrase may carry a number of meanings (polysemy); differently spelled words may sound alike (homophony); words that differ in derivation, meaning, or even pronunciation may be spelled the same way or represented by the same ideographic character (homography).[1] Sentences with univocal lexical forms, moreover, may yet be ambiguous because of confusion about how they are to be punctuated. In addition, even when a sentence contains but a single lexical and grammatical structure, it can still be insufficiently specified for purposes of clear communication—for example, "he hit the man with the stick" or "she is a Chinese art expert"—instances of what linguists gloss as 'grammatical homonyms' or 'structural ambiguity.' Aristotle's *De sophisticis elenchis* indicated the grounds for all this long since: "For names are finite and so is the sum-total of formulae, while things are infinite in number. Inevitably, then, the same formula and a single name have a number of meanings."

1. Yuen Ren Chao estimates that about 15 percent of the characters in a running Chinese text have alternate pronunciations, usually associated with differences in meaning and function (1959, 3).

Another source of ambiguity in language is the tendency for words to acquire associations. Even words that are highly univocal in what they denote inevitably accumulate a wealth of connotations. Commonplace words like 'window' or 'bridge' are rich with personal and collective meanings of this sort. Rilke's ninth *Duino Elegy* alludes plaintively to this:

> Are we perhaps *here*, only to say: House.
> Bridge. Fountain. Gate. Jug. Fruit tree. Window.—
> at most: Pillar. Tower. . . . But to *say* them, mind you,
> *so* to say them, as the things within themselves never
> could have intended.

The human mind, moreover, inclines to exploit the possibilities for ambiguous expression which are inherent in language. We feel compelled to produce constructions such as metaphor, allegory, pun, irony, and paradox in order to express feelings and articulate realities which are too subtle for straightforward univocal representation. Although sober philosophers once taught that metaphoric constructions are idiosyncratic if not pathological forms of language use, now they affirm that metaphor permeates normal everyday language, thought, and action.

Cultures differ with regard to the scope they allow for the exercise of those ambiguities which inhere in speech and thought. To be sure, every culture insists on certain areas of univocal precision, according to the practical exigencies of the people who speak its language. Arabic, for example, is famous for the variety of terms it provides for designating different kinds of camels. But apart from such practical necessities, there is a wide range of variability in attitude toward the use of ambiguities generally. At the extremes, one type of culture puts a premium on the use of ambiguities in conversation and literary forms generally, while the other type disparages the use of ambiguities at all levels of communication.

Ambiguity in Premodern Cultures

The movement against ambiguity led by Western intellectuals since the seventeenth century figures as a unique development in world history. There is nothing like it in any premodern culture known to me.

Studies of the traditional cultures of Asia and Africa reveal time and again cases where ambiguous modes of expression are at the very least benignly tolerated. Indeed, most if not all of the literate civilizations have considered the cultivation of ambiguous locution to be a wonderful art. Generations of Westerners have been struck, for example, by the privileged position of ambiguous expressions in the civilization of China. With a lexicon built so largely of concrete, multipurpose terms, the Chinese language is ill-suited to making sharp distinctions and analytic abstractions; and Chinese speakers like to evoke the multiple meanings associated with concrete images. Traditional Chinese produced an ornate literary style that blends a complex variety of suggestive images and creates subtle nuances through historical allusions. Mastery of such a style became one of the specially prized arts of classical China. In highly stylized contests Chinese courtiers vied with one another in palavers by inventing verses or singing songs that were filled with "diplomatic double meanings" (Granet 1958, 292–94). Despite enormous differences between them, both Confucianism and Taoism were noted for disseminating precepts open to multiple interpretations.

Many of the linguistic customs of China are found in Japan as well. The love for evocative concrete terms reached its pinnacle in the highly prized forms of condensed poetry known as *tanka* and, especially, *haiku*. As with Chinese, Japanese language use promoted ambiguity by constructing sentences in which the subject was often omitted. In addition, Japanese added the distinctive particle, *tenioha,* which expresses delicate shades of emotion and thereby suggests rich overtones of meaning. Japanese Buddhists continued the ambiguous and obscure interpretations of Buddhist texts evolved in China, and Zen teaching perfected the art of ambiguous response: a question like "What is the essence of Zen Buddhism?" would elicit such answers as "The wind blows and the sun heats" or "An oak tree in the garden."

Hindu traditions cultivated a garden of ambiguities with different cognitive equipment. Instead of idealizing concrete objects with their multiple associations, Hindu thought was inclined to regard concrete objects as less real than many abstract ideas, and to see particulars as illusory manifestations of universals. Paradigmatic for the polysemy this gives rise to, the Hindu notion of *atman* refers both to the individual ego and the Universal Self. It has been a Hindu goal to erase the distinctions between self and others, and to attain truth, *satya,* by negating all forms of conceptual discriminations.

Because of this fondness for the abstract, one scholar has written:

The Indians tend to pay more attention to the unknown and the

undefined. . . . This attraction for the unknown resulted in a
fondness for concealing even the obvious; their way of thinking
tended to prefer the dark and obscure over that which was
clear. (Nakamura 1960, 31)

Such an orientation underlies the Indian fondness for riddles and the
profusion of allegorical expressions in the Upanishads and other
writings. Even when Indian philosophers pursue their arguments in
accord with the rules of logic, they prefer to make use of riddles and
allegories.

In that remarkable outlier of Indian civilization, traditional Java,
Clifford Geertz found a number of patterns that evince a studied
cultivation of ambiguous expressions. In the *prijaji* or gentry culture
of Java, the term *alus* signifies a person who speaks flawless high
Javanese, and *alus* refers as well to a clever poetic conceit.
Similarly, the term *rasa* is used to refer to a general principle of
life—whatever lives has *rasa,* and whatever has *rasa* lives—yet
again "*rasa* is applied to the words in a letter, in a poem, or even in
a speech, to indicate the between-the-lines 'looking north and hitting
south' type of allusive suggestion that is so important in Javanese
communication" (Geertz 1960, 238). For the Javanese gentry,
communication that is open and to the point comes across as rude,
and *prijaji* etiquette prescribes that personal transactions be carried
out by means of a long series of courtesy forms and complex
indirections.

Jacques Berque (1961) has attempted to interpret those "chaotic
inflections" of Arabic discourse that appear in the Arabs' penchant
for metaphors, allegories, associations by resemblance and contigu-
ity, and dissemblance, as in expressions of rage that merely signify
alibis or gestures of appeasement that are pure camouflage. He
views them in the context of a deep tension in Islamic culture
between the ideal of unity and the reality of historical diversities,
much as Nakamura connects the Hindu love of allegory to a tension
between particular and universal. Berque relates that tension to the
fascination with which Muslim literati examine the ambiguities of
Arabic and, in particular, to their penchant for distinguishing
between the figurative and the deeper, actual meanings of Koranic
passages.

In one African variant of Islamic culture, that of the Somali
nation, a love for ambiguity appears particularly notable in the
political sphere. David Laitin reports that the Somali boast that *af
somaaliga wa mergi,* "the Somali language is sinuous," because it

permits words to take on novel shapes that accommodate a richness
of metaphors and poetic allusions. Political arguments and diplomatic messages take the form of alliterative poems, mastery of
which is a key to prestige and power. These poems typically begin
with long, vague, circumlocutory preludes, introducing the theme at
hand, which is then couched in allegory. Of these poems, Laitin
writes:

> A poetic message can be deliberately misinterpreted by the
> receiver, without his appearing to be stupid. Therefore, the
> person for whom the message was intended is never put in a
> position where he has to answer yes or no, or where he has to
> make a quick decision. He is able to go into further allegory,
> circling around the issue in other ways, to prevent direct
> confrontation. (1977, 39)

The classical traditions of Western civilization appear scarcely
less hospitable to ambiguous expressions. The Jews created a Book
whose sparse detail has been a standing invitation for evocative
interpretations. Generations of Talmudic scholars and then Kabbal-
ists spent lives in savoring the wisdom and the mysteries of
polysemous words and phrases. Jesus and his followers loved to
represent spiritual truths in terms of familiar worldly images and
events. Christian preachers over the centuries have delighted in
unraveling the strands of thought entwined in his parables. Medieval
dramatists and Renaissance poets proclaimed moral truths through
elaborate allegories. The Platonic tradition made much of the
multiple meanings of words, both in their dual capacity as referents
to sensible and ideal objects and as signs whose meanings shift in the
course of dialectical inquiry. Ciceronian rhetoric made much of the
paradox as a device for startling and persuading one's audience, and
figures of all sorts were celebrated in handbooks of classical
rhetoric. These were all manifestations of those modes of expression
and thought that writers like Locke and Condorcet sought to combat
in prescribing a curriculum that excluded the classics.

The fact that ambiguity was cultivated in so many forms in so
many traditional cultures suggests that ambiguous expressions serve
a number of social and cultural purposes. These purposes should be
examined before one endorses without reservation the modern
project of eradicating ambiguity. To facilitate such an examination,
I should like to compare two cases that represent sharply contrasting attitudes toward ambiguity—the culture of the Amhara of
Ethiopia and that of the United States of America.

Ambiguity in Amhara and American Cultures

Within the universe of traditional cultures where, we have seen, ambiguity as such is probably never the object of focused aversion, Amhara culture presents a case where the love of ambiguity appears particularly pronounced. This is so much the case that one is considered a master of spoken Amharic only when one's speech is leavened with ambiguous nuances as a matter of course. Even among other peoples in Ethiopia the Amhara have been noted for extremes of symbolism and subtlety in their everyday talk.[2]

The Amhara's basic manner of communicating is indirect, often secretive. Amharic conversation abounds with general, evasive remarks, like *Mĭn yeshallāl?* ("What is better?") when the speaker has failed to indicate what issue he is referring to, or *Seṭagn!* ("Give me!") when the speaker fails to specify what it is he wants. When the speaker then is quizzed about the issue at hand or the object he desires, his reply still may not reveal what is really on his mind; and if it does, his interlocutor will likely as not interpret that response as a disguise.

This pattern of indirection in speech governs Ethiopian literature. The written literature of Ethiopia is suffused with parable and protracted symbolism. In what is perhaps the most characteristic expression of the Amhara genius, moreover—a genre of oral literature known as 'wax and gold'—the studied use of ambiguity plays a central part.

Wax and gold (*sam-ennā warq*) is the formula with which the Amhara symbolize their favorite form of verse. The form consists of two semantic layers. The apparent, superficial meaning of the words is called "wax" (*sam*); their hidden, deeper significance is the "gold" (*warq*).

In its generic sense, the expression *sam-ennā warq* refers to a number of poetic figures which embody this duplicity of meaning. The use of such figures distinguishes the Amhara equivalent of true poetry from the ordinary verse in which everyday language is merely embellished with rhyme and rhythm. In the genre known as *qenē,* the original and most elegant kind of *sam-ennā warq* poetry, the lines are composed in Ge'ez (the ancient and liturgical language of Ethiopia) and depend primarily on religious symbolism. But *sam-ennā warq* constructions also appear in many types of secular

2. The following paragraphs incorporate material published previously in my *Wax and Gold* (1965).

verse in the vernacular Amharic and, indeed, frequently inform
ordinary Amharic discourse.

Masters of the art of *qenē* composition have analyzed these poetic
figures into about a dozen different types. *Sam-ennā warq* in its
more specific sense refers to one of these figures—the prototype of
them all. It consists of an explicit comparison in which the subjects
being compared—the "wax" and the "gold"—are presented in
apposition, while their predicates are rendered jointly, by a single
verb which carried both a "wax" and a "gold" meaning. This
terminology stems from the art of the goldsmith, who constructs a
clay mold around a form created in wax and then, after melting and
draining off the wax, pours the molten gold into that form. So, for
example, if the poet's aim is to praise a hero like Emperor Menelik,
he creates a "wax" model, like "the lion," in terms of whose
actions the "gold," Menelik, is depicted: "The lion crushed the wolf
Italy."

The following Amharic couplet exemplifies the *sam-ennā warq*
figure:

> Etsa balas balto addām kanfareshe
> Madhānē ālam lebbē tasaqqala-lleshe.

> Since Adam your lip did eat of that Tree
> The Savior my heart has been hung up for thee.

In this secular couplet the "wax" of Adam's sin and Christ's
crucifixion in his behalf has been used as a mold in which to pour a
love message. A literal translation of the "wax" of the couplet is:

> Because Adam ate of the apple from the Tree of Knowledge
> The Savior of the World has been crucified for thee.

To appreciate the "gold" of the couplet, one must know that the
verb meaning "was crucified," *tasaqqala,* may also mean "is
infatuated with." A literal translation of the "gold" content would
be:

> Because of your (tempting) lips
> My heart is infatuated with thee.

In other figures, the duplicity of the message is rendered less
explicit. In figures known as *hĭber* and *merĭmer,* the "wax" and
"gold" are combined in the same word or phrase instead of being
put side by side. These figures thus correspond to the English pun.
For example:

Abbāt-ennā innātesh sigā naw irmātchaw
Ānjat tabayāllash āntchi-mmā lijātchaw.

Your father and your mother have vowed to keep from meat
But you, their very daughter, innards do you eat.

"To eat someone's entrails" is an Amharic idiom which means "to
capture his heart." The hidden meaning of the couplet is thus: "You
made me love you."

Ethiopic verse becomes most obscure in the figure known as
wesṭa wayrā, "inside of olive tree." Here only the "wax" is given,
and the listener must work to unearth the "gold." Often this can be
done only when the circumstances under which the verse was made
up are known. At times the author of a *wesṭa wayrā* verse may even
refuse to reveal anything that would help the listener grasp its
hidden meaning.

The expression *wesṭa wayrā* alludes to the fact that the inside of
the olive tree is of a different color from its bark. The implication is
that the inner sense of a *wesṭa wayrā* poem is concealed by a veneer
which conveys a quite different sense. For example:

Ya-bāhetāwi līj sifalleg le'llennā
Ya-kristosen mesht telānt washama-nnā
Qeṭal betābalaw hono qarrama-nnā.

The son of a hermit, high rank to display,
Made love with Christ's wife yesterday;
When she fed him leaves he wasted away.

The surface meaning of this tercet describes an ambitious man who
had relations with the "wife of Christ" in order to raise his status,
for in Ethiopia having relations with a woman of high rank is one
way to gain prestige. Instead of advancing his position, however,
this man lost all his power when the woman fed him (medicinal)
leaves.

The esoteric meaning, the "gold," on the other hand, refers to the
experience of a hermit. His "son" is intended to symbolize his
hunger, and "Christ's wife" symbolizes fasting. The "inside"
interpretation, then, is that the hermit's hunger is heightened by its
relation with fasting, but it diminishes when he is fed leaves, the
hallowed diet of a hermit.

The ambiguity symbolized by the formula "wax and gold" colors
the entire fabric of Amhara life. It patterns the speech and outlook
of every Amhara. When he talks, his words carry *double entendre* as

a matter of course; when he listens, he is ever on the lookout for latent meanings and hidden motives. As an Ethiopian anthropologist once told me, wax and gold is far more than a poetic formula; it is the Amhara "way of life."

The American way of life, by contrast, affords little room for the cultivation of ambiguity. The dominant American temper calls for clear and direct communication. It expresses itself in such common injunctions as "Say what you mean," "Don't beat around the bush," and "Get to the point." A Nigerian novelist summed up his impressions of the American style after living more than twenty years in the United States as follows: "Americans tend to be direct and literal rather than allusive and figurative, stark rather than subtle. They are happier dealing with statistics than with nuances" (Echewa 1982, 13).

Intellectual discussions in the United States commonly reflect the assumption that the meaning of a word must be precisely determined before it can be used seriously. The dominant philosophical orientations are given to insisting on the univocal definition of terms. Few American thinkers would be disposed to challenge Abraham Kaplan's straightforward judgment: "Ambiguity is the common cold of the pathology of language" (Kooij 1971, 1).

Poetry, the last refuge of ambiguity, has received relatively little attention in American culture. The poetry that is commonly prized is likely as not to be of a fairly literal sort; and the American way of understanding a poem is often that of translating the "meaning" of the poem into univocal prose.

To lampoon public figures for their alleged equivocation has long been a favored American pastime. George Washington became a culture hero to a large extent because of the perception that he studiously avoided misrepresentations of any sort. A nineteenth-century American patriot, General John Wilcott Phelps, expressed a characteristic attitude in writings that praised the candor and openness of Americans, and scored the machinations of secret societies as a threat to republican institutions:

When men resort to the use of ambiguous expressions, vague similes, parallels, signs, symbols, grips, etc., it is reasonable to infer that they have some object in view that will not bear the light. The borrowing of the livery of the devil, to serve Heaven in, will ever excite suspicion, and impair the confidence of men in each other. Honest intentions should receive honest modes of expression. (1873, 219)

The Functions of Ambiguity and Univocality

These opposed attitudes toward ambiguity reflect contrasting patterns in Amhara and American value systems and social institutions. The shape of those patterns and affinities becomes evident when we examine the properties of ambiguous expressions and the diverse purposes they serve.

Comments by Amhara who have thought about the matter provide a useful starting point for identifying those purposes. *Wesṭa wayrā,* that most obscure of the wax-and-gold figures, they tell us, is ideally suited both for expressing deep philosophical insights and for insulting one's enemies with impunity. In other words, ambiguous discourse functions generally as a preferred medium either for revealing realities or for obfuscating them. These functions may be divided further according to whether the realities in question are those of the external world or those of the communicating subject.

When ambiguous locutions are used to represent external realities, their properties of evocativeness serve a distinctively *illuminative* function. When ambiguity is used to represent the inner realities of a subject, its property of allusiveness serves an *expressive* function. When ambiguity is used to conceal the beliefs and intentions of a subject, its property of opaqueness serves a *protective* function. When ambiguity works to obfuscate external realities, its property of vagueness serves a *socially binding* function.

Ambiguity as a Medium of Enlightenment

In the cultures of India and China, as Max Weber observed, knowledge is highly respected, not in the sense of knowing the things of this world—the everyday events of nature and of social life, and the laws that govern them—but as philosophical knowledge of the meaning of life and of the world (1958c, 330). The same holds true for Ethiopia. In all these cultures, as in so many phases of Western culture, it has been felt that this sort of knowledge finds its natural medium in some sort of ambiguity, whether the form be spiritual parable, philosophic paradox, lofty allegory, subtle symbolism, or "wax and gold."

The prestige of wax and gold among the Amhara is attributed in part to what is considered its philosophic value. Amhara traditionalists extol wax and gold as a unique creation of their culture. One of them has written that *qenē* is as distinctive of Ethiopia's spiritual culture as *ṭeff* (a species of grass grown as a cereal grain only in Ethiopia) is distinctive of her material culture (Moges 1956, 117).

They further maintain that Ge'ez *qenē* contains a uniquely profound sort of wisdom. Instruction in this occult art of verse composition has traditionally been regarded as propaedeutic to the study of religious texts. This is partly because Ge'ez grammar, which must be known in order to understand these texts, is normally taught only in the schools of *qenē*. The more philosophic reason given, however, is that by affording exercise in fathoming secrets it "opens the mind" and thereby enhances the student's ability to approach the divine mysteries.

What is the basis of this virtually universal appeal of the ambiguous? It is, first, that we experience reality as complex, full of overtones and cross-currents which razor-sharp univocal statements do not capture, whereas ambiguous expressions favor the representation of this richness of reality in an economical way. It is, moreover, that when we confront words which first mean one thing, and then mean something else, we feel that we are moving from appearance to reality; we experience a progression from a mediocre truth to a higher, or deeper, truth. It is, finally, that encounter with the ambiguous creates an inner confusion, a tension which is relieved when the two meanings are synthesized or when the deeper meaning has been secured.

A more inclusive sense of reality, a sense of mystery, and the experience of oneness that accompanies release of tension—these are the attributes of mysticism. Ambiguity is par excellence the handmaid of mysticism, a type of cognitive orientation primarily concerned with the meaning of life and of the world.

The connection between ambiguity and mysticism is the obverse of the connection between univocality and rationalized science. What we may call the mystical approach differs from the scientific approach in at least two fundamental respects. The truth sought by mysticism is not knowable or communicable by conventional methods. It is not susceptible to formulation in precise propositions, and often—as was maintained by many Asian sages—it can best be communicated by silence. At the most, it can only be alluded to by ambiguous formulations. For science, on the other hand, the mysterious and incommunicable realities of life are relegated to a residual category outside its purview. Scientific truth is restricted to what can be formulated in clear definitions and precise propositions.

Another difference between mysticism and "scientism" concerns their opposing relations to the natural world. Mysticism involves a kind of surrender to the universe, an intimate participation in the oneness of reality, whether this reality be located in a realm of miracle and fantasy, as in India, or in surrounding nature and the events of daily life, as in China, or wherever. Science, in both its ratiocinative and its empirical dimensions, involves an opposition between the knower and the known, some sort of confrontation in which the attempt is made to make subjective knowledge conform to external reality. Whether its aim be purely cognitive or utilitarian, the scientific approach works to dominate reality, while mysticism aims toward fusion with some transcendental reality or else a state of harmonious oneness with the universe.[3]

If ambiguity is favored by those oriented intellectually to savoring the mysteries of life and pragmatically to a state of harmonious fusion, then one strand of the Amhara-America contrast is at once illuminated. The foundations of American religious culture were laid by those who subscribed to the Protestant turning from otherworldly orientations, a development so vividly portrayed by Max Weber. Within Puritanism, moreover, they subscribed overwhelmingly to its ascetic rather than mystical branches. The latter was precluded not only by the establishment of ascetic Covenant Puritanism as the mainstream version of Puritanism in America by the 1640s, but also by the need to adopt a strenuous this-worldly discipline to build and maintain frontier settlements. Mystical modes of piety could scarcely be tolerated where Indians, famine, climate, and wilderness provided unfamiliar enemies to battle against. The persisting exigencies of a frontier mentality were conducive to making the impulse to gain mastery over nature a core motif of American culture. Indeed, the impulse to dominate nature developed in the United States to a degree the world had never before experienced. I would argue, then, that a strong practical orientation to dominate nature and an intellectual orientation toward gaining cognitive mastery over the world contributed to the American aversion toward ambiguity.

In Ethiopia, on the other hand, a strict conservatism that eschews any departure from inherited techniques and a passive fatalism that declares man's efforts to better himself futile precluded the development of a highly instrumental orientation toward the world. Intellect was applied instrumentally to worldly matters only to the extent

3. This contrast has recently received an important elaboration by Fritjof Capra (1984). Science, writes Capra, "aims for clear definitions and unambiguous connections, and therefore it abstracts language further by limiting the meaning of its words and by standardizing its structure in accordance with the rules of logic." Mystics, by contrast, "well aware of the fact that all verbal descriptions of reality are inaccurate and incomplete [strive for] a direct experience of reality [that] transcends the realm of thought and language" (19, 29).

required by a subsistence standard of living and a minimum of social order. Beyond that, the Amhara mind devoted itself chiefly to contemplating the mysteries of life—and enjoying the subtleties of social intercourse.

Ambiguity and Expressiveness

Univocal verbal communication is designed to be affectively neutral. It aims for the precise representation of fact, technique, or expectation. Univocality works to strip language of its expressive overtones and suggestive allusions.

Ambiguous communication, by contrast, can provide a superb means for conveying affect. By alluding to shared experiences and sentiments verbal associations can express and evoke a wealth of affective responses. The exploitation of ambiguity through wit and jokes can convey a wide array of feelings. The clandestine ambiguities of ironic messages have the capacity to transmit sentiments of enormous power.

Puritanical, utilitarian, commercial, legalistic, and, more recently, bureaucratic and scientific pressures have dried out many of the springs of affectivity in American social intercourse. They have promoted an asceticism in language that in many spheres comes close to defining the indulgence of verbal nuance as a forbidden pleasure.

Traditional Amhara culture exhibits none of those pressures that in the United States have worked to reduce the expression of affect in human communication. Although the Amhara maintain a posture of dignified reserve in most of their social interactions, the subtle expression of affect appears prominently in their social intercourse. Utilitarian or strictly cognitive considerations rarely dominate attention so much that ambiguity is out of place. Whether in the religious constructions of the literati, the political innuendos of lords, the clever repartee of litigants, the improvizations of minstrels, or the banter of soldiers and peasants, "wax and gold" provides a commonly used medium of entertainment. The enjoyment of verbal ambiguities plays a significant role in conversations and stories.

Ambiguity as a Medium of Self-Protection

Univocal expressions enable, if not force, speakers or writers to communicate openly and clearly, and to hold back nothing of their intentions. Ambiguous expressions have the contrary property of enabling their users to conceal, more or less deeply, what is really on their minds. Such concealment may be in the passive vein of withholding information for the sake of privacy or secrecy, or in the more active mode of seeking to deceive others for the sake of tact or some defensive strategy.

One might expect, therefore, to find a marked aversion to ambiguity in societies or groups that place a high value on openness as opposed to secrecy. Secrecy is favored in societies organized on a strongly hierarchical basis. Sharply stratified societies make considerable use of secrecy—elites in order to maintain their privileged status through possession of esoteric knowledge, nonelites in order to defend themselves against intrusive encroachments. Egalitarian societies have an affinity for the value of openness and publicity.

Because of the strongly egalitarian cast of American society, secrecy has typically played a very small part. As Edward Shils has observed, "The United States has been committed to the principle of publicity since its origin" (1956, 37). Communication among Americans is characteristically direct and open. In this century, at least, the thin bastions of privacy have been invaded to the extent that people tend to feel entitled to know what is on everyone else's mind. Americans resent esoteric knowledge of any sort as symptomatic of "undemocratic" snobbishness.

This attitude has been linked to a distinctively American emphasis on univocality in the movement to codify the law. While the tradition of common law inherited from England did not place much weight on clarity and univocality—Blackstone delighted in ambiguity and loved the "mysterious science" of the law—the Jacksonian democrats who sponsored codification saw beneath ambiguity arbitrariness and behind arbitrariness, aristocratic privilege.

Amhara society, by contrast, has been described by all observers as pervaded by a hierarchical ethos, one in which even servants are proud to have servants and where the desire for a title of some sort figures as one of the greatest social passions. And Amhara social structure represents what could be described as an ideal type of "secretogenic" social structure. The nobility have traditionally gained or lost position through notoriously secret intrigues. Literati have maintained their superiority in good part through their monopoly of esoteric knowledge (including the knowledge of how to write). The peasantry have resorted to secrecy, and equivocal and evasive communication, in order to defend themselves against exploitation.

Among the Amhara, accordingly, everyone is assumed to be harboring secrets. The Amhara define a close friend as "someone

with whom one can share secrets." The popularity of wax-and-gold
locutions becomes yet more understandable. Indeed, the word
mistir, often used to designate the "gold" meaning of an obscure
stanza, is in fact the Amharic word for "secret."

One might also expect to find an aversion to ambiguity related to
sentiments that favor the value of impersonal honesty, as opposed to
deception. The extent to which deception is tolerated or even
appreciated in societies or groups reflects, I believe, the degree to
which universalistic standards are institutionalized. The modern
Western notion of truth, along with sincerity and univocality, is a
rare sociological flower. The medieval ideal of truth was not truth as
we know it, in the sense of being in accord with impersonal and
objective standards, but was construed as personal fealty: "being
true" to one's lord or companion. Where particularistic standards
are paramount, there is no obligation for anyone to be honest for the
sake of honesty, and accordingly no generalized sanction against
deception or equivocation as such.

In American society, universally valid moral precepts have taken
precedence over particularistic obligations. This means that cognitive standards have precedence over appreciative standards, and
that in turn entails a concern for intellectual integrity. The American
ethos does in fact idealize intellectual integrity and, closely related
to that, unequivocal communication. This appears, for example, in
popular legends about George Washington and Abraham Lincoln
that portray their exemplary honesty, and in such maxims as
"Honesty is the best policy" and the nearly sacred sense of
obligation to honor the terms of any "deal."

Among the Amhara, where particularistic standards dominate,
integrity as an abstract ideal plays a lesser role. Amhara culture
consequently encourages deceptive modes of communication. Political figures are celebrated not because they "cannot tell a lie," but
for their shrewdness and wit in deceiving opponents. One of the
most notable Amhara culture heros, the nineteenth-century literatus
Aleqa Gabra Hanna, achieved anecdotal fame precisely for his
adroit use of deceptive wax-and-gold equivocations, whether for the
sake of personal gain, to insult others slyly with impunity, to
criticize authorities, or simply to display his virtuosity as a wit.

Deception shades readily into tact and etiquette in personal
relations, and these values seem especially prominent in societies or
groups where particularistic standards are combined with a hierarchical ethos. Particularism implies that consideration of impersonal
honesty must be subordinated to the aesthetics of a personal

relationship, and emphasis on hierarchy means that persons are to be treated according to what fits their status, not according to what they have or have not accomplished. For these reasons, too, ambiguity serves the Amhara well, enabling him to express compliments he does not mean, and avoid direct utterances that might injure the sentiments of others. The contrast with the direct, outspoken, unmannered but honest American could scarcely be more striking.

Ambiguity and Vagueness

Univocal communication has the properties not only of being literal, affectively neutral, and public, it is also precise. Ambiguous expressions, by contrast, can be vague. And vagueness in social intercourse is depreciated when it is important that norms, roles, and beliefs be defined specifically.

Role specificity of an extreme degree has developed in the United States since the middle of the nineteenth century, as a result of extensive occupational specialization and the rationalization of activities in most spheres of life. Job descriptions have come to enumerate in unambiguous terms the duties and facilities appropriate to each office. This simply accentuates a pattern common to all industrialized societies, which rely on a methodical division of the integrated activities of continuously operating offices, on clearly defined spheres of competence, and on a precise enumeration of official responsibilities and prerogatives.

Amhara social organization, by contrast, exhibits a great deal of functional diffuseness. Kinship, political, and religious roles carry multiple functions. The boundaries of responsibilities and prerogatives associated with them are not clearly defined, and there is considerable overlapping among roles. This pattern of diffuseness encourages the vagueness of ambiguity in communication. For example, the term for father, *abbat,* applies equally to one's natural father, guardian father, political lord, religious confessor, and king.

This kind of vagueness, and the social diffuseness it subserves, may be seen to have a kind of socially binding function. That is particularly important in societies of small scale where people carry out their lives with a relatively small number of face-to-face consociates. By contrast, the compartmentalization promoted by functionally specific relationships serves in societies of larger scale and more complex organization to promote the improved performance of specialized roles.

Laitin's analysis of ambiguity in Somali makes a kindred point about the effect of ambiguous locutions in avoiding political confrontations. As mentioned earlier, in traditional Somali political culture debate usually takes the form of highly metaphorical arguments preceded by long circumlocutory introductions. As Laitin sees it, these poetic forms

> serve a very important function in Somali politics; they allow for sufficient public ambiguity concerning the issue at hand as to allow the person who cannot get his way to leave without losing face. In a small scale society, this is most important, because it is very difficult for a clansman to avoid seeing members of his political contract group all the time. (1977, 207)

It is probably impossible for politics to be carried out in any community without the use of ambiguous language. The American system of political parties has long been celebrated for providing an agency through which varieties of special and divisive interests might be aggregated behind relatively vague party orientations.[4] Yet a countercurrent of confrontational politics has been prominent in American political history, and the recent emergence of a politics that defers to groups advocating single, special causes does seem to reflect a deep American commitment to specific, unambiguous claims. This reflects yet another dimension along which American patterns contrast with Amhara culture, where the public articulation of specific interests has never been favored and the art of politics is overwhelmingly an art of nonconfrontational maneuver.

The distinctions I have been making are represented schematically in figures 1 and 2.

Ambiguity and Modernity

I have argued that a predilection for ambiguity appears in most traditional cultures but that in Amhara culture the penchant is manifest to an extraordinary extent. Conversely, I believe that a flight from ambiguity characterizes the culture of most modern

4. In recent studies of the "art of ambiguity" practiced by politicians (which he, however, finds harmful to electoral democracy) Page (1978) has argued that political candidates have deliberate recourse to ambiguous talk, not in response to their perception of the interests pursued by rational actors but as a way to exert strategic control over the types of information and campaign issues they wish to bring before the public.

Figure 1
The Functions of Ambiguous Discourse

	External Realities	Internal Realities
Cultural functions	Enlightenment through intuited indeterminacy	Expressivity through evocative allusions
	(mysticism)	(metaphor)
Social functions	Bonding through diffuseness	Self-protection through opaqueness
	(solidaristic symbolization)	(secrecy, deception)

Figure 2
The Functions of Univocal Discourse

	External Realities	Internal Realities
Cultural functions	Cognitive mastery through determinateness	Disciplined expression through literalness
	(secular science)	(prosaic language)
Social functions	Discrimination through specificity	Self-disclosure through transparency
	(specification of claims)	(publicity, honesty)

societies but that in the United States this tendency has been manifest to an exceptional degree.

The several strands of aversion to ambiguity in the United States recall the special role played by Puritanism in the shaping of American culture. Puritanism worked in many ways to combat the uses of ambiguity. Newtonian science, the great fountainhead of univocality among Enlightenment intellectuals, found support and legitimation in the Puritan ethos, as Merton and others have shown. Puritanism turned the mind from otherworldly orientations and from mysticism, the natural haven for ambiguous thoughtways, to the utilitarian application of intellect to the problems of this world. It discouraged aesthetic pleasures, including the enjoyment of ambiguous figures in repartee. In place of the latter it favored plain talk. Puritanism stressed the moral imperative of honesty and the political imperative of publicity, values that came to be cherished to a remarkable degree in American society.

Apart from what may be considered the distinctive coloring of American culture by the Puritan ethic and by such other factors as the exigencies of frontier settlement and an insistent populism, the fate of ambiguity in the United States probably reflects above all the fact that the institutions and ideals of modern culture are seriously dependent on unambiguous modes of expression. Modern science, technology, commerce, occupational specialization, bureaucratic management, and the formal rationalization of legal procedures and much else are all unthinkable without resources for clear and distinct communication. Insofar as ambiguous patterns are prominent in traditional cultures like that of Ethiopia, they must present an obstacle to the modernizing aspirations of their new elites.

During my sojourn in Ethiopia in the late 1950s I found that tension between traditional proclivities for ambiguity and modern demands for univocality had indeed surfaced as a troublesome issue. I found modern-educated Ethiopians anxious to secure greater clarity in the way that administrative responsibilities were specified. I found an undercurrent of chafing at the devious, equivocal talk that seemed de rigueur for political action of any sort. I found a special sensitivity to cognitive standards and honesty flowing from a certain embarrassment about traditional patterns of deceptiveness. That this issue was on the minds of Ethiopian youth seemed to be indicated by responses to a questionnaire I administered to seven hundred secondary and college students in 1959: when asked to identify the best character trait of all, by far the largest number indicated ''honesty''—a conspicuous departure from traditional norms—and a number mentioned ''honesty'' when asked to name what they would most like their children to have that they did not themselves have.

Regarding the use of the Amharic language itself, I found that many Ethiopians who spoke Amharic regularly at home, and enjoyed the ambiguities of wax-and-gold expressions, often preferred to speak English at work, to avoid what some complained of as the excessive and burdensome subtleties of Amharic. Comparable contrasts have been noted elsewhere; one observer who had access to cabinet meetings in Tanzania noted that the use of English facilitated clear, precise decisions, whereas when the officials spoke Swahili, with its expansive, often imprecise, style of exposition, they often reached less clear decisions.

Also commonly, I found journalists and writers attempting to adapt Amharic to a modern idiom, ''honest, straightforward, sensible, grammatical, and plain.'' Again, changes of this sort have been reported for a number of other modernizing societies, such as Japan—where increasingly strict and precise modes of expression have been grafted onto the traditional, highly ambiguous, Japanese style (Nakamura 1960, 484).

In short, something akin to what I described as the flight from ambiguity seems no less essential to modern societies than the institutions of money and banks, electronic communications, written legal codes, and highway systems. Such a change, however, can be viewed in either of the two ways that any aspect of modernization can be conceived: as a substitutive *replacement* for an outmoded pattern, or as a newly specialized *addition* to a previously less differentiated pattern.

Many of the seminal statements about modernization have viewed it as a process of evolutionary or progressive supersession. Comte viewed theological and metaphysical orientations as archaic forms that would be wholly replaced by the patterns of positive science. Marx imagined that capitalist forms of ownership and production would be wholly replaced by socialized forms. Weber seemed to suggest that traditional forms of authority would be wholly replaced by rational-legal forms, and some followers of Parsons have taken him to imply that particularistic-ascriptive patterns would be superseded by universalistic and achievement patterns in modern societies.[5]

My own view is that the question whether any kind of social change takes the form of A followed by B, or of A followed by a + b, in which the original pattern differentiates into a continuing feature and a contrasting emergent feature, can only be answered empirically. But I think one is justified in taking a skeptical stance toward proponents of some novel form who claim that their new creation has come to replace any prior dispensations, even though belief in the absolute virtue of a new approach often figures in the motivation to pursue it.

In the case of ambiguity, there can be no doubt that the institutions of modern society and culture require an enormous increase in the resources of univocal communication. As our examination of the American case has intimated, univocal discourse serves functions that are indispensable to any high-tech society. Univocal discourse advances our capabilities for gaining cognitive mastery of the world, both by the determinateness that it lends to the representation of external phenomena and the control over internal sentiments by which it disciplines verbal communications. Univocal discourse also provides resources essential to life in complex societies by facilitating the precise designation of specific rights and responsibilities and

5. Mayhew has produced an important critical revision of this Parsonian implication in his "Ascription in Modern Society" (1968).

by constituting a symbolic coinage of the realm—unequivocally understood tokens and measures that are available to a wide public.

On the other hand, if univocality is essential to modernity, ambiguity is no less so. Just as, contrary to the projections of a Comte, a Marx, or a Weber, there remains an important role to be played by theological and metaphysical thinking in regimes dominated by positive science, for private ownership and production in the most socialized of economies, and for primordial ties and traditions of ritual despite a hegemony of rationalized institutions, so, contrary to the projections of a Condorcet, there remain spheres of representation and expression that are best served by the resources of ambiguous language. These spheres include, on the side of interiority, the need for expressivity under a regime of computerese and other formal rationalities, and the need to protect privacy in a world of extended central controls. In the domain of external realities, moreover, these include the need for mediating the experience of community in a society built of highly specialized units, and the persisting need, in a culture informed by disenchanted representations of the external world, for symbolic forms that mediate the experience of transcendent unities.

A theme central to critiques of modern culture in recent decades has been the danger to our humanity posed by the ascendance of a monolithic idiom of language use. Richard Weaver scored this development by bemoaning the triumph of "journalese," characterized by "words of flat signification . . . and with none of the broadly ruminative phrases which have the power to inspire speculation." As Weaver further observed:

> The essential sterility of such a style is one of the surest signs
> we have that modern man is being desiccated. For the 'modern'
> style is at once brash and timid; brash enough to break old
> patterns without thinking, and timid before the tremendous
> evocative and constructive powers immanent in language.
> (1958, 77)

George Orwell could think of no more horrifying denouement for modern man than a language constituted by words to which one and only one specific meaning was permitted. In the last few decades, moreover, the formal rationalities of bureaucratic organization, on the one hand, and high-tech computerism, on the other, have amplified the extension of univocalese to a degree that even the humane mind of a Weaver or the fevered imagination of an Orwell could scarcely conjecture. If the ambition of modern culture to create a fuller life for human beings is to retain full credibility, it must unleash the tremendous evocative and expressive powers immanent in language no less than its capabilities for precise and disinterested representation.

The extension of centralized political control and political technology are fatefully consequential not only for our habits of language use, they make possible an extraordinary degree of surveillance and control over personal lives. In the modern societies where this kind of threat has been realized in its most malignant form, the totalitarian societies of eastern Europe, the ambiguities of oral wit and certain literary genres have provided desperately embraced safety valves. The productions of Polish playwrights, Romanian novelists, and Russian poets have been widely celebrated for facilitating the assertion of personal autonomy under conditions of stark political repression. The much milder version of repressiveness that obtains in modern democratic polities may be countered tonically by comparable ambiguous forms, forms that express the plaint of modern souls against the DO NOT FOLD, MUTILATE, OR SPINDLE mentality.

However much the bureaucratic administration of modern society relies on univocal messages, moreover, modern political communities remain unthinkable without the sinews of ambiguous language. This is true, to begin with, for the fundamental process of modernization itself. The problems of "cultural management" faced by the developing nations have been dealt with only by an almost deliberate effort to exploit the ambiguity of traditional symbols. Time and again the historical record demonstrates the futility of attempting the revolutionary implementation of a clear and distinct ideal in human society. No matter how bold and sweeping the program, traditional patterns persist tenaciously. The only real alternatives are whether they are to be maintained in isolation from the modern culture or whether traditional and modern patterns can be successfully fused to produce a novel synthesis. To my knowledge no one has refuted Almond's (1960) argument that the latter alternative contributes significantly to political stability over time. For that to take place, however, traditional symbols have had to be interpreted with sufficient ambiguity to permit their fusion with modern ones.

The contribution of ambiguity to the process of political modernization is but a special case of the crucial role of ambiguity in the life of all modern political systems. The formal rationalization of law, far from putting an end to ambiguity, has rendered its uses more indispensable than ever. The codification of legal norms, through case law, statutory law, and constitutional law alike, simply provides a complex of verbal formulations that need continuously to be interpreted and reinterpreted. In the words of Edward Levi, "It is only folklore which holds that a statute if clearly written can be completely unambiguous and applied as intended to a specific case" (1948, 6).

The benefits of the inherently ambiguous character of legal rules are twofold. The ambiguity of the categories used in the legal process permits the infusion of new ideas, and thus enables societal regulations to adapt to an inexorably changing environment. And it permits the engagement of parties who submit contending interpretations of legal notions to participate, through the open forum of the court, in the continuous reestablishment of a rule of law that stands as their common property and their warrant of real community. In Levi's analysis,

> If a rule had to be clear before it could be imposed, society would be impossible. The mechanism [of legal reasoning] accepts the differences of views and the ambiguities of words. It provides for the participation of the community in resolving the ambiguity by providing a forum for the discussion of policy in the gap of ambiguity. (1948, 1)

It is not only through the language of the law that ambiguity serves to promote community. In the modern world this takes place preeminently through a style of political language that Murray Edelman describes as "hortatory language." This is a mode of language use in which commonplace terms, like 'justice,' 'freedom,' and 'public interest,' are invoked to elicit the support of particular audiences for certain policies. Edelman finds this style distinctively significant for modern political practice because of the modern emphasis on participation and rationality. "In spite of the almost total ambiguity of the terms employed," he writes, and "regardless of the specific issue discussed, the employment of this language style is accepted as evidence that the public has an important stake and role in political decisions and that reason and the citing of relevant information is the road to discovering the nature of the stake" (1964, 135). Even in a language style that puts a premium on univocal talk, the language of bargaining, Edelman suggests that ambiguity has a role to play, both by permitting a degree of feinting and feeling out of positions in the early stages of negotiation, and by providing a means of getting agreement on unambiguous central issues.

In many ways, then—by enhancing adaptiveness to change, by facilitating negotiation, by mobilizing constituencies for support and for action, by inviting participation in the definition of communal beliefs, by permitting different elements of the polity to share each other's response precisely in situations where conflict would otherwise occur, by providing symbols that are constitutive of the identities of communities of many kinds—ambiguous talk makes modern politics possible. It does so by tempering the assertion of particular interests and parochial understandings with symbols whose common use, in the face of diverse interpretations, provides a mooring for social solidarity and a continuing invitation to engage in communal discourse. And that continuing invitation, finally, engages us as well in quests for meanings that transcend whatever univocal determinations we have achieved at any moment. In the words of my epigraph, "We proceed as if we were faced with a choice between the univocal and the ambiguous, and we come to the discovery . . . that the univocal has its foundations and consequences in ambiguities" (McKeon 1964, 243). Indeed.

3

The Flexibility of
Traditional Cultures

In the previous chapter I depicted the patterning of Amhara and American attitudes toward ambiguity as a contrast between polar types. That mode of representation tends to produce useful empirical insights and theoretical constructions. Yet it runs the risk of leading author and reader to ignore important tendencies in any culture thus depicted that run counter to the dominant patterns so sharply etched. For all their love of ambiguity, the Amhara could not long survive without certain communications they value for being clear, precise, and determinate. For all their aversion to ambiguity, the Americans have enjoyed ambiguous formulations in certain spheres of life; consider the widespread affinity for puns among Americans, an inclination thoroughly incorporated by the advertising and entertainment industries. The danger Merton cited when criticizing the tendency of sociological analysts to confine their attention to the dominant attributes of a role or social relation (1976, 16) inheres a fortiori in characterizations of entire societies or cultural patterns.

We stand particularly vulnerable to that danger when representing cultures that are commonly described as traditional. This is because the ideas we have learned to orient ourselves to traditional cultures incline us to portray them in monochromatic terms.

The Doctrine of Uniformity

Just as the themes of innovation and diversity recur in virtually all discussions of the nature of modernity, so the idea of *sameness* informs most efforts to specify the most general characteristics of traditional culture. The content of a traditional culture is thought to be similar throughout a population, or *uniform*; it is held to be similar over time, or *persistent*. Internally, the parts of a traditional culture are thought to be similar, the culture as a whole integrated, or *consistent*. Much evidence to the contrary notwithstanding, the images of uniformity, persistence, and consistency dominate our perception of traditional cultures.

Such images clearly dominated my own thinking when I set out, some twenty-five years ago, to study tradition and innovation in Ethiopian culture. I felt delighted and relieved to have found among the highland-plateau Amhara, the politically and culturally dominant ethnic group of the country, what appeared to be a pure specimen of an intact traditional culture. While change and diversity were conspicuous in the capital city, rural Amhara preserved a culture that had been virtually the same for a millennium. I set out at once to locate Amhara culture in time and space, and to determine its core content as a base against which to consider the problems of modernization. In so doing, I did not remain blind to variable elements in Amhara culture; but such elements often were set aside in my mind, chiefly because the intellectual constructs I was using to fashion my body of facts oriented me in the opposite direction.

Such constructs inclined me to think, for example, that once I had identified the elements of Amhara culture, it could be presumed that all Amhara shared them. A respectable source for this doctrine was Emile Durkheim, who held it a fundamental characteristic of premodern societies that their members possess the same ideas, sentiments, and values. Durkheim's theory that this common consciousness provides grounds of solidarity in such societies still contains a solid kernel of truth, and the assumption of uniformity had the practical value of assuring me that the lessons learned in one part of Amhara land could be applied in other parts. It was helpful to expect, and convenient to find, the same norms of deference, religious rituals, and poetic forms during briefer forays into Gondar and Gojjam that I had become familiar with during more extended work in Manz.

Yet all told, I was led to conclude that there is more disunity among the Amhara than solidarity, and it is clear that to the Amhara themselves their culture does not appear as a uniformly distributed set of patterns. They see their fellow Amhara as bearers of considerable cultural variety, a variety which sometimes irritates them, sometimes entertains them, sometimes leaves them cold. They make much of nuances of cultural diversity among themselves:

different attitudes toward fasting between the highlanders and lowlanders, differences in norms regarding theft among provinces, differences in ego ideals among families. And even to a dull outsider areas of considerable cultural variation become manifest once the stereotype of uniformity has been cracked.

Sources of Diversity

This variation flows from at least three sources: cultural specialization, competitive accentuation of differences, and differential enculturation.

In any society groups that perform different functions and enjoy different statuses tend to develop somewhat specialized cultural orientations. Nobility, clergy, and peasantry are three such groups in Amhara society. These status groups merge imperceptibly into one another but nonetheless possess distinctive cultural elements. For example, cosmological beliefs of the learned clergy differ in many respects from those of the uneducated. Patterns of morality and etiquette are not the same for nobility and commoners. Linguistic patterns both express and constitute considerable variation of this sort. Amharic is understood from one end of Amhara land to the other, yet to speak of its use as uniform is greatly to exaggerate the case. Church literati known as *dabtara* make use of an ornate and literary style, sometimes referred to as "*dabtara*'s Amharic." The nobleman's use of Amharic is quiet and reserved, the peasant's raucous and aggressive. Still other groups such as minstrels, merchants, and shepherds have evolved their own special argots.

Cultural elements shared by members of a certain status group but not by the whole population are what Ralph Linton (1936) called *Specialties*. Linton maintained that Specialties exist in the most primitive of cultures; they should be expected a fortiori in societies, like that of the Amhara, which have attained what has been called an "intermediate stage" of societal evolution—societies which possess a written tradition that is esoteric and limited to specialized groups (Parsons 1966). For societies of this type, one must at the very least take into account the differences between what Redfield (1956) called the "Great Traditions" and the "Little Traditions" and move on to explore other dimensions of variation between elite and nonelite cultures. Failure to do so has led some observers of Amhara culture to conclude, for example, that the typical Amhara food is a kind of pancake made from a cereal grass called *teff* and mead a frequent beverage, whereas these are typical only for well-to-do strata. Peasants more frequently consume pancakes made of barley and drink, almost exclusively, not mead but barley beer.

Apart from such rather visible and well-established axes of variation, there are other more subtle and spontaneous kinds of cultural variety. There are not only Specialties, but also what Linton called *Alternatives*—traits shared by a number of individuals but not by all, and not even by all members of a recognized status group. Among the Amhara, Alternatives are evident in such areas as poetry, religious doctrines, wedding customs, and customs regarding land tenure.

One might predict that Alternatives of this sort would emerge in any society from the supposition that human aggressive and competitive strivings are universal. In this view certain of my field observations, which at the time seemed only entertaining, now take on greater significance. As I went from one part of Amhara land to another, I often noted that inhabitants of one region sought to distinguish themselves from others by referring to their strong adherence to one or another aspect of Amhara culture. People in one area boasted of their scrupulous respect for the inalienability of land-use rights, others boasted of their distinctively elegant use of Amharic, still others of unusually pious adherence to certain religious practices. In each case, the values in question were associated with a claim to superiority over other Amhara. In other cases, the competition revolved around the most suitable version of some generally accepted cultural form. Thus, canons for the esoteric type of religious poetry known as *qene* are often regarded as standard for all practitioners, yet the masters in different areas have developed distinct styles and approaches to the art. To the casual observer the beliefs and rites of the Ethiopian Church seem quite uniformly accepted, yet Amhara of different regions have waged bitter disputes over subtle doctrinal differences.

A third source of diversity in traditional cultures is that individuals learn the culture of their group in different degrees and in different ways. This point was made dramatically during one of my trips within Manz, a region which prides itself on consistent observance of religious prescriptions for fasting, when I encountered a group of Amhara embroiled in a strenuous argument over whether a certain day was to be observed as a fast day or not. Initially I was stunned—I had already learned what their tradition said on the question, and here they were disputing which alternative was to be preferred! This kind of observation, doubtless familiar to all careful ethnographers, reminds us that the transmission of culture is inher-

ently precarious and never perfect. The very fact that the adult
members of every society have different genetic constitutions and
have grown up in markedly differing family environments guarantees that they will be disposed to make differential selections and
interpretations of any body of culture. As recent work in the field of
human development suggests, moreover, not all members of a
particular society attain the same stage of development with respect
to the internalization of its culture. In sum: cultural elements may be
partially learned, incorrectly learned, or transformed in the learning,
and the degree of confusion over what is proper tradition should
never be underestimated.

The Doctrine of Persistence

Even if one admits a certain amount of cultural variation among
the members of a traditional society, it is possible to perceive that
differentiated culture as relatively persistent over time. The image of
traditional culture as essentially changeless is immediately congruent with stereotypes about Ethiopian culture which have gained
wide currency. These stereotypes were prefigured by Gibbon's
famous line that, following the advent of Islam, "the Ethiopians
slept near a thousand years, forgetful of the world, by whom they
were forgotten." Toynbee went on to categorize the strictly preserved culture of the Amhara as a "fossil in a fastness," remarking
that

> the survival of her Monophysite Christianity in the borderland
> between Islam and paganism, the survival of her Semitic
> language between the Hamitic and Nilotic language-areas, and
> the stagnation of her culture . . . are all peculiarities which
> derive from . . . the virtual impregnability of the
> highland-fastness in which this Monophysite fossil is ensconced
> (1935, 365).

It has been common for other writers (prior to the 1974 revolution)
to refer to Amhara culture as petrified.

Similar pictures have been drawn of other non-Western cultures.
Max Weber may be cited as one source for such an image. Weber
did much to promote the concept of traditionality, and he defined it
in terms of the long-term persistence of culture traits. By traditional
action he meant action that follows long familiar custom; by
traditional authority, that grounded on the sanctity of ancient
norms, norms that "have always existed." This idea of the change-

less character of traditional culture coincided with much that I observed in studying the Amhara. I encountered much resistance among the rural Amhara to innovations proposed by modern-educated men. The customs and beliefs I recorded were remarkably similar to those reported by writers in earlier centuries; I was to find, for example, after noting down some legends in the region of Alo Bahr in Manz that the exact same legends had been reported more than a century earlier by the British missionary Krapf.

Precisely because Amhara tradition lends itself so readily to being described as rigid and petrified, however, one needs to be doubly cautious in adopting the image uncritically. In fact, of course, there are numerous indications of culture change in any century for which we possess documentation, and Toynbee's allegation that Ethiopia is a country without a history can be respected only if it is altered to read: the writer's knowledge of Ethiopian history is incomplete. Of the many grounds for asserting that change is constantly underway in even so apparently changeless a culture as that of the Amhara, I shall mention four: the scope for authoritarian innovation, spontaneous rationalization, diffusion, and the shifting status of cultural complexes.

Sources of Change

One source of change is already implicit in the very notion of traditional authority as conceived by Weber: the scope for free arbitrary action accorded anyone holding authority on a traditional basis. A number of Ethiopian emperors have used this discretionary power to institute or promote changes of considerable significance. The official conversion of the Aksumite kingdom to Christianity in the fourth century was largely due, it seems, to the decision of Emperor Ezana. Zara Yaqob in the fifteenth century altered the face of ecclesiastical ritual by instituting new liturgies and religious holidays, and other emperors have intervened decisively in the reshaping of doctrine. Emperor Iyasu and others at Gondar created the conditions for a notable renascence of religioaesthetic culture, and Menelik in the early years of his reign decreed such innovations as the adoption of smallpox vaccination and the growing of eucalyptus trees. Innovations in official protocol have been decreed at various times and places by authorities at various local levels.

Another way to see how the cake of custom was continually being broken is to regard the interest shown by some Amhara in rationalizing their technology and other cultural resources. To those for

whom Amhara technology reflects unswerving commitment to the
ways of the fathers, Lebna Dengel's urgent appeal to the King of
Portugal for technical assistance in 1527 must seem bewildering:

> I want you to send me men, artificers, to make images, and
> printed books, and swords and arms for all sorts for fighting:
> and also masons and carpenters, and men who make medicine,
> and physicians, and surgeons to cure illnesses; also artificers to
> beat out gold and set it, and goldsmiths and silversmiths, and
> men who know how to extract gold and silver and also copper
> from the veins, and men who can make sheet lead and
> earthenware; and craftsmen of any trades which are necessary
> in kingdoms, also gunsmiths. (Beckingham 1961, 505)

The sentimental attachment to traditional practitioners and folk
medicine notwithstanding, European medical techniques were readily adopted whenever available from the sixteenth century on
(Pankhurst 1965)—by the royal families at least, and these always
provided models for imitation by the nobility and then by others.

In the area of technology that most deeply attracted them, the
Amhara manifested a continuous interest in improving weaponry
through the centuries. The largely correct notion that their painting
was restricted to a highly conventionalized treatment of religious
subjects overlooks significant stylistic changes between the fourteenth and sixteenth centuries and that secular subjects came to be
depicted in a more naturalistic style during the Gondarine period
(seventeenth and eighteenth centuries) and increasingly during the
last century (Chojnacki 1964). And the image of the routine transmission of religious beliefs in Amhara culture is contradicted by the
occasional creation of rationalizing tracts, like the Confession of
Faith which Emperor Galawdeos composed to combat the ideas of
Jesuit missionaries, as well as the oral argumentation addressed to
the defense of theological positions—apologia which not only re-
affirmed but extended and modified existing beliefs.

Isolated though the Amhara have been, they have not been wholly
out of contact with other peoples at any point or impervious to the
diffusion of culture traits. The normal but not exclusive path has
been from the courts of the emperor and highest nobility downward.
Arabic loanwords, Maria Theresa dollars, the use of coffee, and the
acceptance of photography represent a sample of cultural items that
gradually made their way into Amhara culture, often after some
lively initial resistance.

There is, finally, a kind of change in traditional culture which involves not the creation or adoption of new cultural elements but a shifting in the relations among existing elements. Such change is exemplified by the shift toward greater importance of the court clergy over the monastic clergy in the thirteenth and fourteenth centuries, the fluctuating importance of the values associated with the emperor and the imperial court during the last three centuries, and the increased importance of religious and literary values at Gondar during the Gondarine period.

The Doctrine of Consistency

Even if one's focus on traditional society is sharp enough to apprehend change as well as diversity, a fully realistic picture may still be impeded by the conviction that all this variability can be subsumed under certain basic culture patterns, which are closely and harmoniously interwoven. Robert Redfield's conceptualization of the folk society, as one in which "patterns are interrelated in thought and in action with one another, so that one tends to evoke others and to be consistent with the others" (1947, 299), has long inspired such a conviction. Although his ideal type of folk culture was based on analysis of the most primitive isolated tribal community, it has tended to guide much thinking about all premodern societies. Thus Riesman's "tradition-directed" people live in societies marked by a comparatively "tight web of values" (Riesman 1950, 13).

It is tempting to portray the Amhara as having lived in such a beautifully integrated system. And the overwhelming impression that Amhara ecology, social structure, personality, and culture are harmoniously adapted to one another seems to justify an extravagant portrait of that sort. But the aesthetic gratification to be obtained thereby would be gained at the expense of some corner of the truth. It would also be misleading for purposes of analyzing Ethiopia's modernization. A tightly consistent culture must seem both more resistant to change and more fragile when pushed toward modernity than one with many inconsistencies, for inconsistencies provide more bases for leverage toward change and ways of cushioning sudden lurches in the direction of cultural transformation.

Sources of Inconsistency

Even in the most primitive cases, however, there seem to be grounds for arguing that inconsistencies are inevitable. One stems from the concept of culture lag: since change is inexorable, new cultural items are likely to appear which do not fit perfectly with the rest of preexisting culture. Such discrepancy may be illustrated among the Amhara, for example, by the introduction of money and a primitive market economy. Since the prevailing values continued to denigrate the role of the trader, commercial trading has traditionally been restricted largely to non-Amhara.

Apart from the assumption of change, moreover, the general theory of social systems indicates that the diverse functions needed in every society must be supported by values that are ultimately discrepant and not reducible to a single core pattern. Indeed, I would argue that the one-sided and exclusive elaboration of *any* single cultural theme would produce an unworkable system. Of the manifold value conflicts which may be identified in Amhara culture, I shall mention two: aggressiveness versus reconciliation, and piety versus intellectuality.

Masculine aggressive prowess is highly valued among the Amhara. Martial ability, excellence in litigation, and political shrewdness are some of the main forms it takes, and these virtues have been important in maintaining the political and land-tenure systems of the Amhara. The value of aggressive masculinity is inculcated during the socialization of boys and widely celebrated in folk verse and anecdote. But other ideals and norms are upheld which serve to curb the effects of masculine aggressiveness. Fasting, for example, is felt to be a particularly important part of the Amhara round of life, because it curbs the human inclination to be aggressive and provocative. The value of aggressiveness is also counteracted by the ideals of justice and reconciliation, values associated with the teachings of the church and with the activities of elders and judges. The call to be a judge or mediator is one that is hallowed in Amhara custom. These contrasting sets of values are held by the same individuals, who now praise one local ruler because of his toughness and capacity to exploit others, now another because of his sense of justice and ability to neutralize conflicts; now idealize one emperor because of his military achievements, now another because of his Solomonic wisdom and diplomatic finesse.

Among the clergy, certain men are renowned for their mastery of the oral and written traditions of the Ethiopian Church. Through years of study, under conditions of considerable personal privation, they have become adepts in the composition of subtle poetry and interpreters of the great books of Amhara tradition. The Amhara esteem their attainments: witness the many honorific titles indicating grades of comprehension of this intellectual lore. The Amhara remain nonetheless highly ambivalent about such attainment, and a strong anti-intellectual strain is evident in Amhara tradition. This is manifest in such traditional traits as the association of learning with madness, disdain for the practice of writing, and the belief, often justified, that the literati who command this knowledge tend to be men of sensuous indulgence and immoral behavior. Contrasted with the literati are those truly religious men, the pious, both clerical and lay, who typically have little or no learning but are models of ritual observance and ascetic practice. It is an Amhara axiom that the truly religious person does not ask too many questions or probe too deeply into mysteries, which are the province of God and not to be trespassed upon.

Against the model of a highly consistent web of values, then, set the reality of a life where experience of conflicts of value is manifold, constant, and endemic. That this experience is not so troubling for traditional Amhara as for moderns is probably true. The obsessive rationalism of modern culture makes value conflict at best perplexing, at worst abhorrent. The Amhara, and members of other traditional societies, are less involved in such conflict, partly because of a lesser degree of self-consciousness, partly because of a greater capacity for tolerating ambiguity. The latter trait, as we have seen, is developed to an unusually high degree in Amhara culture and appears pronounced in traditional cultures generally, owing to their extensive use of analogical reasoning, metaphorical thought, and equivocal expressions. But the absence of cultural *Angst* should not be taken to indicate the presence of a totally consistent order of meanings, in which, like T. S. Eliot's perfect sentence,

> every word is at home,
> Taking its place to support the others,
> The word neither diffident nor ostentatious,
> An easy commerce of the old and the new,
> The common word exact without vulgarity,
> The formal word precise but not pedantic,
> The complete consort dancing together.

If Amhara culture is at all representative of traditional cultures in these respects, the following propositions should command support:

The contents of premodern culture are not uniformly shared throughout any population. Specialization, competition, individuality, and differential enculturation produce diversity in any culture.

The contents of premodern culture do not persist unchanged. The innovative power of traditional authorities, impulses toward rationalization, diffusion, and the shifting relative status of cultural complexes generate many kinds of change.

The contents of premodern cultures do not form a tightly consistent whole. Culture lag and functional differentiation account for basic inconsistencies in all cultures.

These propositions invite us to reconstruct the basic concepts we use to think about traditional culture. When challenged, no scholar would defend a view of the tradition he or she knows as monolithic and static, but the ideas implanted in our minds about tradition have a life of their own. The tenacity of the old ideas may reflect not only imperfect understanding of traditional cultures, but a regressive need for projecting a simple, undifferentiated state of things onto some external object. Overcoming such a need is part of the maturational process which Westerners must undergo if they are to relate realistically to non-Western cultures. The properties of diversification, change, and complexity which we associate with modernity may represent not so much a revolutionary difference in the human condition as an accentuation of characteristics with which members of premodern societies have always been familiar. To recognize this we must develop new models for analyzing traditional cultures—models which make diversity and flexibility essential, rather than peripheral, aspects of an analytic scheme.

4

Emile Durkheim,
Univocalist Manqué

Emile Durkheim has long figured as an archetype. The first sociologist to exhibit a passion both for theoretical rigor and metric precision, he inspired generations of social scientists driven by a quest for the univocal. Yet perhaps it is time to rethink his meaning as a role model. The figure of Durkheim stands to instruct now less as a priestly exemplar of univocalism than as a hapless prophet of ambiguity: a scientist whose practice diverges from his precepts because his self-understanding reflects an imperfect notion of what he actually professes. No less than his prodigious record of scholarly accomplishment, Durkheim's enduring claim to stature may be said to consist in a heroic embodiment of contradictions endemic in the pursuit of post-Newtonian social science.

Lire le Durkheim

To ask what Durkheim really signifies is scarcely a novel move. The literature does not want for displays of diametrically opposed views of Durkheim held by different authors. We have been shown that some find him a cognitive relativist, others a determined positivist (Gieryn 1982, 108–11); a champion of science, or a moralizing metaphysician (LaCapra 1972, 5); a committed nominalist, or a philosophical realist (Nye and Ashworth 1971); methodologically brilliant or methodologically weak (Pope 1976, 2–4). Durkheim has been defined now as a conservative, now a liberal, now a socialist; now as a friend, now a foe of modern individualism; now an ardent secularist, now a mystical religionist (Lukes 1972, 3).

Some stress the consistency of Durkheim's thought across his career, others find it full of changes (Bellah 1973, xiii).

Divergent readings of this order are by no means unusual for classical authors; the capacity to elicit divergent readings counts as one defining feature of a classic. This is because classics touch on profound themes that resonate varyingly with different readers. Also, classic works—not to say the entire oeuvre of a classic author—are so complex that most readers lack the time and patience to master them more than fragmentarily. Durkheim surely touched on profound themes of modern life—vocationalism, community, moral disorientation, secularization, suicide—in ways that were bound to elicit differing responses. And his oeuvre is sufficiently complex that one might have predicted the epidemic of "one-eyed readings of Durkheim" that Gieryn (or LaCapra, as "partial and highly selective readings") diagnosed. Yet once one has allowed for such points, there remains something naggingly problematic about the experience of reading Durkheim. It is that Durkheim expresses himself—through a rhetoric of univocalism, a way of starting with crisp definitions, a bent for sharply drawn typologies—in a style that leads one to expect his ideas to be distinct and transparent, whereas critical readers have identified an uncommonly ambiguous quality in his thought and writing.[1] Despite Durkheim's emphasis on the need to sanitize scientific discourse by divesting it of the ambiguous words of everyday language, he remained conspicuously oblivious to the multiple meanings he ascribed to his favorite constructs—society, individualism, anomie, social facts. As a result readers find themselves lured into unwarranted confidence in the conclusions advanced by Durkheim and those who build on his work.

Nowhere can this ill effect of Durkheim's ostensible flight from ambiguity be demonstrated more dramatically than in what is often taken as one of the great success stories in the history of sociology, the progressive development of anomie theory from Durkheim to Robert Merton. Merton's "Social Structure and Anomie" has often been described as the most widely quoted paper in the field of

1. Steven Lukes (1972) is particularly adept at detecting this quality. See the many listings under "Ambiguities in Durkheim's Thought" in his Subject Index. The verdict of Charles Tilly is rather harsher: "It turns out that sociologists always have one more version of Durkheim to offer when the last one has failed. It develops that many of the key ideas in Durkheim are either circular or extraordinarily difficult to translate into verifiable propositions. . . . The challenge of refuting Durkheim becomes more difficult and less engaging. Isn't that outcome in itself a serious condemnation of a major sociological tradition?" (1981, 108).

sociology. It has spawned studies that number in the hundreds. Among the notable, and attractive, features of that seminal paper was its claim to represent a line of scholarly continuity with a classic author—notable only because the field of sociology has suffered a peculiarly disjunctive history. After reviewing the relevant writings, however, one may conclude that much of the claimed continuity is questionable and indeed that Durkheim and Merton together introduced considerable confusion into the research tradition concerning anomie at the same time that they created and inspired it.

Ambiguities in Merton's Theory of Anomie

At a panel of the 1977 meetings of the American Sociological Association devoted to reviewing the state of anomie theory and research, each of the four papers presented either asserted or exhibited the fact that lack of consensus about the meaning of anomie was a conspicuous feature of the field. Although two of those papers (Byrne; Johnson and Turner) connected the work of Robert Merton with some of that semantic disarray, this linkage has yet to be systematically examined.

Merton's "Social Structure and Anomie" is the vehicle through which one of Durkheim's most distinctive conceptual contributions made its way into modern sociological research. This paper established what has been called "the dominant paradigm for the study of anomie" (Kytle 1977, 3).[2]

Although years later Merton (1964) would tell us that Durkheim's notion was much on his mind when he composed the first version of "Social Structure and Anomie," on reading the 1938 version now, one is hard put to understand why Merton even used the term anomie in the first place. Although parts of the discussion bear a faint family resemblance to Durkheim's conception of anomie, the notion is not at all thematic in the paper. The paper claims to be and actually is about something rather different: the social-structural pressures toward deviate or nonconformist behavior. 'Anomie' is employed with the utmost casualness in two brief passages, without explication and with no mention of Durkheim. In the second passage Merton implicitly defines the term: "Predictability disappears and what may properly be called cultural chaos or anomie intervenes"

2. This may be one of the few instances where someone has used the word paradigm in a way that corresponds both to Merton's sense of the term and some of Kuhn's key meanings.

(1938, 682). Anomie so understood is in that passage said to be a consequence of the lack of coordination between the "means" and the "goals" phases of social structure.

In the ensuing decades Merton went on to rework that formulation at three junctures (1949, 1957, and 1964). To read that sequence of statements is to find a pattern of steadily increasing semantic confusion combined with an increasingly explicit identification with Durkheim as well as increasing divergence from the main tenets of Durkheim's own theories of anomie and deviant behavior. These different usages of 'anomie' in Merton's writings may be represented schematically as follows:

1. Unpredictability, cultural chaos (1938)
2. Normlessness (1949; 1957)[3]
3. Deviant behavior (1949)[4]
4. Group confusion due to value conflicts (1957)[5]
5. Breakdown in cultural structure; disintegration of value systems (1957)[6]
6. Perceived isolation and inefficacy (1957; relabeled 'anomia' in 1964)[7]

    3. "As this process of attenuation [of institutionally prescribed conduct] continues, the society becomes unstable and there develops what Durkheim called 'anomie' (or normlessness)" ([1949] 1968, 189 [128]). Although this sentence substitutes for the 1938 sentence just cited, it conveys a slightly different notion of anomie: normlessness is similar to but not the same thing as unpredictability or chaos. Note also: "As initially developed by Durkheim, the concept of anomie referred to a condition of relative normlessness in a society or group" ([1957] 1968, 215 [161]).
    4. 'Anomie' and 'deviant behavior' are used interchangeably in the following passage: "The social structure we have examined produces a strain toward anomie and deviant behavior. . . . The strain toward anomie does not operate evenly throughout the society. Some efforts have been made in the present analysis to suggest the strata most vulnerable to the pressures for deviant behavior . . . . Potential deviants may still conform in terms of these auxiliary sets of values. But the central tendencies toward anomie remain" ([1949] 1968, 211–12 [146–47]).
    5. "Simple anomie refers to the state of confusion in a group or society which is subject to conflict between value-systems, resulting in some degree of uneasiness and a sense of separation from the group" ([1957] 1968, 217 [163]).
    6. "Anomie is then conceived as a breakdown in the cultural structure, occurring particularly when there is an acute disjunction between the cultural norms and goals and the socially structured capacities of members of the group to act in accord with them. . . . Acute anomie [refers] to the deterioration and, at the extreme, the disintegration of value-systems, which results in marked anxieties" ([1957] 1968, 216–17 [162–63]).
    7. The scale of anomie "incorporates items referring to the individual's perception of his social environment. . . . More specifically, the five items comprising this preliminary scale refer to (1) the perception that community-leaders are indifferent to

7. A residential condition measured by high delinquency rates and high proportions of nonwhite residents and renters (1957)[8]
8. Estrangement; withdrawal of allegiance from prevailing social standards (1964)[9]
9. Estrangement from goals and rules manifested by others (1964)[10]
10. Aggregation of measures of private estrangement from standards (1964)[11]

Some of these variations pose less difficulty than others. It is hard to believe that Merton meant us to take anomie$_3$ as a serious definition; the context generally makes clear that he intended to present anomie as a cause of deviant behavior, not to make the two notions equivalent. Anomie$_6$ was an attempt to incorporate the anomie scale of Leo Srole, who measured anomie in terms of the individual's perception of being isolated and powerless. Following Srole, Merton later distinguished that phenomenon from anomie by designating it 'anomia.' Anomie$_7$ reflected an effort to find objective indicators for anomie that Merton presented with some reservations, if not with as many as he should have.

---

one's needs; (2) the perception that little can be accomplished in the society which is seen as basically unpredictable and lacking order; (3) the perception that life-goals are receding rather than being realized; (4) a sense of futility; and (5) the conviction that one cannot count on personal associates for social and psychological support" ([1957] 1968, 218 [165]).

8. "Through factor analysis of eight properties of census tracts in an American city, [Bernard Lander] has identified two clusters of variables, one of which he designates as 'an *anomic* factor.' By this he means that this cluster of variables—having the values of a high delinquency rate, a large percentage of non-white residents in the area and a small percentage of dwellings occupied by the owners—seems, on inspection, to characterize areas of relative normlessness and social instability" ([1957] 1968, 218 [165]).

9. "[When] appreciable numbers of people become estranged from a society that promises them in principle what they are denied in reality . . . this withdrawal of allegiance from one or another part of prevailing social standards is what we mean, in the end, by anomie" (1964, 218).

10. "It is not one's private estrangement from the goals and rules laid down by society that constitutes anomie—that, as we have seen, is the individual attribute of anomia—but the visible estrangement from these goals and rules among the others one confronts" (235).

11. "Measures of anomia for individuals in a particular social unit . . . can of course be aggregated to find the rate or proportion having a designated degree of anomia. This aggregated figure would then constitute an index of anomie for the given social unit" (229).

What is most troublesome in these papers is that Merton vacillates between telling us how important it is to distinguish between the psychological and sociological senses of anomie and failing to maintain that distinction. In the 1957 paper, for example, Merton stresses the qualitative distinction between the psychological and sociological meanings of anomie but then on the very next pages presents them as states on a single continuum. On this page he identifies the psychological concept with "simple anomie" ("confusion in a group or society which is subject to conflict between value-systems") and the sociological concept with "acute anomie" ("the deterioration and, at the extreme, the disintegration of value-systems"). This indicates, he observes, that "anomie varies in degree" ([163] 217). But confusion in a group is not transparently a psychological phenomenon, nor does a more extreme version of a psychological phenomenon turn it into a sociological one.

Similarly, in the 1964 paper Merton returns to an insistence that anomie be understood to refer to a property of social systems, not to the state of mind of any individual within the system. In this vein he endorses Srole's move to use 'anomia,' not 'anomie,' as a separate term for referring to an individual's state of mind. Accordingly, Merton contrasts anomia, defined as "one's private estrangement from goals and rules laid down by society," with the more objective condition of anomie, defined now as "the visible estrangement from [society's] goals and rules among the others one confronts" (235). Nevertheless, as though trying to repudiate this subjective/objective distinction before he so cleanly articulates it, Merton proposes a few pages earlier (229) the following operational definition of anomie: anomie is indicated by the aggregation of measures of anomia for the individuals in a collectivity—as though "visible" estrangement were equal to a plurality of private estrangements!

Although Merton failed to acknowledge the ambiguities of anomie in his own work, in the 1964 paper he did express some sense of the ambiguity of the anomie concept in the literature. At one point he questions his own assumption that the concept of anomie is really understood in the same way by practicing sociologists, and goes on to note the "familiar fact" in the use of language that "a word that has not been strictly defined in the first instance tends to become blurred with frequent use" (226).

This pertinent observation leads one to ask: How in fact did Durkheim define anomie? And if anomie was not strictly defined in the first instance, why did Merton—otherwise so scrupulous in his conceptual work—fail to spot that confusion early on and instead treat the concept himself in such an apparently cavalier fashion?

Ambiguity in Durkheim's Theory of Anomie

As Merton was to do some forty years later, Durkheim began a period of original work using the notion of anomie by altering the basic sense of the term as given by a previous sociologist. He adapted it from a French sociologist of religion, Jean Marie Guyau, who used 'moral anomie' to signify the ideals of human dignity and freedom which had come to replace the dogmas of traditional religions. Although Durkheim found much to applaud in Guyau's book on religion—he reviewed it in *Revue philosophique* in 1887— he found Guyau's interpretation too intellectualistic and questioned whether 'moral anomie' could stand as the moral ideal of the future.

In 1893 Durkheim presented his first constructive use of the term in a context dealing with structural differentiation in modern societies. He used 'anomie' to designate a condition where specialized social organs were not in sufficiently close or prolonged contact to permit the spontaneous emergence of norms to regulate their transactions. The paucity or total absence of moral regulations made it easier for those transactions to flare into violence, most notably in the escalated conflicts between capital and labor. In describing the division of labor, anomie signified a state at the low end of a continuum of social regulation; at the other extreme, the forced division of labor signified a condition of excessive regulation. Under anomie, conflict flared because regulation was missing; under the pathology of excessive constraint, conflict was made impossible; under what might be called nomic regulation, Durkheim's idea of a normal state, established norms regulated the expression of conflict.

In later writings Durkheim continued to use anomie to refer to a state of little or no moral regulation. But its more concrete meaning shifted significantly in three respects, namely, with respect to (1) the object of the insufficient regulation; (2) the source of that under-regulation; and (3) the relation of anomie to the conditions of modern life.

In his 1897 book on suicide, Durkheim used anomie to designate the regulation not of social relations among groups, but of passions within individual actors. In *Suicide* Durkheim linked the weakness of regulatory norms with an expansion of individual desires, a condition of insatiable appetite that induced intense unhappiness. The anomic malaise discussed in *Suicide,* moreover, manifested itself not as the failure of novel structures to develop new norms, but either as the ineffectuality of existing norms under drastically altered circumstances, or else as the introduction of new values that embody a high degree of permissiveness. Anomie produced by the obsolescence of norms was illustrated by situations in which individuals suddenly cast into a lower social position find themselves habituated to old norms that are too loose to help them accommodate to the level of self-restraint they now must practice. Durkheim also illustrated the concept by cases where individuals are propelled abruptly into a higher social position, possessing such power and wealth that they no longer feel bound by previous moral limits and find no ready scale of values to curb new appetites stimulated by their rise in fortune. A rather different type of anomie appears in two other cases Durkheim considers—'conjugal anomie' and the chronic anomie of modern trade and industry. In these cases it is neither the absence of norms nor the obsolescence of norms that constitutes anomie; rather, it is a shift in the content of the values embodied in existing norms. Conjugal anomie, for Durkheim, refers to a state where the regulation of individual passions becomes weakened because the legalization of divorce has the effect of weakening the institution of marriage. The chronic anomie of trade and industry refers to the liberation of the economy from the constraints of religion, state, and guild. This has produced an economic system guided only by an endless quest for greater prosperity, such that the desire for constant improvements in the standard of living has become legitimized; a society where "the doctrine of the most ruthless and swift progress has become an article of faith" (1951, 257).

Durkheim's view of the relation between anomie and modern society also shifted somewhat between 1893 and 1897. In considering the anomic division of labor Durkheim held that anomie simply reflected the lag between the emergence of new structures and the creation of suitable norms governing their relations. His expectation was that in due course such norms would evolve; the anomic division of labor was a temporary abnormality, a symptom of growth. Yet in considering the anomie of trade and industry in *Suicide,* he observed that the moral state of wishing constantly to improve one's economic condition had come to be considered normal by society. Indeed, describing the modern era as one in which men are inoculated with the precept that their duty is to progress, he observed that "the entire morality of progress and perfection is thus inseparable from a certain amount of anomie"

(1951, 364). Excessive anomie, leading to surging suicide rates, was abnormal; but some core of anomic orientations had to be viewed as a normal feature of modern industrial society. In the 1902 preface to *The Division of Social Labor,* however, Durkheim reverted to the strong view of anomie as pathological, and to a view of its object as social relations rather than individual passions: "if anomy is an evil, it is above all because society suffers from it, being unable to live without cohesion and regularity" (1933, 5); yet in this passage he altered its sense once again, defining it here as a consequence of "unprecise and inconsistent" regulation, rather than of not yet emergent, obsolete, or substantively permissive norms.

Enough has been said to indicate some of the main ambiguities in Durkheim's conceptualization of anomie. He used it interchangeably to refer to the deregulation of intrapersonal desires as well as intergroup relations, although it is clear, for example, that employers and employees whose relationships have not been institutionally regularized can as personalities be morally regulated, and that psychopathic individuals can function in social relationships that are subject to institutionalized norms. He defined anomie now in terms of the absence of norms, now as the obsolescence of norms, now the presence of permissive norms, now the presence of inconsistent or imprecise norms. He viewed it as a pathological abnormality but also to some extent as a normal feature of modern industrial society.

The vagaries of Durkheim's interpretation of anomie have troubled some readers. They did not appear problematic to Merton. This was scarcely because of any tendency toward conceptual fuzziness on Merton's part. On other topics—when analyzing functionalism, constructing his paradigm for the sociology of knowledge, formalizing reference group theory, or formulating propositions in the sociology of science—Merton has proved circumspect to a fault when treating classic authors and conceptual issues. Perhaps Merton was more casual than usual when dealing with Durkheim's discussion of anomie because he did not want to be constrained by the context which a more painstaking dissection of the Durkheimian passages would necessarily have imposed. Just as Durkheim recast Guyau's notion of moral anomie in order to launch into his own project of diagnosing the moral malaise of Western civilization, so Merton may have needed to recast Durkheim's conception of anomie in order to launch his own project of diagnosing the structural pressures toward deviant behavior in modern American society.

In the course of this effort, at any rate, Merton produced
formulations that deviated from Durkheim's views in three significant respects—without noting that he was in fact doing so. First,
whereas Durkheim repeatedly argued that the commission of crime
was a socially normal phenomenon, properly understood as symptomatic of an intact moral order, Merton preferred to view crime and
other forms of deviant conduct as symptoms of a condition of
normlessness. Second, where Durkheim viewed the modern malady
of infinite strivings as an expression of chaotic impulsiveness,
Merton rejected any instinctual grounding for appetitive strivings
and considered such a malady to reflect only culturally transmitted
goals.[12] Third, what became for Merton the primary dynamic in the
relation of anomie to deviant behavior—frustration from constricted
opportunities faced by those oriented to the pursuit of secular
rewards—was in no way a manifestation of anomie as Durkheim
viewed it. Rather, constricted opportunities represented forms of
excessive constraint that Durkheim depicted as polar opposites of
anomie: the forced division of labor and the fatalistic type of suicide.
If Merton finally located the social problem of anomie in the
estrangement from prevailing social standards, Durkheim saw that
problem as the *absence* of prevailing standards.

At the time he first wrote "Social Structure and Anomie," Merton
later recalled, he found himself stimulated by Durkheim's analysis
and determined to extend Durkheim's seminal ideas by "construing
systematically the character of anomie in terms of social and cultural
variables" (1964, 215). Given this intention, it is conceivable that
Merton might have had some reason not to deal as fully as would
now seem indicated with the contradictions between his own

12. To be sure, one could read Merton as hinting at some divergence from
Durkheim on this point when he opens the 1938 version of "Social Structure and
Anomie" by criticizing the tendency in sociological theory to attribute the mal-
functioning of social structure "primarily to those of man's imperious biological
drives which are not adequately restrained by social control." One suspects,
however, that Merton was alluding to sociologists influenced by Freudian theory at
the time, and that he was interpreting Durkheim as a source of support for his
emphasis on the societal structuring of human goals. Although certain passages in
Durkheim lend themselves to such an interpretation—as when he insists that notions
about what constitutes luxury vary with the moral ideas of society—I consider
Durkheim's dominant argument to place more stress on the psychobiological foundations of desire, as when he speaks of a "natural erethism" or of the adult male's need
for marriage because "the unmarried man . . . aspires to everything and is satisfied
with nothing," and more generally when he contrasts our "egoistic . . . sensory
appetites" to those moral controls that emanate from society (1951, 253, 271; [1914]
1960).

formulations and those of Durkheim. Merton and those who followed him paid a high price for that inattention. Above all, perhaps,
they found themselves chronically beset by a tendency to vacillate
between construing anomie now in psychological terms and now in
social-structural terms. And yet, even though in some strict sense
the principle of cumulative inquiry suffered in the process, Merton
did succeed in producing an original, insightful, and seminal formulation regarding the sources and directions of deviant behavior by
drawing on Durkheim in a way that misconstrued him.

Let us turn now to examine the question of what it was about
Durkheim's formulations of anomie that enabled Merton to deal so
casually with them. Otherwise put: Why did Durkheim not strictly
define anomie in the first instance and thereby impose greater
stringency on the manner in which subsequent scholars would
represent his ideas?

The Strain toward Ambiguity in Durkheim's Thought

It should be noted, first of all, that anomie was one of a small
cluster of related concepts that circumscribed the central core of
Durkheim's entire research program. These included the terms
'society,' 'individualism,' and 'social fact,' whose multiple ambiguities Steven Lukes has so perspicuously dissected. These notions
figure no less prominently in Durkheim's practical aspirations than
in his theoretical work. Indeed, Stephen Marks has plausibly argued
that much of Durkheim's intellectual program during his last two
decades related to a quest "to discover fruitful ways to engineer the
crisis of anomie out of existence" (1974, 330).

Concepts in which thinkers invest so heavily are bound to carry a
number of meanings. This follows from the fact that the more
involved persons are with any sort of object, the more meanings that
object will have for them. In the intellectual domain it stands to
reason that the more intense our involvement with a certain idea, the
greater the semantic load terms used to carry that idea will have to
bear. The load may get so heavy that some of those meanings come
to be distributed to other terms. This is analogous to what often
transpires in interpersonal transactions, where sociolinguists have
observed that the more intense and intimate the relationship between two people, the greater the number of discrete terms of
address they employ when talking to one another. Thus, someone
preoccupied with the notion of freedom may come to assign some of

its various meanings to related terms such as 'liberty,' 'autonomy,' 'independence,' or 'liberation.' More often, however, the very same term is likely to be used to carry a whole raft of differing meanings.

That their central terms have been highly polysemous has been true, I dare say, for every major figure in the sociological tradition. This was the case for Simmel with his concept of forms, for example, and for Weber with his concept of rationality. Unlike Durkheim, both Simmel and Weber expressed awareness of the ambiguity of their central notions. Durkheim differed from them because he was committed to an ethic of univocalism and because he subscribed to the syllogism:

To be scientific means to be univocal;
I am a scientist;
therefore my formulations are univocal.

There is more, however, to the ambiguity of Durkheim's conception of anomie and related concepts than his failure to realize their inexorably polysemous character. The ambiguous character of Durkheim's work was in fact overdetermined. This is so in two senses I shall consider here, one substantive and the other epistemological.[13] The substantive source of the pervasive ambiguities in Durkheim's thought was the complicated meaning that the notion of society held for him. It has been said that the symbolism of *la société* had such an intoxicating effect on Durkheim's mind that it hindered clear analysis. If so, the vulnerability was inherited. Intoxication over the concept of society marks a long tradition of French social thought which Durkheim merely codified and extended. In a paradigmatic earlier synthesis, Auguste Comte had combined three heady brews, all of which reflect a passion for 'society' among French writers and which together produced a perennially confusing potion.

The first, derived from Montesquieu, was ontological. It may be termed the postulate of *social realism*. This was the notion that 'society' refers to a distinct order of phenomena with determinate properties that cannot be identified and explained merely by reference to the properties of individual actors.

13. There may well be other reasons. Lukes suggests that Durkheim's embattled desire to advance the claims of sociology as a science expressed itself in a reliance on metaphors for social phenomena drawn from thermodynamics and electricity, metaphors which actually led him to misrepresent his own ideas and confuse his readers (1972, 34–36).

The second, articulated by Rousseau, was social-psychological. It may be termed the postulate of *social morality*. This was the notion that the nature of human individuals is such that they are animated by the pressure of biological appetites and egoistic strivings, and that it is through the agency of 'society,' and that alone, that they are imbued with moral propensities as well.

The third argument, derived from Condorcet,[14] was ethical. It may be termed the postulate of *societal normality*. This was the notion that the proper criterion for moral judgments is the appropriateness of a given practice or institution for the scientifically ascertained normal state of a determinate stage of development.

These primitive notions were each developed in a more differentiated and focused manner by Durkheim. Indeed, one can say that each of the three central ideas I have posited as the theoretical core of the French tradition became the rhetorical focus of Durkheim's argument in his three major substantive monographs. The postulate of social realism was clearly the enveloping theme of *Suicide,* which begins by identifying an explanandum, suicide rates, as constituting a type of fact that represents, both in its constancy and its variability, distinctive properties that can only be identified at the societal level of analysis; reviews a series of extrasocial and social factors that might be hypothesized to account for variations in suicide rates; and concludes by asserting the demonstrated superiority of explanations that adduce strictly social causative factors.

The postulate of social morality was the more general theme of Durkheim's last monograph, on religion, as of a number of related writings from his later years. In pursuing the question of what are the essential characteristics of the religious beliefs and practices of Australian tribesmen, he came to argue that just as society provides both the object to which religious symbols ultimately refer and the set of forces that predispose humans to create and revere such symbolism, so society constitutes the reference point of moral beliefs and sentiments and the agency for inculcating them in otherwise nonmoral organisms.

The postulate of societal normality formed the rhetorical focus of *The Division of Social Labor.* Holding that the principal objective of every science of life is to define and explain the normal state and to distinguish it from pathological states, Durkheim sought in his first

14. Durkheim himself would later credit Montesquieu for having demonstrated the need to ground morality in the character of a given state of societal organization, just as he acknowledged Montesquieu for having laid, by his conception of social realism, the groundwork for sociology by determining its subject matter, nature, and method.

substantive monograph to determine whether or not high levels of specialization were morally supportable by asking two questions: Does the division of labor contribute to the well-being of society, and do phenomena associated with the division of labor that are commonly considered objectionable represent normal or pathological conditions? Durkheim's aim in that work was to demonstrate that moral questions could be treated in a superior manner through positive science, one which examined types of societies and determined their normal and pathological states. He sought to correct Montesquieu's view that some types of societal organization are intrinsically abnormal by eliminating normative criteria outside the societal level and thus arguing that each type of social organization has its own perfect form, which is equal in rank to the perfect form of the other types.

If it is true that Durkheim's three principal books are devoted respectively to each of what I have called the three central postulates of the French tradition of social thought, it is also true that Durkheim was himself devoted to all three throughout his career. This multiple commitment resulted not only in a chronically ambiguous conception of society and social facts, but in a duality of purpose that accounts for what have often been cited as contradictory tendencies in Durkheim's thought.

The nub of the matter is that Durkheim ran into contradictions by relating these postulates to his perception that the Europeans of his day exhibited an abnormal deficiency in the moral regulation of their personalities. They were afflicted by desires freed of all restraints— the malady of infinite aspiration, which could be nothing but "a source of constant anguish" (1973, 40). From the postulate of social morality, Durkheim derived the argument that the only way to instill a new order of moral regulation was to enhance the attachment of individuals to their local groups and societies. To do that in a rationalistic era meant that the reality of society as a naturally given entity had to be scientifically demonstrated. It is this point that accounts for the urgency with which Durkheim defends the scientific character of sociological investigations. As with Comte, his insistent "positivism" reflected the wish not merely to establish a respectable place for sociology in the academy, but seriously to use the authority of science to attract allegiance to society and its moral imperatives:

Moral behavior has as its end entities that are superior to the individual, but that are also empirical and natural—as are

minerals and organisms. These entities are societies. Societies
are part of nature. . . . We can only dedicate ourselves to
society if we see in it a moral power more elevated than
ourselves. But if the individual is the only real thing in society,
whence could it derive that dignity and superiority? (1973, 266,
257)

The notion of social facts was the main vehicle Durkheim used to
drive home the scientific validity of societal realities. But Durkheim
meant different things by the notion of social fact. At times he used
it to signify institutionalized norms; at other times, to denote
aggregated properties of individuals. Although the former sense
better represented what he had in mind, by referring to society as an
emergent order of reality, the latter sense, because of its quantitative character, enabled him to make the most scientifically persuasive case for social realism. It was the stability of the rank order of
the suicide rates of different nations over decades that Durkheim
cited to establish conclusively the reality of social facts.

Because he moved back and forth indiscriminately in these two
different ways of representing social facts, it was natural for him to
move back and forth casually between construing anomie as a
property of poorly institutionalized social relationships and anomie
as a distributional property of deregulated individuals. This is a
confusion that Merton would repeat decades later by viewing
anomie now as a condition of the cultural structure, now as an
aggregation of individual measures of anomia.

What is more, Durkheim's commitment to a rhetoric of scientific
naturalism constrained him to make an effort to find objective
indicators when applying the postulate of societal normality. In
attempting to decide whether or not modern anomie was pathological, then, he had to ask whether it was an unavoidable characteristic
of life within the species of society found in modern Western
Europe. His conclusion:

Among peoples where progress is and should be rapid, rules
restraining individuals must be sufficiently pliable and
malleable. . . . As soon as men are inoculated with the precept
that their duty is to progress, it is harder to make them accept
resignation. . . . The entire morality of progress and perfection
is thus inseparable from a certain amount of anomy. (1951, 364)

Thus the imperatives of social realism and societal normality
constrained Durkheim to see modern anomie as a relatively normal
phenomenon, at the same time that his sense of the need for the

internalization of social norms as a condition of adequate individual
functioning made him protest again and again about the evils of the
anomic malady of infinite aspirations.

It was not simple carelessness, then, that accounts for the
pervasive ambiguity of Durkheim's key terms. It was a culturally
rooted infatuation with the notion of society that endowed it with an
abundance of meanings, plural meanings that invariably became
attached as well to any related terms. And it was that same
infatuation, finally, that may illuminate what might be called an
epistemological determination of ambiguity in Durkheim—an internal resistance, based ultimately on a commitment to social realism,
to his own program for univocal antisepsis.

For if it was Durkheim who stood out among the founders of
modern social science for his concern about reducing the fuzziness
of sociological concepts, it was none other than he who first
proclaimed the social *dangers* of carrying such a policy too far. The
fact is, Durkheim asserted in his lectures on moral education, that

> there is a turn of mind which is an extremely serious obstacle in
> the formation of the feeling of solidarity . . . it is something we
> might call oversimplified rationalism. This state of mind is
> characterized by the fundamental tendency to consider as real
> in this world only that which is perfectly simple and so poor
> and denuded in qualities and properties that reason can grasp it
> at a glance and conceive of it in a luminous representation,
> analogous to that which we have in grasping mathematical
> matters. . . . In modern times, Descartes has been the most
> illustrious and distinguished exponent of this attitude. Indeed,
> we know that for Descartes nothing is real unless it can be
> clearly conceptualized . . . and that for him nothing can fulfill
> this function if it cannot be reduced to mathematical simplicity.
> (1973, 250–51)

Durkheim went on in this lecture to score this Cartesian penchant
for oversimplification for having become an integral element of the
French mind, and to stress the threat it posed to moral practice by
hindering the appreciation of society as an "enormously complex
whole." In his view, the teaching of science could be a signal
corrective in countering this "dangerous view of reality." From that
it followed that a primary mission of sociology would be to replace
the mental construct of "a system of mathematical points" with a
view of society as "tangled complexes of properties that interpenetrate each other" (250).

Again, if it was Durkheim who instructed social scientists to make a *tabula rasa* of the notions of social facts they had formed in the course of their lives, and to circumvent ambiguity by methodically circumscribing the order of things of which they intended to speak, so too it was Durkheim who acknowledged that this was an utterly unrealistic policy and that the words of everyday discourse, albeit ambiguous, contained a fundament of wisdom:

> We must not lose sight of the fact that even today the great majority of the concepts which we use are not methodically constituted; we get them from language, that is to say, from common experience, without submitting them to any criticism. The scientifically elaborated and criticized concepts are always in the very slight minority. Also, between them and those which draw all their authority from the fact that they are collective, there are only differences of degree. A collectivity representation presents guarantees of objectivity by the fact that it is collective: for it is not without sufficient reason that it has been able to generalize and maintain itself with persistence. (1915, 486)

Finally, if it was Durkheim who proclaimed that it was desirable and possible to define scientific terms in such a way that they correspond to the intrinsic properties of real things, and to establish taxonomic systems that reflect the "most essential characteristics" of species being classified (1938, 80), so it was Durkheim who first dared to develop the notion that the social construction of the forms of understanding extend even to the precincts of science itself. So, too, it was he who pointed out that the same "social fact may be characterized in several different ways" and that "it is only important to choose that characteristic which appears the best for one's purpose; and it is even quite possible to use, concurrently, several criteria, according to the circumstances" (1938, liv).

In reaching, like Comte, for a rigorously positive scientific approach in order to compel belief in the reality of a naturally existing supraindividual entity, Durkheim found himself committed to a rhetoric for social science that appealed for clear and distinct conceptions, fresh definitions of terms, and the correspondence of such terms to real things. Yet the actual properties of that supraindividual entity he so loved turned out to be such that its complexity made it refractory to Cartesian simplifications, and its natural expressions in the form of collective representations comprised linguistic terms that were tenacious as they were full of sense, and produced social constructs that finally constituted the ultimate categories of scientific understanding.

As Nye and Ashworth observed when commenting on Durkheim's entrapment within another philosophical dualism, "Even if we do define Durkheim as a failure we ourselves who live in his shadow can take no credit for having 'gone beyond' him" (1971, 146). Perhaps it is time to define Durkheim as a success for showing us the irrefutable claims of both univocality and ambiguity in our discourse about society, and time for us to learn how to enjoy their dialectical tension.

5

Useful Confusions
Simmel's Stranger and His Followers

Owing to the undisciplined way in which classic authors have been incorporated into American sociology, their works often suffer distortions of two types. They have been criticized or even rejected out of hand simply when certain of their statements have been treated in isolation or patently misunderstood. Conversely, they have been cited as authorities for ideas that deviate from anything they have written, through a process sometimes glamorized as "inventive misinterpretation." One need not search long to find both kinds of distortions associated with such famous constructs as Comte's 'positivism,' Marx's 'alienation,' Toennies' *'Gemeinschaft,'* Durkheim's 'anomie,' and Weber's 'charisma' or 'bureaucracy.'

The aim of what follows is not to bemoan such abuses (which, after all, are but local instances of the universal and inexorable process of misunderstanding in human relations) but to show—through inspection of a case involving selections from the literature related to Georg Simmel—how such distortions and the confusions they produce can yield points of departure for fruitful theoretical developments.

Out of a total corpus equivalent to some fifteen volumes, Simmel is perhaps most widely known among anglophone social scientists for his six-page excursus on "the stranger." What is less well known is that this "classic essay" originally appeared as a note, a mere digression, in a long chapter on "Space and the Spatial Ordering of Society" (1908, chap. 9). Yet while the short excursus has been translated more often than any other of Simmel's writings, the bulk of the chapter from which it is drawn—a pioneering analysis of the

ways in which the properties of physical space provide both
conditions for and symbolic representations of different types of
social interaction—has still not been translated into English. Nor
has it, to my knowledge, been drawn upon in the recent upsurge of
scientific work in proxemics, the study of spatial relations. The
excursus itself, however, as a stimulus both to studies on the role of
the stranger and to work on the related concept of social distance,
has probably been cited more often than any other of Simmel's
writings. Such citations occur in nearly every methodological genre,
from ethnographic reportage, cross-cultural comparison, and historical reconstruction to laboratory experiment, survey research,
and mathematical model building. The abundance of materials in
this literature might give the impression of a rigorous and cumulative
tradition of inquiry, an impression conveyed by Alex Inkeles when
he wrote some years ago that there exists "a special and well-
developed sociology of the stranger" (1964, 12).

Careful inspection of that literature reveals a different picture. Far
from the superbly critical treatment of Simmel's work which one
finds in Coser's formalization of Simmel's chapter on conflict,
Hazelrigg's analysis of Simmel's propositions on secret societies,
Mills's conversion of Simmel's ideas into hypotheses about small
groups, or Merton's selective incorporation of Simmel's conceptions about group properties in general, one finds in the literature
that draws on the excursus, both treatments of social distance and of
the stranger proper, a sprawling and confused assortment of statements (an illustration, perhaps, of the special advantage which
latecomers, in science as in technological modernization, have over
early birds, since the exemplary scholars to whom I just referred did
their work on Simmel a good quarter-century after the traditions of
research on the stranger and social distance had been established).

Ambiguities in the Reception of Simmel's Essay
on the Stranger

The literature on the stranger exhibits four distinct areas of
confusion. First, Simmel's concept of the stranger has been equated
periodically with the "marginal man," which signifies a quite
different social type. Second, his concept has often been identified
with the newly arrived outsider, another distinctly different type.
Third, his analysis of the role of the individual stranger has been
taken indiscriminately to refer to ethnic communities as well.
Fourth, the significance of the variety of ways in which Simmel used

the metaphor of simultaneous closeness and remoteness has been obscured. Let me now document each of these points briefly and then suggest how clarification of these issues can lead to more interesting theory in this area.

The first of these confusions was created by Robert E. Park, a man who did more than anyone else to make Simmel's work known in American sociology in the 1920s and, indeed, produced the first English translation of "Der Fremde." In his seminal essay "Human Migration and the Marginal Man" Park cited Simmel's definition of the stranger and proceeded to delineate a concept of the marginal man as its equivalent—an equivalence illustrated by his remark that "the emancipated Jew was, and is, historically and typically the marginal man. . . . He is, par excellence, the 'stranger,' whom Simmel, himself a Jew, has described with such profound insight and understanding" (Park 1928, 892). Commenting on this adaptation, Alvin Boskoff observed that

> Park borrowed the concept of the stranger [from Simmel] and applied it to the phenomena of migration and culture contact in complex society. Briefly, Park suggested that various kinds of deviant behavior (crime, delinquency, illegitimacy) reflected the experience of persons who, by migrating, had given up old values but had not adequately acquired the norms and skills of their new setting. (1969, 282–83)

It should be clear, however, that in the borrowing Park altered the shape of the concept: his "marginal man" represents a configuration notably different from Simmel's "stranger." Thinking of the experience of ethnic minorities in zones of culture contact in American cities, Park conceived the marginal man as a racial or cultural hybrid—"one who lives in two worlds, in both of which he is more or less of a stranger"—one who aspires to but is excluded from full membership in a new group. Simmel's stranger, by contrast, does not aspire to be assimilated; he is a potential wanderer, one who has not quite got over the freedom of coming and going. Where Park's excluded marginal man was depicted as suffering from spiritual instability, intensified self-consciousness, restlessness, and malaise, Simmel's stranger, occupying a determinate position in relation to the group, was depicted as a successful trader, a judge, and a trusted confidant.

In an extended study of marginal men Park's student Everett Stonequist indicated his awareness that Park's marginal man was not identical with Simmel's stranger. He observed, first, that marginality need not be produced by migration, but could also come about through internal changes like education and marriage. More explicitly, he stated:

> The stranger, [Simmel] writes, first appears as a trader, one who is not fixed in space, yet settles for a time in the community—a "potential wanderer." He unites in his person the qualities of "nearness and remoteness, concern and indifference." . . . This conception of the stranger pictures him as one who is not intimately and personally concerned with the social life about him. *His relative detachment frees him from the self-consciousness, the concern for status, and the divided loyalties of the marginal man.* (1937, 177–78; emphasis mine)

Stonequist went on to note that the distinctive properties of the stranger identified by Simmel are lost if an individual moves into the position of being a marginal person.

In spite of Stonequist's clarity, a tendency to confuse the marginal man with Simmel's stranger persisted.[1] Thus, more than a decade later, Hughes uncritically repeated Park's view that Simmel's passages on the stranger referred to the phenomenon of the marginal man. Boskoff, with comparable carelessness, glossed Simmel's stranger as "vulnerable to internal uncertainties" (1969, 282). Seeking to "reexamine the ubiquitous concept of 'marginal man,'" Peter Rose did so by asking "how the 'stranger' in the midst of alien territory adapts to community life." After interviewing exurban Jews in several small towns of upstate New York, Rose concluded that their position could be described more aptly as one of duality than as one of marginality; for they felt "we have the best of both." Rose thought his findings refuted the view of "Stonequist [sic], Park and others who have characterized the Jew as a disturbed marginal man, an eternal stranger [here Rose footnotes Simmel!] unable to reconcile the traditions of his people with the counterforces of the majority world" (1967, 472). In making this point, Rose, like Hughes and Boskoff, was misreading Simmel through Park's distorting lens. What he in fact found was that the Jews in question were not adequately characterized by Park's concept of marginality but that they might indeed be characterized in terms of Simmel's concept of the stranger.

1. One exception to this tendency was Ernest Mowrer's *Disorganization: Personal and Social* (J. B. Lippincott 1942), whose chapter "The Nonconformist and the Rebel" faithfully reproduces Stonequist's distinction between strangers and marginal men.

If Stonequist's distinction between marginality and strangerhood was made only to be lost, it was inadvertently recovered by Paul C. P. Siu. In his investigation of Chinese laundrymen in Chicago, originally carried out as a study of "marginality," Siu was dismayed to find that "none of the Chinese laundrymen I studied could be considered a marginal man." In this case, however, Siu did not use those findings to invalidate Simmel's concept of the stranger. Rather, he returned to Simmel to raise the question whether the marginal man might not more aptly be viewed as one of many possible variant types of stranger. Siu then proposed a new type, the sojourner—who, in contrast to the bicultural complex of the marginal man, clings to the culture of his own ethnic group—adding a few notes on still another type of stranger, the settler (1952, 34–44). The way was thus opened for a more differentiated view of phenomena previously lumped together under the diffuse categories of strangerhood or marginality.

A related step, albeit in a different direction, had been taken around the time of Stonequist's study. Margaret Mary Wood's *The Stranger: A Study in Social Relationships* drew freely on Simmel, but adopted a definition that was clearly differentiated from Simmel's:

> We shall describe the stranger as one who has come into face-to-face contact with the group for the first time. This concept is broader than that of Simmel, who defines the stranger as "the man who comes today and stays tomorrow, the potential wanderer, who although he has gone no further, has not quite got over the freedom of coming and going." For us the stranger may be, as with Simmel, a potential wanderer, but he may also be a wanderer who comes today and goes tomorrow, or he may come today and remain with us permanently. (1934, 43–44)

In other words, Wood's topic was not the sojourner but the newly arrived outsider, and her concern was with those internal adjustments by which different types of groups adapt to his arrival in their midst. Her work might well have laid the groundwork for an extensive sociology of the stranger, in which Simmel's formulations would properly have been understood as referring to a special type; but, as McLemore (1970) stresses in a spirited review of some of the literature related to Simmel's essay, subsequent sociologists of the stranger continued to cite Simmel as the primary point of reference for the topic and, even when citing Wood, tended to miss the distinction between Wood's newly arrived outsider and Simmel's stranger. Thus Greifer, in the course of reconstructing the evolution of ancient Jewish attitudes toward the stranger, defines the stranger as one who "has come into face to face contact with the group for the first time," and in the next sentence refers to this stranger "*as described by Georg Simmel*" (1945, 739; emphasis mine); Grusky (1960) similarly confuses the new arrival with Simmel's stranger by using the latter concept in describing the position of a newcomer in a line of administrative succession.

In this context, it is instructive to examine an experimental study which claims to draw inspiration from Simmel, "The Stranger in Laboratory Culture." In this study Nash and Wolfe (1957) sought to create in an experimental setting a role which approximated Simmel's description of the stranger. However, the hypothesis they tested sprang from the ideas of Park, Stonequist, and others concerning the peculiar creativity of the marginal man. What they found was that "strangers" proved to be less innovative than other participants in the experiment. In spite of its experimental rigor the value of this study is limited by a double conceptual confusion. It seeks to verify Simmel's formulations about the stranger by using hypotheses devised, not by Simmel, but by others concerned with a different social type, the marginal man; and to do so by constructing an experimental role modeled, not on Simmel's "stranger," but on the still different type of the newly arrived. Nash and Wolfe were led by their unexpected findings to draw a distinction between persons socialized in a marginal situation and persons introduced into such a situation briefly as adults. The distinction seems useful, and broadly parallels the distinctions noted above between the marginal man and the newly arrived—neither of which, it should be clear, replicates Simmel's own concept of the stranger.

In a study more faithful to Simmel's formulations, "Aggressive Attitudes of the 'Stranger' as a Function of Conformity Pressures," Zajonc (1952) recovered the distinction between the stranger and the newly arrived. Linking Simmel's ideas about the stranger's relative independence from local customs with frustration-aggression theory, Zajonc hypothesized that insofar as strangers are expected to conform to host culture norms and find those expectations disturbing owing to conflicts with values brought from their home culture, they will tend to express aggression against those norms; and that their special position as strangers makes it easier for them to voice such criticism and further reduces the need for them to conform by devaluing the norms in question. "This relationship," Zajonc notes, "hinges upon the unique role of the stranger, and it *consequently cannot be expected to hold for the newly arrived''* (emphasis mine). His second hypothesis, then, is that "attitudinal aggression as a result of frustration in conformity will be greater for strangers with long residence [Simmel's 'stranger'] than for those with short residence [the 'newly arrived']." His findings support this hypothesis.

If the materials just reviewed reflect a tale of distinctions lost and distinctions regained, other studies which remain fairly faithful to Simmel's own conception of the stranger suggest a story of distinctions still struggling to be born. One such distinction concerns whether generalizations about strangers are to refer to a category of persons or to members of a collectivity. The former usage appears, for example, in several papers which examine the effects of social detachment on moral and cognitive orientations. Coser (1964), noting that "what Georg Simmel said about the stranger applies with peculiar force to the eunuch: 'He is not radically committed to the unique ingredients and peculiar tendencies of the group,'" has argued that the detachment of the eunuch-stranger from all group involvements makes him an ideal instrument for carrying out a ruler's subjective desires; and then extended the point to cover uncastrated but politically impotent aliens, such as the court Jews of Baroque Germany and Christian renegades who served the Ottoman sultans. A kindred theme is examined in papers by Daniels (1967) and Nash (1963) which consider the ways in which the stranger's lack of social affiliations affects the degree of objectivity which social scientists can have in field research.

In other writings whose authors are no less concerned to associate their work with Simmel's essay, strangers are referred to chiefly as members of ethnic communities. In *Immigrants and Associations,* for example, Fallers assembled a collection of papers on Chinese, Lebanese, and Ibo immigrant communities. Generalizing from these papers, Fallers observes that stranger communities exhibit a typical pattern: "a socially segregated and hostilely-regarded community of kinship units, knit together and defended by associational ties" (1967, 12). Similarly, Bonacich (1973) set forth "A Theory of Middlemen Minorities" to account for the development and persistence of communities of this sort. The possibility that free-floating individual strangers and those organized in ethnic communities might have quite different properties cannot be explored so long as the same concept is used to refer indiscriminately to both sets of phenomena.

Other distinctions of considerable analytic importance are sub-
merged beneath the ambiguous concept of 'distance' which Simmel
used with such memorable effect in his excursus. The stranger
relationship, Simmel tells us, involves a distinctive blend of closeness and remoteness: the stranger's position *within* a given circle is
fundamentally affected by the fact that he brings qualities into it that
are derived from the *outside*.

Generations of readers have been haunted by the imagery of
distance contained in this and related passages. Some have been
lured by the promise implicit in the metaphor of social distance—
that social relations could somehow be represented in mathematical
terms analogous to those used to represent physical space—into
constructing instruments for the measurement of social distance.
Although certain sociologists have become aware of the highly
ambiguous character of the metaphor of social distance—one could
cite, for example, the four distinct social-distance scales of
Kadushin (1962) and the two still different social-distance scales of
Laumann (1966)—none has sought to specify and relate the particular dimensions of social distance represented in the position of the
stranger.

A step in that direction, however, was taken by McFarland and
Brown (1973) in their paper "Social Distance as a Metric." They
write that Simmel's stranger was

> described as having elements of both nearness and distance.
> The nearness comes from features held in common with the
> observer, and the distance comes from the observer's
> awareness that the features held in common are common to all
> men or at least to large groups of men. Simmel's use of the
> concept does not lend itself either to quantification or to a clear
> analogy with physical distance since in his usage two people
> can simultaneously be "near" and "distant." His concept of
> social distance actually seems to be a mixture of two different
> concepts: features held in common, and the degree of
> specificity or generality of these common features. (1973, 215).

This univocalist interpretation does injustice to Simmel's
excursus in two respects. For one thing, it attends to only one of the
meanings of distance actually used in Simmel's essay. As Simmel
himself observed in a different context, there are "very manifold
meanings encompassed by the symbol of 'distance'" (1908, 321; see
also Simmel 1955, 105). In the stranger essay, Simmel employs his
formula concerning the mixture of nearness and remoteness in at

least *three* quite different senses. He says, first, that "the appearance of this mobility within a bounded group occasions that synthesis of nearness and remoteness which constitutes the formal positions of the stranger" (1971, 145). In this passage, Simmel is referring to distance in the sense of *interaction as proximity:* the stranger is near in that he interacts with numerous members of the group, he is remote in that he does so incidentally and not by virtue of well-established expectations based on ties of kinship, community, or occupation.

In another passage, discussing the quality of objectivity inherent in the position of the stranger, Simmel goes on to equate the distinction between remoteness and nearness with "indifference and involvement." In this context, distance is used to refer to the degree of *emotional attachment* between actors. It is only toward the end of the essay that he comes to the usage which McFarland and Brown single out, distance in the sense of the degree of *generality of features held in common.*

In rejecting Simmel's usage, since it conceived of people as being simultaneously near and far in the same relationship, McFarland and Brown further underestimate the scientific fruitfulness of the Simmelian formulation. On the contrary, I would argue that Simmel's paradoxical formulation not only makes great social-psychological sense but is indeed the key to opening up a proper sociology of the stranger.

If people can be close or remote from one another in many ways, it is the compresence of characteristics of closeness and remoteness along any of those dimensions—the very dissonance embodied in that dualism—that makes the position of strangers socially problematic in all times and places. When those who should be close, in any sense of the term, are actually close, and those who should be distant are distant, everyone is "in his place." When those who should be distant are close, however, the inevitable result is a degree of tension and anxiety which necessitates some special kind of response.

Two psychological mechanisms appear to underlie this universal need—separation anxiety and group narcissism. The common observation that "the child's dread is brought into existence by the approach of a 'stranger'" (Freud 1949, 86) can be grounded in a primal experience: the infant's dread of losing its mother aroused by the appearance of a strange person in her place. In that paradigmatic situation, one who should be distant appears to be taking the place

of one who should be close, and the result is immediate apprehension.

Compounding this primal anxiety is the response represented by
Freud's formulation concerning the narcissism of small differences:

> In the undisguised antipathies and aversions which people feel
> towards strangers with whom they have to do we may
> recognize the expression of self-love—of narcissism. This self-
> love works for the self-assertion of the individual, and behaves
> as though the occurrence of any divergence from his own
> particular lines of development involved a criticism of them and
> a demand for their alteration. (1949, 55–56)

To translate all this into the terms of a more general group
psychology: group members derive security from relating in familiar
ways to fellow group members and from maintaining their distance
from nonmembers through established insulating mechanisms. In
situations where an outsider comes into the social space normally
occupied by group members only, one can presume an initial
response of anxiety and at least latent antagonism. A systematic
sociology of the stranger might therefore organize itself around the
types of response to this frequent social dilemma.

Logically prior to the question of the host's response, however, is
the question of how the stranger himself seeks to relate to the host
group. One thing to be learned from our brief review of the literature
is that the stranger concept has been used to refer to a number of
distinct social phenomena, phenomena which may have quite different properties. Some of these differences reflect the variety of
modes of acceptance which stangers try to elicit from host groups.

Wood affords a point of departure for formulating these distinctions when she points out that "for us the stranger may be, as with
Simmel, a potential wanderer, but he may also be a wanderer who
comes today and goes tomorrow, or he may come today and remain
with us permanently." If, however, sociological interest in the
stranger concept is to understand it as referring to a distinctive type
of relationship—as Wood herself, like Simmel, maintains—then
perhaps the critical variable here is not the length of time spent in
the host community, but the type of relationship which the stranger
aspires to establish with the host group. In other words, the stranger
may wish merely to *visit* the host community, remaining an outsider
throughout his visit; or he may desire *residence* in the host community without becoming assimilated into it—to be in the group but

Figure 3
A Typology of Stranger Relationships

Host's Response to Stranger	Stranger's Interest in Host Community		
	Visit	Residence	Membership
Compulsive friendliness	Guest	Sojourner	Newcomer
Compulsive antagonism	Intruder	Inner enemy	Marginal man

not of it; or he may aspire to gain *membership* as a fully integrated participant in the host community.

Whatever his aspirations, the appearance of an outsider is likely to arouse some feelings of anxiety and antagonism. More accurately, perhaps, it could be said to arouse pronounced ambivalence: positive feelings related to the proximity, negative feelings related to the fact that one who should be distant is close by. The host's response will therefore be described as compulsive, reflecting the reality of a persisting ambivalence underlying all stranger relationships and the related fact that these relationships are invested with a particularly high degree of affect. It will be compulsively friendly if positive feelings predominate, compulsively antagonistic if negative ones are dominant.

Taking this dichotomy into account enables us to incorporate Stonequist's distinction between marginal men and strangers readily and, indeed, to classify each of the three types of stranger orientations just distinguished according to whether it is reciprocated in a primarily positive or primarily negative form. The typology of stranger relations shown in figure 3 may then be generated by cross-classifying the two variables in question.[2] Each of these types, finally, should be further distinguished according to whether it is taken to refer to strangers as *individuals* or as *collectivities*.

This typology provides the basis for developing an analytic paradigm, one organized here with respect to three basic questions which appear to define the main areas of interest in this field:

1. What are the characteristic properties of each of these types of stranger relationship?
2. What factors are associated with the process by which persons enter into one or another of these types of relations?

2. The resulting characterization of the Marginal Man is congruent with that of Merton who, cross-classifying two somewhat different variables, depicts the Marginal Man as one who aspires to belong to a group but is defined as ineligible for membership by the group (1968, 344).

3. What factors account for the changes which move persons from one of these types of relation into another?

The following outline is designed to provide a means for organizing existing empirical materials and for articulating a set of specific questions for future research.

Beyond Ambiguity: A Paradigm for the
Sociology of the Stranger

1. Characteristics of each type of stranger (Guest, Intruder, Sojourner, Inner Enemy, Newcomer, Marginal Man)

    a. Individual strangers
       i. Personal characteristics (detachment, insecurity, etc.)
       ii. Typical relations with host (used as confidants, king's men, etc.)
    b. Stranger collectivities
       i. Internal characteristics (high levels of participation in voluntary associations, etc.)
       ii. Typical relations with hosts (residentially segregated, used as scapegoats, etc.)

2. Factors affecting assumption of each type of stranger status

    a. Factors affecting aspirations of stranger
       i. Reasons for leaving home (alienation, boredom, calling, disaster, economic hardship, political oppression, etc.)
       ii. Conditions of entrance into host group (amount of prestige, movable resources, special skills, etc.)
    b. Factors affecting response of host
       i. Extent of stranger-host similarity (ethnicity, language, race, region, religion, value orientations, etc.)
       ii. Existence of special cultural categories and rituals for dealing with strangers
       iii. Criteria for group or societal membership (classificatory kinship, religion, citizenship, professional certification, etc.)
       iv. Conditions of local community (age, size, homogeneity, degree of isolation, etc.)

3. Factors affecting shifts in stranger status

    a. Factors affecting orientations of strangers
       i. Changing conditions at home
       ii. Changes in stranger's control of resources in host community
    b. Factors affecting response of host
       i. Changes in criteria of group membership (from tribal affiliation to national citizenship, etc.)
       ii. Changes in local community conditions (increasing unemployment, political unrest, etc.)

The 'Stranger' Literature Reconsidered

The precise nature of Simmel's contribution in the excursus on "Der Fremde" can now be specified. It deals almost exclusively with the question of the characteristics of the status of the individual Sojourner. For the most part these concerned his relations with the host group: his freedom from its conventional constraints, the fluidity of his relations with host group members, and the ease with which he establishes a confidant relationship with them. Wood did, in fact, make the point that the characteristics enumerated by Simmel should *not* be presumed to exist in all stranger relationships, but only in those in which the stranger does not seek to become a regular group member. Nor would they obtain when the host group expresses a compulsively antagonistic attitude toward the stranger, though Simmel's account does call attention to the host's underlying ambivalence toward Sojourners.

Much of the literature on strangers is concerned with the characteristics of Sojourner communities. Thus, Fallers speaks of the tendency of Sojourners to form a great number of interlinked voluntary associations. Wood describes the tendency of oldtimers within Sojourner communities to be anxious about those newly arrived from their homeland, because the latter may not appreciate the precarious circumstances under which the Sojourners live and by some untoward act may trigger an antagonistic reaction from the host group. Becker (1950) writes that such communities tend to form counterideologies which depict themselves as superior or chosen in defense against the low regard in which they are held by the host community.

Other literature on a variety of kindred subjects may be connected fruitfully by reference to the above typology. Thus, the sociology of tourism belongs to consideration of the stranger as Visitor. The Sojourner category would encompass most of what has been discussed as "middle-man minorities." The analysis of the Newcomer would include materials on problems of succession in large organizations, as well as studies on the assimilation of immigrants. The Marginal Man would include such problematic positions as that of the Homecomer, as described by Schutz (1945), and the kindred phenomenon of the *estranged* native, discussed by Skinner (1963; 1979) and Tiryakian (1973). I know of no studies concerning the range of motivations involved in becoming a stranger, though Michels long ago (1925) enumerated some points which bear on the question. It seems likely, however, that the type of status acquired by strangers will be significantly affected by whether the stranger views the host commmunity as an asylum from political or religious persecution or natural disaster, as a market for special skills and services, as a reference group attractive because of special moral or other cultural features, as a group of infidels to be converted, or as a source of stimulating adventures.

Some cultures may know very well how to deal with Guests, but lack any institutionalized procedures for accommodating Sojourners. Some may be able to integrate legitimate immigrants as Newcomers, but can only define short-term visitors as Intruders. There is a huge and fascinating range of variability here, all the way from the custom of those northern Australian tribesmen who reportedly speared any stranger from an unknown tribe unless he came accredited as a sacred messenger, to that of the ancient Jews, who were told to leave the gleanings of their harvests for the poor and the strangers, and that "if a stranger sojourn with thee in your land, ye shall not vex him; but the stranger that dwelleth with you shall be unto you as one born among you, and thou shalt love him as thyself; for ye were strangers in the land of Egypt" (Leviticus 19:9–10; 33–34)—an ethic toward Guests, if not Sojourners, likewise highly developed in Arabian culture and represented among the Amhara by the concept *ye-egziabher ingida,* a "guest of God."

The potential interest of this topic may be illustrated by considering the quite disparate ways in which different ethnic groups within Ethiopia relate to strangers. In this respect, as in so many others, the traditional patterns of the Amhara and the Oromo (Galla) stand in sharp contrast. Although the Amhara, guided by their concept of the "guest of God," are customarily inclined to receive legitimate visitors with extremely considerate hospitality, they find it difficult to integrate Newcomers, and often even Sojourners, into their local communities—a process which Oromo communities in many parts of the country are reported to do almost effortlessly. I attribute this difference in good part to the different criteria for local group membership in the two traditions. In a traditional Amhara community full-fledged status is related to the possession of *rist,* rights to the use of land inherited through an ambilineal descent system, and no outsider, lacking genealogical affiliations through which he might establish some legitimate claim to *rist,* can expect to acquire that status. Oromo traditions, by contrast, derive from a style of life that historically (and among the Borana, today) may be described as serially sedentary. Local camps were formed and reformed periodically on a voluntary basis; neighbors were chosen with respect to qualities of cooperativeness and personal friendship (Levine 1974, chaps. 8–10).

Wood's book provides a wealth of propositions on this topic in a section titled "The Stranger and the Community Pattern." There she considers the differential effects on reception of strangers produced by such factors as whether the host communities consist of natives or foreigners; whether they are frontier settlements or retarded districts; whether homogenous in culture or highly diverse; whether rural areas, small towns, or large cities.

The topical salience of the sociology of the stranger reflects those dramatic shifts in the position of strangers experienced in many new states of Africa and Asia following their independence. In many instances, Guests were redefined as Intruders; Newcomers of long standing were turned into Marginal Men; Sojourners became transformed into Inner Enemies, and subjected to harassment, expulsion, and even assassination. There is need for studies that illuminate the dynamics of these fateful changes, studies that will consolidate and extend the pioneering analyses of this topic by Skinner and Bonacich in the papers cited above.

Finally, it should be noted that the sociology of strangerhood articulated by this paradigm is limited by its adherence to one essential feature of Simmel's conception: the depiction of stranger-hood as a "figure-ground" phenomenon, in which the stranger status is always defined *in relation to a host*. Other kinds of phenomena, however, have been linked with this concept, namely, those in which *both* parties to a relationship are labeled strangers. In this usage, strangerhood is defined simply as a function of the degree of unfamiliarity existing between the parties. In Lofland's elaboration of this notion (1973), individuals are strangers to one another simply when they lack personal and biographical information about one another. Following this definition, Lofland and others have produced some interesting insights by analyzing the modern urban milieu as a "world of strangers" (see also Packard 1972). Applying a similar model at the collective level, relations between ethnic groups have been conceived in terms of attitudes and transactions between stranger communities, and analyzed with respect to the degrees of stereotyping, prejudice, and receptivity that obtains in their relationships (Williams 1964).

Important though such topics are, there is a danger that in characterizing the content of strangerhood so broadly what has always been most fascinating about this subject may become obscured. The continuing relevance of Simmel's essay is its focus on what happens when people bring into a group qualities not endemic to it. "The stranger," writes Edward Tiryakian, "brings us into contact with the limits of ourselves. . . . He makes us aware of ourselves by indicating the boundaries of selfhood" (1973, 57). The experience of and responses to this mixture of closeness and remoteness, of threat and excitement, is a distinctive social formation which continues to demand attention wherever there are firmly bounded groups and others who step across their boundaries.

In a sense, it is only at this distance that it has been possible to specify exactly what Simmel was doing in "Der Fremde." As noted above, he was dealing almost exclusively with one small and determinate segment of the sociology of strangerhood, with the question of the properties of the relations of individual sojourners with their host groups. To locate Simmel's contribution with this degree of precision is to define the broader area of related questions with clarity and deeper understanding. Would this not have been extremely difficult, if not impossible, before the stimulating ideas from his essay had been applied and misapplied in so many ways? At this distance, one could in fact argue that the misinterpretations and distorted readings of his work were just as fruitful for advancing that understanding as the incontestably accurate ones.

The case just examined suggests one way to resolve the dilemma of how to deal with the terminological problem posed by a commonplace term that carries a plurality of determinate meanings. One solution, advocated by Riggs (1979), is to avoid using the many-valued homonym when convenient synonymous terms are available. Another solution, advocated by Albrow (1970), is to retain the polyvalent term because it possesses a utility akin to that of a family name, namely, it suggests a fact of relationship, of some historical and logical connection among problems. The above typology of stranger relationships shows the attractiveness of pursuing *both* options: a taxonomy of discrete names to avoid future confusion, an embracing category of strangerhood to connote a network of family relations.

6

Ambivalent Encounters
Disavowals of Simmel by Durkheim, Weber, Lukács, Park, and Parsons

"Whoever is not for me is against me" is
only a half-truth. Only the indifferent person is against me—one whom the ultimate
questions for which I live move neither to a
For nor an Against. But whoever is against
me in a positive sense, one who ventures
onto the plane where I exist and combats
me on that plane—that person is in the
highest sense *for* me.

    G. Simmel

Emile Durkheim (1858–1917), Max Weber (1864–1920), Georg
Lukács (1885–1971), Robert Park (1864–1943), and Talcott Parsons
(1902–79) have more in common than their preeminence in shaping
the consciousness of sociologists. Before arriving at the views for
which they are best known, they went through periods of intense
ferment during which they moved beyond the disciplines in which
they had been trained, devoured materials, changed views, and
clarified central themes. Along the way, each of them became
engaged for a while with the writings of Georg Simmel (1858–1918).
The distinctive manner in which each of them came to terms with
Simmel—how they understood, appropriated, rejected, and misunderstood his teachings—throws light on the distinctive features of
the five traditions they came to represent. Their experience illuminates, no less, the richly ambiguous Simmelian legacy—including,
perhaps, what it has to suggest about the little understood process of
interaction between readers and authors.

Durkheim

Simmel was introduced to France in 1894, shortly after his first
substantial works appeared in Germany. Three of his essays were
published in French journals that year, as was Bouglé's lengthy
review of his books on morality, philosophy of history, and social
differentiation. Durkheim thus encountered Simmel's work at a time
when he was struggling to codify his own sociological views, just
after completing *De la division du travail social* and his first
formulations on the subject matter and methods of sociology. At

once attracted by the work of his German contemporary, Durkheim translated Simmel's essay on the persistence of social groups and published it in the very first issue of *l'Année sociologique*. Although he found its prose style unduly complicated, Durkheim wrote (to Bouglé in the fall of 1897) that the essay was "lively, agreeable to read and certainly in the general spirit of the *Année*" (Lukes 1972, 405).

It is easy to see why Simmel aroused Durkheim's interest. An admirer of German social science ever since he visited some German universities a decade earlier, Durkheim thought that Simmel's work paralleled his own effort to establish sociology on firm scientific grounds by positing a phenomenal domain consisting of irreducibly *social* facts. How, after all, could Durkheim be anything but enamored of passages in Simmel's essay like "On peut voir combien il est juste de présenter la société comme une unité *sui generis,* distincte de ses éléments individuels"?—even to the extent of rendering Simmel's German locution, "als eine besondere Einheit," in the words of his own beloved idiom, "une unité *sui generis*" (1897, 73; 1898, 591). Since Simmel clearly manifested "a sense of the specificity of social facts" (Lukes 1972, 404), as Durkheim observed in his first letter to Bouglé on the matter, he could only welcome the German philosopher as an ally in the enterprise.

The more Durkheim considered the matter, however, the more he realized that Simmel's way of formulating the specificity of social facts, and hence the task of sociology, was at odds with his own emerging position. In statements made a few years later, Durkheim took pains to distance himself from Simmel's approach, by insisting on an alternative definition of social facts, recasting the notion of social forms, and faulting Simmel's methodology.

The principle advanced by Simmel for marking the domain of the social was a distinction between the relational patterns involved when persons interact with one another, the *forms* of association, and the reasons that bring them together, the *contents* of their association. Only the forms of association were defined as the proper object for sociological investigation. Simmel thus conceived social facts to be not concrete, naturally existing entities, but analytic variables, organizational features of human social life to be identified through a process of mental abstraction.

Durkheim's program of positive sociology, by contrast, depended on the assumption that social facts constitute a universe of naturally existing, concrete entities—"les faits sociales sont des choses"—

and this property alone secured the basis for treating them as the object of study for a rigorous empirical science. In a vigorous critique of Simmel's view first published in 1900, Durkheim rejected the distinction between the forms and contents of social life for being too abstract and arbitrary. Conceptual distinctions, he argued, must separate facts "according to their natural distinctions; otherwise, they are bound to degenerate into fantastic constructions and vain mythology" (1960, 356). Since the contents of social life are not less social than are the external forms of the collectivity, there is no basis in the nature of things for the distinction drawn by Simmel.

What is more, the effect of Simmel's proposal to direct sociology to the study of social forms alone would be to restrict the scope of the discipline unjustifiably. Durkheim sought not to find a sharply delimited jurisdiction for his science but to make sociology the master social science, to which scholarly work on particular sectors of society, like law, religion, and economy, would make specialized contributions. He found it useful to distinguish two elements in social life, not for the purpose of delimiting the field of sociology but in order to divide its various branches. Instead of Simmel's distinction between form and matter, Durkheim proposed a distinction between form and function, to which would correspond the subdisciplines of social morphology and social physiology.

Durkheim formalized the category of social morphology in 1899, just as he was working out his negation of Simmel's conception. He meant it to designate a branch of sociology dealing with matters demographic and ecological: the size and density of populations, the boundaries and communication networks of their territories. A note on the subject prefaced his review of a book by Friedrich Ratzel, whose project he endorsed but whose rubric, "political geography," he sought to replace with social morphology, "which has the advantage of placing in sharp relief the unity of the object on which all this research bears, namely the *tangible, material forms of societies* or, in other words, the nature of their substratum" ([1899] 1978, 89, emphasis mine).

Expanding on this notion in his critique of Simmel, Durkheim wrote: "We propose to call the science that has for its object the study of the material forms of society 'social morphology.'" The term 'form,' which, as used by Simmel, has only a metaphorical significance, is here used in its proper sense. In this view, "every morphological phenomenon consists of material adaptations that acquire a definite form" ([1900] 1960, 362).

The notion of social morphology solved several problems for Durkheim. As the study of "material forms of society," it enabled him to collapse Simmel's distinction between form and matter, thereby negating whatever restrictions on the scope of sociology were implied by Simmel's proposal. Indeed, it enabled him to *enlarge* its scope by incorporating work such as Ratzel's and so to subsume demographic and geographical studies as subdivisions of sociology. It enabled him to argue that his way of regarding forms was scientifically sound, for categories of social phenomena like territory and population are based on empirically accessible "natural" distinctions.

What exists in nature, Durkheim continued, is not only the material forms of society, but also the social life that flows from or is sustained by them. Beside the morphological phenomena, there are the functional phenomena, the subject of social physiology. A few years later Durkheim would further subdivide the province of social physiology into the study of various functional complexes: religion, law, morality, economy, language, and art ([1909] 1978, 83). In the critique of Simmel he merely spoke in general terms about this domain, stressing the socially imperative character of the beliefs and practices that pervade the lives of persons. Summarizing the argument, he states: "Social life is nothing but the moral milieu that surrounds the individual" ([1900] 1960, 367). We see here another fundamental point of conflict between the views of Durkheim and Simmel. For Simmel, social facts are morally indifferent. They consist of properties of the structures and processes which organize human relations. Normative regulation may enter into these relations, but only incidentally, not as a defining characteristic. Nothing could be more antithetic to the view of social life Durkheim had crystallized by that time. For Durkheim, society had come to signify above all else a moral community. Societies were the embodiment and the source of human morality, and the dimension of normative regulation was one of their essential features. Thus, Durkheim faulted Simmel for failing to appreciate the crucial dimension of *regulation* on the effects of money in social life (1902, 145), just as he could not abide Simmel's proposal to exclude normative phenomena from the domain of the truly "social": "It is by its law, its morality, its religion, etc., that a society is characterized. There is just no justification for putting their study outside of sociology" ([1903] 1975, 140).

The construct of social morphology has especial methodological significance for Durkheim as well, inasmuch as the "social substratum . . . is the object most immediately accessible to the sociologist because it takes on material forms that we can perceive with our senses" ([1900] 1960, 360). This concern, too, reflected a strand of argumentation against Simmel that Durkheim developed at a number of points. Durkheim also objected to Simmel's conception of sociology because the notion of social forms was too vague and indefinite, making it impossible to draw disciplinary boundaries in anything but a highly subjective manner. In addition, he faulted Simmel for presenting proofs that consist merely of explanation by example; for using concepts that are imprecise and excessively elastic (1903a, 647); for presenting propositions that cannot possibly be subjected to rigorous proof (1903b, 649); and for carrying out, in the *Philosophy of Money,* a form of "bastard speculation, where reality is expressed in terms necessarily subjective as in art, but abstract as in science" (1902, 145). Simmel's substantive studies were speculative meditations, not refractions of an integral scientific system—"philosophical variations on certain aspects of social life, chosen more or less at random according to the leanings of a single individual" ([1900] 1960, 359).

The unsystematic way in which Simmel tended to present concepts, marshal observations, and select problems offended Durkheim's penchant for rigorous methodology no less than did Simmel's seemingly artificial delimitation of the domain of sociology. Scientific method applied to societies entailed, for Durkheim, two kinds of work: comparative history, involving the careful accumulation of facts about concrete societies and institutional sectors, and statistics, involving studies of the frequency distributions of various traits and their correlation with diverse variables. There was no way he could muster sympathy for Simmel's methodological penchant: the intuitive grasp of the essence of forms and their properties.

In the first years of this century, then, Durkheim quite abandoned his initial sympathy for Simmel. In 1902 he commented ruefully on the whole condition of German social science: whereas in the past he had gained a great deal from German writers, their work at the time reflected nothing but intellectual stagnation ([1902] 1975, 400). His summary judgment of Simmel was expressed the following year, in an article titled "Sociologie et sciences sociales": "The extreme indeterminacy for which we reproach M. Simmel is not simply implied . . . in his principles; in fact, it characterizes all of his work" ([1903] 1975, 143). Later versions of the article simply omit the whole discussion of Simmel; after 1904, Durkheim made no reference to Simmel ever again.[1]

What little discussion has been focused on Durkheim's critique of Simmel has linked it with his disposition toward intellectual "imperialism."[2] However much Durkheim may have been disposed to counter any competitive threats to his leadership of the field of sociology, the fact of a fundamental incompatibility between their theoretical orientations cannot be denied. The principles and methods for sociology that Durkheim espoused simply could not be reconciled with those followed by Simmel. Although both agreed on the crucial importance of defining an ontological domain of specifically social facts, they diverged radically on how to conceive those facts and how to proceed to study them.

Broadly speaking, the pattern of Durkheim's experience with Simmel—a phase of sympathetic interest, followed by critical confrontation, resulting in rejection and subsequent neglect—was exhibited by each of the other authors to be considered below. What is more, all of them experienced their most intense critical engagement with Simmel's ideas at a relatively advanced point in their careers— Durkheim, Weber, and Park in their early forties, Lukács and Parsons in their early thirties—when they were on the verge of crystallizing their mature orientations as social theorists. In each case, however, both the aspect of Simmel's work found appealing and the reasons for eventual disavowal were different.

Weber

Weber became interested in Simmel during the first years of this century, when he was recovering from his period of acute depres-

1. Durkheim would leave it to Bouglé to have the *Année*'s final word on Simmel. Reviewing *Soziologie,* Bouglé indicated his own clear awareness that Simmel's "social forms . . . are far from something that can be reduced to spatial determinations, to the material structure of groups, to what one has proposed here to study under the rubric *"social morphology."* Going on to express his appreciation of the suggestive psychological insights of the "brilliant" author of this work, Bouglé concludes on a Durkheimian note: for sociology to become a scientific discipline, it must afford more scope than Simmel does to "objective" historical comparisons (1910, 17, 20).

2. Thus Lukes writes of Durkheim's "sociological imperialism" and his "imperialistic positivism" when discussing Durkheim's refutation of other sociological approaches (1972, 392–405), and Jaworski (1983) interprets Durkheim's critique of Simmel as a bid to undermine the latter's rapidly growing international reputation and to depreciate the German contribution to social science while presiding over the efflorescence of French sociology.

sion. His initial admiration was expressed in a number of appreciative remarks in essays published between 1904 and 1906. He observed, for example, that "Simmel's . . . theses are invariably artfully developed and technically refined," and praised the "uncommon subtlety" of his formulations and his "brilliant depiction" of the spirit of capitalism (1975, 258, 272[3]; 1905: 15). Around 1908, Weber, like Durkheim, sought to come to terms with Simmel in the form of a pointed critical essay. Thereafter, except for cursory remarks in the 1913 "Kategorien" essay and a few terse critical comments written in the last two years of his life, Weber made no further references to Simmel in his published work.

It was not Simmel's discussion of social facts or of the foundations of sociology that stimulated Weber's interest, however. During the first years of this century Weber still viewed himself as an economic historian, showing little sympathy for the efforts of sociologists. Rather, what drew Weber to Simmel was his work in epistemology. Not inclined to pursue philosophical investigations himself, Weber depended on the work of others for epistemological analyses that would serve his interest in reorienting scholarship in the social sciences. One of his concerns was the need to separate the promulgation of value judgments from scholarly research. Upon acceding to the editorship of the *Archiv für Sozialwissenschaft und Sozialpolitik* (along with Edgar Jaffé and Werner Sombart) in 1904, Weber prefaced a methodological editorial essay on "objectivity" in the social sciences with the statement that everything of importance in it was based on the work of the modern logicians, naming Simmel along with Windelband and Rickert as the authorities in question. On several other issues Weber expressed positions that had previously been articulated by Simmel. Although Weber drew as well on Dilthey and Rickert for philosophical support in some of these matters, on certain points he explicitly sides with Simmel as against Dilthey or Rickert (1975, 253, 252). Even when he neglects to cite Simmel, his formulations are very close to those of Simmel, when the latter discusses such matters as the inadequacy of the search for general laws as a goal for the social sciences; the importance of the values and interests of the investigator in determining the selection

3. The two-part essay on Knies, together with a 1903 essay, "Roscher's Historical Method," comprised "Roscher and Knies: The Logical Problems of Historical Economics." In citing that work here, I give page references to the 1975 English edition when I follow the Oakes translation, and to the 1922 German reprint, in *Gesammelte Aufsätze zur Wissenschaftslehre*, when I have supplied my own translation.

of scholarly problems; the fruitfulness of hypothetical constructs in historical analysis; and the limited utility of historical materialism in providing one set of such synthetic constructs.

Where Weber explicitly focuses his attention on Simmel is in the central section of "Knies and the Problem of Irrationality," published in two parts in 1905–6. In producing this essay Weber labored tortuously to cast off the confused statements about the cultural sciences that two decades of extravagant polemics among Germanic scholars had produced. The resolution he achieved there was to establish the central methodological orientation he followed the rest of his life.

Weber's chief problem in that essay is to refute the positivist claim that there are no essential differences between the methodologies appropriate to the natural sciences and to the cultural sciences without succumbing to many of the untenable arguments that earlier critics of positivism had made, arguments "which fairly glitter in the variety of their colors and forms" (1975, 184). His point of departure is the view of Karl Knies that what distinguishes human action from the naturally given conditions of action is that the latter are subject to rationally determinable general laws, whereas the concrete action of persons is *free and irrational*. These properties of voluntarism and incalculability were held to give human action and the disciplines studying it a special dignity that natural events operating according to mechanical causality wholly lacked. Knies' views on the irrationality of human action, Weber notes, were fairly widely shared at the time. Weber had, I believe, two urgent reasons for seeking to refute them, reasons related to the projects that preoccupied him at the time. One was his ambition to sustain an argument about the subjective meanings lying behind the rise of modern capitalism. The other was his desire to propound an ideology that justified the work of social science by an appeal to its potential contribution to enhancing human freedom by helping to make action more rational.[4] Weber proceeds to refute this position vis-à-vis irrationality by showing that natural events are neither less unpredictable nor less complex than human conduct, and that indeed human conduct has a specific property that renders it more calculable than natural processes: the property of being informed by understandable motives. "Because of its susceptibility to a meaningful *interpretation*—and to the extent that it is susceptible to this

---

4. This point is elaborated below in chapters 7 and 8.

sort of interpretation—individual human conduct is in principle intrinsically less 'irrational' than the individual natural event'' (1975, 125).

Weber's whole argument against Knies thus depended on his formulation of a plausible conception of interpretation. Such a conception could not be set forth as a vague notion of intuition, but had to be so formulated that it could meet the standards of objectivity in scholarship. The interpreting historian can secure objectified knowledge, Weber argues, by employing the categories in which concrete reality is experienced by human actors. The implication of this point, he continued, can only be dealt with by a *"theory of 'interpretation,'* a theory which apparently at this point has hardly been explored at all'' (1922, 91).

This is the moment when Weber turns to Simmel. "By far the most fully developed logical analysis of the elements of a *theory of 'understanding' [Verstehen]* appears in the second edition of Simmel's *Probleme der Geschichtsphilosophie''* (1922, 92). Weber proceeds then to incorporate much of Simmel's discussion of *Verstehen,* accepting some points, refining or disagreeing with other points, referring the reader back to Simmel for still others. For example, he illustrates one point by referring to Simmel's discussion of the proposition that "one does not have to be Caesar in order to understand Caesar" and cites "Simmel's acute observation that, in general, 'clearly outlined' and 'unique' personalities can be 'understood' more deeply and unambiguously'' (1975, 258, 259). He concludes his discussion of *Verstehen* with very Simmelian language: "Historical interpretation . . . is concerned with a task with which we have an everyday familiarity; that of 'understanding' concrete human action in terms of its motives" (1975, 197).[5]

Of all these allusions to Simmel, Weber's most pointed reference and extended discussion concern Simmel's distinction between two forms of understanding, between what Simmel himself called objective or immanent understanding and historical understanding.[6] "First of all, it is Simmel's merit to have distinguished clearly—within the widest universe that the concept of 'understanding' *[Verstehen]* . . . can encompass—the objective 'understanding' of the *meaning [Sinn]* of an utterance from the subjective 'interpreta-

5. Thus, Simmel: "Our understanding of the Apostle Paul and Louis XIV is essentially the same as our understanding of a personal acquaintance" ([1915] 1980, 95).
6. On this distinction in Simmel's work on history, see Oakes (1980, 68–83).

tion' *[Deutung]* of the *motives [Motive]* of a (speaking or acting) person. In the first case we 'understand' what has been said *[das Gesprochene]*, in the latter the speaker (or actor) *[den Sprechenden oder Handelnden]*" (1922, 93; emphasis in original). In his later discussions of *Verstehen,* Weber would carefully retain this distinction.

A few years after Weber completed the essay on Knies, his relationship to Simmel changed. Three related events took place in 1908. First, Simmel was proposed for a chair in philosophy at Heidelberg. Weber exerted himself strenuously on Simmel's behalf, and was furious about the anti-Semitic sentiments that prevented Simmel from receiving the appointment. Another development was Weber's move to align himself more closely with sociology, by taking part in efforts to establish a German sociological society. Until that time he tended to belittle the work of sociologists; in the Knies essay he referred to them sarcastically with quotation marks and derided them for their "blind enthusiasm" for a valuational approach to mental phenomena and for their domination by the foolish prejudice of "naturalistic dilettantes" who hold that mass phenomena are somehow less a matter of acting individuals than are the deeds of heroes (1922, 53, 48; 1975, 240, 100). In the latter passage, however, Weber assumed that Simmel's views were like his own. Simmel thus provided him with a model of a professed sociologist not bound by the organicist evolutionary thinking that dominated the field at the time. Dilthey had recently noted, as Weber was aware (1975, 251), that Simmel's sociology stood out as an alternative acceptable to those who could not abide the sociologies of Comte, Spencer, Schäffle, and Lilienfeld. According to Werner Sombart, Weber's move to affiliate himself with sociology was partly inspired by his association with Simmel.[7]

At the same time that Weber was drawn closer to Simmel professionally, he felt constrained to clarify his stance regarding Simmel's work and to distance himself intellectually. He thus began to write a critique of Simmel's style of work in the two major sociological writings that had just appeared, the second edition of *Philosophie des Geldes* (1907) and *Soziologie* (1908). The essay was never published, apparently because Weber did not want to jeopardize Simmel's chances for obtaining a professorial appointment; only a fragment survives.

7. Oral communication from one of the participants in Sombart's seminar in Berlin in the 1920s, Professor Ludwig Lachmann.

The essay begins by reporting the ambivalent responses aroused by Simmel's work:

On the one hand, one is bound to react to Simmel's works from a point of view that is overwhelmingly antagonistic. In particular, crucial aspects of his methodology are unacceptable. His substantive results must with unusual frequency be regarded with reservations, and not seldom they must be rejected outright. In addition, his mode of exposition strikes one at times as strange, and often it is at the very least uncongenial.

On the other hand, Weber continues,

One finds oneself absolutely compelled to affirm that this mode of exposition is simply brilliant and, what is more important, attains results that are intrinsic to it and not to be attained by any imitator. Indeed, nearly every one of his works abounds in important new theoretical ideas and the most subtle observations. Almost every one of them belongs to those books in which not only the valid findings, but even the false ones, contain a wealth of stimulation for one's own further thought, in comparison with which the majority of even the most estimable accomplishments of other scholars often appear to exude a peculiar odor of scantiness and poverty. (1972, 158)

After commenting on the negative responses to Simmel's work by scholarly specialists in Germany, Weber conveys two negative assessments of his own before the fragment ends. Noting that Simmel tends to illustrate sociological matters by drawing analogies from the most diverse provinces of knowledge, Weber comments, "This analogical procedure will be criticized below for the dubiousness of its basic principles." (The promised critique does not appear in the surviving fragment.) The other critical point concerns Simmel's conception of the field of sociology. Stating that sociology is for Simmel "a science concerned with 'interactions' among individuals" (1972, 162), Weber faults that criterion for being too ambiguous and so general that it includes nearly all human phenomena.

It is questionable, however, whether it is the vagueness and elasticity of Simmel's formula that really bothers Weber. When Weber comes finally to propose his own definition of sociology, what he says is nothing if not ambiguous and general—"a science concerning itself with the interpretive understanding of social action and thereby with a causal explanation of its course and conse-

quences'' (1968, 4). It is difficult to see in what way "social action"
is more precise and specific a notion than "interaction." Some light
on Weber's thinking may be provided by a passage from his earlier
essay on objectivity in the social sciences. In justifying the policy of
the *Archiv* in restricting its focus to socioeconomic matters, Weber
writes:

> The belief that it is the task of progressive scientific work to
> cure the "one-sidedness" of the economic perspective by
> broadening it into a *general* social science suffers primarily
> from the weakness that the viewpoint of the "social"—that is,
> of the relationships among persons—acquires sufficient
> specificity to delimit scientific problems only when it is
> provided with some particular substantive *[inhaltlichen]*
> predicate. . . . The concept of the "social," which seems to
> have a quite general sense, turns out to carry—once one
> examines its actual application—a thoroughly peculiar,
> specifically colored, albeit largely indefinite meaning. Its
> "generality" actually rests on nothing but its indefiniteness. It
> provides, when taken it its "general" meaning, no specific *point
> of view* for illuminating the *meaning* of determinate elements of
> culture. ([1922] 1949, 67–68 [165–66]; emphasis in original;
> translation altered)

Simmel, of course, never held that sociology should study "interaction" or "relationships among persons" *in general*. He indicated,
as Weber was well aware, that sociological investigations should be
concerned with particular forms of interaction. He showed a way to
delimit specific scientific problems by directing sociological work to
the analysis of phenomena such as conflict, stratification, division of
labor, and the like. It was to do this by abstracting the relational
properties of human association from their motivating contents
(*Inhalte*). For Weber, however, it was only the contents of social
action that provided lines of specificity. Like Durkheim, Weber saw
the plausible subdivisions of social science as based on diverse
substantive spheres, reflecting such distinctions as economic, political, and religious interests. But where Durkheim insisted on fusing
forms and contents because the latter were no less *social* than the
forms of interaction—that is, motivations and norms were socially
shaped—Weber found it important to fuse them because the contents alone were the source of *meaning* in action, and it was only the
possibility of understanding the meanings of actors that gave social
science a distinctive agenda and methodology.

Although by 1908 Weber was thus disposed to repudiate Simmel's way of defining the field of sociology, he maintained a cordial personal and professional relationship with Simmel. Because of the compatibility of Simmel's "value-neutral" approach to sociology and his rejection of organicist approaches as well as his intellectual gifts and philosophical attainments, Weber moved toward closer association with Simmel as a sociologist and agreed to serve with him on the governing board of the German Sociological Society when it was set up in January 1909. In promotional material that he drafted for the society, Weber stressed general themes in language that Simmel could not but find congenial: the importance of separating value judgments from the research, scientific discussions, and publications of the society, and a focus on "understanding the unique structure which we call society, its nature, its forms, and its development" (Wiese 1959, 11). (Both Weber and Simmel resigned from the society in 1912, chiefly over the issue of value neutrality.)

In 1909 Weber also assumed editorship of the *Grundriss der Sozialökonomik,* for which he eventually came to produce his monumental *Wirtschaft und Gesellschaft.* In the course of that work Weber felt called to work out his own statement about the discipline of sociology. The statement appeared in two versions, one published in *Logos* in 1913 and the other as the opening section of the part of *Wirtschaft und Gesellschaft* written in 1919–20. Compare the language used by Weber in these two versions to differentiate his approach from that of Simmel:

> Attention is directed to the discussion of Simmel (in *Probleme der Geschichtsphilosophie).* . . . The pedantic complexity of these formulations bespeaks the wish to separate sharply the *subjectively* intended meaning from the objectively valid meaning (thereby deviating somewhat *[teilweise]* from Simmel's method). ([1913] 1922, 403)

> On the concept of "understanding" compare . . . particularly some of Simmel's discussions in the *Probleme der Geschichtsphilosophie.* . . . The present work departs from Simmel's method (in his *Soziologie* and his *Philosophie des Geldes*) in drawing a sharp distinction between subjectively intended and objectively valid "meanings"; two things which Simmel not only fails to distinguish but often deliberately treats as belonging together. (1968, 3–4)

In both of these excerpts, Weber continues to acknowledge his earlier indebtedness to Simmel's theory of *Verstehen* from the *Probleme;* and his central point of objection to Simmel's sociological approach is expressed in identical language. In the first case, however, Weber's divergence from Simmel's approach to sociology seems muted and partial; in the second, it is definitive and complete.

I suggest that the 1913 "Kategorien" essay records a transition in Weber's thinking between a phase of sympathy toward Simmel's sociological approach and a phase of disavowing that approach. In "Kategorien," Weber set forth a schema for general sociology to which, in a chapter of the earlier part of *Wirtschaft und Gesellschaft* he had ascribed the task of "classifying the various kinds of groups according to the structure, content, and means of social action" (1968, 356). The schema is presented in chapters that, he notes, had been written *a long time before (schon vor längerer Zeit)*. And what the schema in fact presents is a typology of forms of human association—voluntary associations; "consensually" organized associations, like markets and language communities; institutions; and formal organizations. Although these categories are linked with volitional variables—the extent to which rules are deliberately formulated, the degree of voluntary participation of group members—in effect the typology (heavily based, to be sure, on ideas from Toennies) presents a kind of Simmelian analysis of forms of human association. In the 1919 material, by contrast, Weber's rhetorical emphasis has shifted to his own well-known typologies of human action orientation.

It is extraordinary that Weber's divergence from Simmel in 1919 is expressed in terms that bear such close resemblance to those for which he praised Simmel in 1905. In the earlier passage he affirmed Simmel's distinction between the subjective interpretation of motives and the objective understanding of meaning; in the later, he faulted Simmel for confusing subjectively intended meaning and objectively valid meaning. The matter may be clarified by noting that the former distinction refers to (two ways of analyzing) the *meanings of actors;* the latter refers to *meanings of forms of social action.* Simmel chose to investigate the "meanings" of conflict, domination, money, and the like as forms of human relationship. Although this type of inquiry is by no means so different from what Weber tried to do when ascertaining the basic structural characteristics of, say, formally rationalized organizations in commerce, judicial systems, and public administration, the language Weber felt constrained to use when describing what he was about—notably different, it seems, from what his substantive sociology frequently accomplished—was to insist on the understandability of subjective meanings as the defining criterion of social action and of the sociological enterprise. Weber understood and accomplished a great deal as a formal, structural sociologist, far more than his metatheoretical commitments permitted him to acknowledge in his methodological writings. But those commitments constrained him to reject Simmel's conceptualization as a point of departure for sociology.[8]

Consider how very differently the two authors came to regard the relevance of *Verstehen* for human studies. For Simmel, *history* requires a theory of understanding inasmuch as historical knowledge is grounded on an understanding of mental processes, and the form of consciousness that constructs history depends on a capacity to understand the human significance of past events. By contrast, *sociology* for Simmel is constituted by a radically different form of consciousness, one that is disposed to apprehend the actual forms of association embodied in the varieties of human relationship (see Simmel 1971, xx-xxxi; Oakes 1980, 46–57). For Weber, a theory of understanding is required to guide *any* sort of analysis of human action. History and sociology thus deal with the same kinds of material. The two disciplines differ only in that history deals with concrete events and their imputed causes while sociology subserves the project of historical explanation by using comparisons to produce generalizations that support such causal imputations. When Weber finally came to make his only published critique of Simmel's substantive work, it was to point out Simmel's failure as a sociologist to identify the *historically specific* character of a money economy under conditions of modern capitalist social organization ([1920] 1958b, 185).

Lukács

In words penned just after Simmel's death in 1918, Georg Lukács was clearly relaying his own experience when he wrote: "For all those thinkers of the last generation with a genuine concern for philosophical questions . . . Simmel was so terribly seductive that there was virtually no one among them who was not laid low for

8. This point has been recognized, among (not many) others, by Lukács: "Max Weber polemicized occasionally against the exaggerated formalism of Simmel, but his own sociology is likewise full of such formalistic analogies. Thus, ancient Egyptian bureaucracy is formally likened to socialism, councils to status groups; and similarly, when speaking of the irrational calling of leaders (charisma), he draws the analogy between a shaman and the social democratic leader K. Eisner, etc." ([1954] 1962, 530).

some period by the magic of his thinking" (1958, 171). Of the five
men considered in this chapter, Lukács had the most intense
relationship to Simmel. He alone was intimate with the full range of
Simmel's thought; his own early work was the most profoundly
shaped by Simmel's ideas; in the end, he was the one who turned
against Simmel most harshly.

While yet a student of philosophy at the University of Budapest,
Lukács began a serious study of Simmel's writings. What appealed
to him primarily was not Simmel's grounding of sociology, nor his
theory of *Verstehen,* but the analysis of modern culture set forth in
the *Philosophy of Money.* This work remained the focal point of
Lukács' interest in Simmel and a point of departure for much of his
own work for more than a decade.

Like many central European intellectuals of the pre-World War I
generation, Lukács felt a deep antagonism to the culture of bourgeois capitalist society, due in part to the pervasive influence of
Nietzsche and the aestheticism of the 1890s. Combined with a
pronounced distaste for politics—not least for proletarian political
movements informed, as they saw it, by the demeaning mood of
ressentiment—their attitude expressed itself mainly in a commitment to the realm of art as an autonomous sphere of life, the one
sphere where authentic individual expression might still be possible
in a world based on the exchange of commodities.

Lukács found much to admire in Simmel's aesthetic approach to
philosophy: his metaphysic of forms, his view of art as a self-
sufficient cosmos, and his frequent use of aesthetic analogies. In a
late reminiscence, Lukács recalled that "when I looked for the
perspectives, foundations and methods of application of philosophic
generalisation, I found a theoretical guide in the German philosopher Simmel" (1970, 7). The dominant perspective Lukács acquired
from Simmel concerned the nature of cultural forms and their
conflict with the domain of subjective individuality.[9]

According to Simmel's conception, all cultural forms originate
ultimately in situations where the undifferentiated unity of immediate experience is ruptured by some sort of stress. At that point the
experiencing self divides into a self-conscious subject and a con-

9. I shall not be able here to detail all the particular ways in which Lukács drew on
Simmel. Lutz has noted the influence of Simmel's book on moral philosophy on
Lukács' early views (Lukács 1967, xxiv), and Rücker has argued that Lukács' key
notion of "totality" was greatly indebted to Simmel's work (cited in Bottomore and
Frisby 1978, 43, n. 77). On the signal importance of *The Philosophy of Money* in
Lukács' appropriation of Simmel, see Bottomore and Frisby (1978, 16–21).

fronted object, one defined in whatever formal mode is appropriate to the problem at hand. This results in the creation of forms tied to the adaptive problems of particular situations. The further crystallization of forms is dependent on a continuing distantiation between subject and object. The most advanced level of distantiation between subject and object is reached when the forms become liberated from their connection with practical purposes and become objects of cultivation in their own right—when, for example, the rhythmic and melodic variations of sound initially formed to aid human communication become transformed into music composed and played according to intrinsic norms.

Although this advanced stage of objectification of forms is no longer *directed* by subjective interests, it relates to the interests of subjects insofar as there is a human tendency toward self-fulfillment through "cultivation." Subjective experience and objectified cultural forms are thus appropriately differentiated, in Simmel's view, when they can be connected in one of two ways: when pragmatic forms serve to satisfy a subject's adaptive needs, and when autonomous forms serve the subject's interest in the free development of personality. In modern society, however, the money economy and the division of labor produce objectified forms at a rate that exceeds the capacities of human subjects to assimilate them. The limitless production of new techniques and artifacts had spawned the "typically problematic situation of modern man":

> his sense of being surrounded by an innumerable number of
> cultural elements which are neither meaningless to him nor, in
> the final analysis, meaningful. In their mass they depress him,
> since he is not capable of assimilating them all, nor can he
> simply reject them, since after all they do belong *potentially*
> within the sphere of his cultural development. (1968, 44)

In the *Philosophy of Money,* Simmel describes this as a phenomenon of the *reification* of cultural objects and their *alienation* from the experience of producing and consuming subjects.

These were the notions that Lukács seized upon to make sense of the oppressive cultural condition of his time and place. He employed them to good effect in his earliest essays on drama, which he sees as symbolic of the crisis in modern life due to the objectification of the process and products of work and the individual person's powerlessness in the face of his own creations. On many points, these early essays closely parallel Simmel's *Philosophy of Money* as both

Bottomore and Frisby (1978) and Arato and Breines (1979) have shown.

Having closely studied and appropriated the main themes of Simmel's cultural sociology in his work in Hungary on the sociology of modern drama, Lukács elected to study with Simmel in Berlin. He attended Simmel's lectures during the 1909–10 academic year, rapidly becoming one of Simmel's favorite pupils and frequenting private seminars at Simmel's home.

Already at that point, however, Lukács was pointed in a somewhat different direction from Simmel, a divergence that widened during the next eight years as both men moved toward the consolidation of their mature philosophical orientations. Simmel went on to deepen his analysis of the foundations of the modern crisis, arguing that the process by which unassimilable cultural forms are created is inherent in the very nature of culture; he thus came to refer to that process, in carefully considered terms, as the "tragedy of culture." Although Lukács was probably never happy with the position of resigned acceptance that Simmel's "tragedy of culture" implied, his writings just after the time in Berlin reveal, if anything, an even closer identification with Simmel's outlook. In 1912 Lukács moved to Heidelberg, where he spent most of the next five years. There he played an active part in the discussion circle that met at Max Weber's house on Sunday afternoons, and contributed regularly to Weber's *Archiv*. The major works he composed during this period, the *Philosophy of Art* (1912–14) and the *Theory of the Novel* (1915–16), bear the strong imprint of Simmel's guiding conception of the "tragedy of culture."[10]

The World War forced Lukács to rethink his positions. Unsympathetic to the belief in German cultural chauvinism and imperialism shared by some of his Heidelberg associates (though no longer, it seems, by Weber himself), Lukács was utterly distressed

10. "In the *Philosophy of Art*, Lukács' concept of *Erlebniswirklichkeit* treats alienation in the manner of Simmel, as an ontological given. Moreover the process and price of development is presented by Lukács of the *Theory of the Novel* in a manner that seems to be completely analogous to Simmel's 'tragedy of culture.' According to Lukács, man has invented the productivity of the spirit and the creation of forms and thereby discovered individuality and an infinitely rich world. But as a direct result he had had to surrender completeness of truth and concreteness of totality; he has been forced to discover deep gulfs between theory and praxis, creator and created, self and world. . . . The step into the world of alienation is conceived not on class lines, but as a function of the productivity of the spirit. As in the *Philosophy of Art*, so in everyday empirical life (the domain of the novel): objectification once again equals alienation pure and simple" (Arato and Breines 1979, 57, 64).

by the war. He turned away from the aloof aestheticism represented by Simmel toward engagement with the conflicts of his time, a process aided by his renewed study of Hegel and Marx from 1916 on. If, as he later recalled, his first serious examination of Marx was carried out "through Simmelian spectacles,"[11] he now began to find in more radically dialectical views of history the ideas needed to deal with his nagging discomfort over the outlook conveyed by Simmel.

If the notions of reification and alienation provided the common bond between Lukács and Simmel, Lukács' emerging critique of Simmel can be seen as a different way of interpreting those phenomena. Where Simmel had formulated the consequences of a money economy in timeless, universal terms and had linked reification and alienation with inalterable metaphysical properties of human life, Lukács would increasingly insist on their connection with the historically specific conditions of society under bourgeois capitalism. Where Simmel had presented his interpretations in the form of abstract sociological and philosophical analysis, Lukács was inclined toward a more active project of social criticism and revolutionary "praxis." Where Simmel's own ultimate values would be expressed solely in terms of the ideal of individuality, Lukács was torn between individualistic and collectivistic value orientations and tended, as early as 1910, to search for a way of making the agent of cultural renewal a collective, universal "We" subject (Arato and Breines 1979, 28, 35).

Lukács' deviation from Simmel accelerated during the last months of 1918. On September 28, Simmel died. On October 2, Lukács published an obituary essay: his farewell to Simmel, in more than one sense. He hailed Simmel for having provided, in the desolate and soulless intellectual landscape of late nineteenth-century materialism and positivism, an oasis of methodological pluralism, an inexhaustible source of sensibility and enthusiasm for the manifold possibilities of symbolic creativity. He credited Simmel with possessing the greatest of philosophical talents—"the capacity to view the smallest and most insignificant phenomenon of everyday life so strongly *sub specie philosophiae* that it becomes transparent, and behind its transparence there becomes visible an eternal formal nexus of philosophical meaning" (1958, 172). And yet, Lukács said, Simmel's work had to be regarded as a blind alley; Simmel was a

11. "Mit dem mir immer klarer werdenden imperialistischen Charakter des Krieges, mit der Vertiefung meiner Hegelstudien . . . beginnt meine zweite intensive Beschäftigung mit Marx. . . . Diesmal war es jedoch ein Marx, nicht mehr durch die Simmelsche, wohl aber durch eine Hegelsche Brille gesehen" ([1933] 1967, 325–26).

stimulator, an "impressionist," not one who brought questions to completion and reached firm conclusions. This was due, he said, to Simmel's "lack of a center." Lukács' summary judgment, then, was that Simmel was an indispensable figure in the history of philosophy, but only a transitional figure, one who would have to be surpassed by those capable of formulating ultimate decisions and a stable, coherent world view.

We can leave it to psychobiographers to speculate whether the death of Simmel, who served Lukács for so many years as a model, freed his energies in a way that facilitated his abrupt move to embrace a firmer world view less than three months later—his "conversion," as most commentators have called it, to Marxism. Certainly his deepening immersion in Marxian literature and the excitement of the revolutionary events of 1917 and 1918 were the major precipitants. The fact is that in November Lukács was approached by Bela Kun, a leader of the newly formed Communist Party of Hungary, and in mid-December he joined the Party.

As an effort to come to terms with Simmel, by affirming his intellectual prowess but repudiating his basic philosophical approach (however defined), Lukács' obituary essay occupies a place in the story of his relation to Simmel analogous to that of Durkheim's 1900 article and Weber's unfinished critique of 1908. In contrast to the others, Lukács went on to transform his criticisms of Simmel in accord with his developing views as a Marxist and a committed member of the Communist Party. Those views evolved in four stages.

In the years just after he joined the Party, Lukács struggled to work out his own interpretation of the Marxian tradition. Eight essays from that period were published in 1923 as *History and Class Consciousness,* a book that continues to be regarded as the germinal work of "Western Marxism." The premise of that work, Lukács tells us, is "the belief that in Marx's theory and method the *true method* by which to understand society and history has *finally* been discovered" (1971, xliii; emphasis in original). This method remains valid even if all of Marx's particular theses prove untenable. The heart of the method is not its stress on the primacy of economic motives, but rather its adopting the point of view of totality, of "the all-pervasive supremacy of the whole over the part," and the related emphasis on the principle of historicity, "knowledge of the historical process in its entirety" (1971, 27, 34).

When applied to that analysis of objectified cultural phenomena which Lukács had previously found in Simmel, this method requires one to link the modern reification of products and mental faculties to the concrete relations of the capitalist society that engenders them. Lukács cites Simmel as the prime example of those bourgeois thinkers who fail to make that connection, thinkers who have no desire to deny or obscure the existence of reified consciousness "and who are more or less clear in their own minds about its humanly destructive consequences," but who nevertheless "remain on the surface. . . . They divorce these empty manifestations from their real capitalist foundation and make them independent and permanent by regarding them as the timeless model of human relations in general" (1971, 94–95). In similar manner, after explaining the rise to prominence in modern philosophy of such antinomies as the opposition between subject and object, individual and society, and form and content, by linking them to the contradictions of bourgeois society, Lukács faults Simmel for accepting such antinomies as given realities:

> In this way the very thing that should be understood and deduced with the aid of mediation becomes the accepted principle by which to explain all phenomena and is even elevated to the status of a value: namely the unexplained and inexplicable facticity of bourgeois existence as it is here and now acquires the patina of an eternal law of nature or a cultural value enduring for all time. (1971, 157)

Instead, Lukács calls for a "mediating" analytic approach, one that identifies "immanent possibilities" not apparent in the immediately given phenomenal reality, and he finds in the emerging consciousness of the proletariat—the true heir to German classical philosophy—the agency that stands to transcend the reification of bourgeois mentality.

After *History and Class Consciousness,* Lukács would make no more substantial references to Simmel until three decades later. His own intellectual journey would henceforth be charted in the mazeway of Communist Party ideological disputes. Having come to view the Party as the living vessel of the proletariat's (and thus humanity's) "moral mission," he came to idolize Lenin from 1926 on, and to replace his messianic vision of an international proletarian revolution by an identification with Stalinism and the goal of building "socialism in one country." As Lukács had used his Hegelianized version of Marxism to discredit his initial Simmelian reading of Marx, so now he accepted the Party's more materialistic position to discredit the idealism of his Hegelian phase. In an

address to the Philosophical Section of the Communist Academy at
Moscow in 1934, Lukács solemnly denounced *History and Class
Consciousness,* repudiating his views therein as "objectively"
counterrevolutionary and simply indicting Simmel (along with Max
Weber and Georges Sorel) as one of the pre-1914 writers who had
reinforced his leanings toward "romantic anticapitalism."

After a decade more in Moscow and another decade back in
Hungary, Lukács turned once again to a more extended consideration of Simmel. This was in the context of his penetrating analysis of
the vicissitudes of irrationalism in German intellectual history, *Die
Zerstörung der Vernunft,* first published in 1954. Lukács' goal in this
book was to depict the road from Schelling to Hitler: the main lines
of thought, in German philosophy and sociology, that promoted a
reaction against reason and thereby helped shape the ideology of
Nazism. In this context, Lukács chose to ignore Simmel's writings
as a sociologist (p. 17), and to focus on Simmel's later writings as a
metaphysician and a proponent of *Lebensphilosophie* (philosophy of
life). In the chapter on Simmel (pp. 386–401), Lukács identifies
several features of Simmel's philosophy that represent a turn against
rationality. First, he notes Simmel's tendency to combat every form
of a realistic representation of reality, his transformation of Kant's
a priori categories into a stance of ultra subjectivism. This kind of
relativistic skepticism "undermines objective scientific knowledge
and creates . . . a space for the most desolate reactionary obscurant-
ism, for the nihilistic mystique of imperialistic decadence. . . . It is
the self-defense of imperialist philosophy against dialectical materialism" (p. 389). This relativism, moreover, opens the door to a
defense of religiosity—for Simmel, a subjectively created "world"
that possesses its own dignity and autonomy alongside science,
philosophy, art, and other such worlds. Lukács sees this conception
as part of the modern tendency toward "religious atheism," the
disposition of intellectuals whom modern science has alienated from
established churches and religions but whose experience of disorientation and emptiness creates some sort of religious need. In
fact, Lukács argues, this need was fostered by the insecurity of
conditions under capitalism in the imperialistic period: where workers experienced that insecurity in the brutal material conditions of
their lives, bourgeois intellectuals experienced it in a more "subli-
mated" form, in the contradiction between "complete freedom, the
intoxicating feeling of being stood entirely on oneself, and an
inconsolable sense of destitution; between the pressure to seek the
norms of every action in one's own ego, on the one hand, and a

growing nihilism with respect to all norms, on the other hand'' (p. 391). Lukács faults Simmel for encouraging this "religious atheism" as a solution to those problems, a solution which he says led to the posture of "heroic pessimism" and "heroic realism" that prefigured the fascist world view (p. 394).

Lukács further takes Simmel to task for replacing Kant's bourgeois-revolutionary morality of universal human equality, not by the new historically progressive morality of socialism, but by a romantic morality of unique individuality that at the time could only have been proclaimed in the name of a parasitic, privileged stratum of intellectuals (p. 398). Lukács sees the metaphysical foundation of all these mistakes in Simmel's mythic concept of "life," one that subsumes all conflicts under a highly abstract notion of transcendence and elevates the "tragedy of culture" into a manifestation of the ultimate contradictions of life itself. This kind of philosophic generalization thus "perverts the anticapitalistic dissatisfaction of intellectuals into self-sufficiency, self-complacency, self-mirroring" (p. 397).

In the final analysis, then,

> the indirect apologia set forth by Schopenhauer and
> Nietzsche—the defense of the capitalist system that proceeds
> by acknowledging and stressing its bad sides, but at the same
> time inflates them into cosmic contradictions—has here openly
> declared its bankruptcy. Simmel is sharp-sighted enough to see
> the inexorability of the contradictions, but he is too much the
> ideologist of imperialist *rentier* parasitism to be done in by this
> insolubility of the contradictions. On the contrary, the esoteric
> moral of his philosophy of life is the deliberate evasion of their
> ultimate consequences. . . . The Simmelian nuance of relativism
> and skepticism thus introduces something new into German
> philosophical consciousness: self-complacent cynicism. (p. 400)

"This unintended cynicism of Simmel," Lukács concludes, "grows into a methodology of highly frivolous dilettantism with Spengler, and therewith invades the scholarly spirit of philosophy in a destructive and dissolving manner. From that point, the development moves rapidly ahead toward fascism" (p. 401).

Thus, from being an enthusiastic student of Simmel (1905–15), Lukács shifted to viewing Simmel first as an interesting transitional figure who afforded no enduring point of view (1918), next as a superficial analyst of the contradictions of capitalist culture (1923), then as a counterrevolutionary influence responsible for promoting the attitude of romantic anticapitalism (1934), and finally as an ideologist for imperialist capitalism who unwittingly contributed to the rise of fascism (1954). In the years around his eightieth birthday, Lukács' tone alters once again: his few references to Simmel seem to express an old man's appreciation for what he gained from the mentor of his youth. In a public letter to Alberto Carocci in 1962, Lukács credits the degree of sociological understanding he acquired from Simmel (and Max Weber) for saving him from such pathetic notions as that of the "great man" approach to history (1967, 658), and in conversations held in 1967 he reflected:

> I do not at all regret today that I took my first lessons in social science from Simmel and Max Weber and not from Kautsky. I don't know whether one cannot even say today that this was a fortunate circumstance for my own development. (1975, 100)

Park

Although Robert Park was some twenty years older than Lukács, it can be said that Park, too, took his first lessons in social science from Simmel, inasmuch as Simmel's lectures on sociology, which he attended in the autumn of 1899, constituted the only formal instruction in sociology Park ever received. Park carefully preserved his notes from those lectures and published them at Chicago three decades later. Like Lukács, Park later credited Simmel with providing him a fundamental point of view at a time when he was searching for a suitable intellectual orientation. What Park found in Simmel, however, was not a theory of cultural forms and a critique of modern culture, but a basic way to think about society—by applying the notion of *forms of interaction*.

What took Park to Berlin was a complex personal quest that by then had crystallized into a wish to understand the role of the news media and public opinion in modern urban society. Park had struggled for years to find a way of expressing his humanitarian identification with the common people and his belief in the capacity of abstract thought to enlighten the path of social evolution, both of which were kindled by earlier study with John Dewey at the University of Michigan. Years of work as a newspaperman had gratified his desire to be close to humble human realities but left his intellectual aspirations unsatisfied. In the early 1890s he rallied, along with Dewey and others, to the idea of publishing *Thought News,* a journal intended to interpret current events according to the insights of philosophy; but the project fizzled. After several years more working as a reporter and city editor, Park left journalism for further academic work, entering the Department of Philosophy at Harvard in order, he wrote in his diary, to study "the philosophical aspects of the effects of the printed facts on the public" (Matthews 1977, 31). That experience turned him against the abstractions of metaphysics and toward an empirical approach to the study of social life. The great prestige of German social science at the time drew him to Berlin. Thus it came about, as Park later recalled, that "it was from Simmel that I finally gained a point of view for the study of the newspaper and society" (Baker 1973, 256).

The lectures Park heard presented a plausible solution to the conflict between organicism and individualism, an issue that had long been on Park's mind. Simmel rejected both notions, arguing that organicism, or sociological realism, illegitimately reified the products of social action, while sociological nominalism makes individuals the ultimate units of analysis only by establishing an arbitrary cutting point, since individual persons themselves are highly composite phenomena. Simmel proposed to resolve that old controversy by shifting the question from a debate about the ultimate nature of reality to a matter of making the definition of objects of study depend on the perspective of observer, on the one hand, and, on the other, the existence of something in reality that corresponds to that interest. With regard to a science of society, the "something in reality" that corresponds to an observer's interests is the existence of reciprocal dynamic relations among individuals or groups. Society was thus for Simmel a name for this phenomenon of social interaction, and the task of sociology was to study the diverse forms of interaction (*Wechselwirkung*) or association (*Vergesellschaftung*).

Simmel's conception not only enabled Park to satisfy both his individualistic and his sociologistic leanings; it also gave him a language in which to articulate the ideas about news and public opinion he had been developing. Although Park went on to Strasbourg and then Heidelberg to complete his doctoral work under Wilhelm Windelband, his dissertation was very much a Simmelian essay. *Masse und Publikum* treated the crowd and the public as two forms of association, constituted by the interaction of large numbers of persons in settings not governed by customary constraints. Both crowd and public are transitional phenomena, offshoots of the breakdown of established social groupings and vehicles for the expression of new collective impulses. While the members of crowds interact through "milling" until some contagious impulse

emerges that then sweeps through them and galvanizes their emotions, the members of publics interact through discussion, critical
analysis, and the reciprocal shaping of opinions. Park's dissertation
enabled him to counter the pessimistic theorists of crowd psychology by arguing that the modern world offers "*two* alternatives to
traditional society, not only the crowd, swayed by the emotion of
the moment, but also the public, emancipated from customary
beliefs but not from the capacity of rational discussion of means and
ends: the enlightened public in which Dewey and the progressives
put their faith was a real possibility" (Matthews 1977, 56).

Park's doctoral formulations gave him a rationale for the publicity
work on behalf of Booker T. Washington and the efforts to improve
the lot of American Negroes in which he would spend the following
decade. They also provided the intellectual capital on which he
would draw heavily when he resumed academic work as a teacher
and scholar at the University of Chicago in 1914. Park went on to
teach a course on "The Crowd and the Public" for many years. He
applied the notion of forms of social interaction in other original
ways, most notably by conceiving the course of relations between
racial and ethnic groups as a natural cycle, moving from competition
and then conflict through accommodation and eventual assimilation.
He drew heavily on Simmel, both for selections and for organizing
principles, in the book of readings published with Ernest Burgess in
1921, the famous *Introduction to the Science of Sociology*. He
exploited Simmelian ideas in his writings on urbanism, social
distance, marginality, and conflict.

In the case of Park, one cannot speak of a moment of repudiating
Simmel that is truly comparable to the critiques of Simmel produced
by Durkheim, Weber, Lukács or, as we shall see, Parsons. Indeed,
in later years Park would refer to Simmel's *Soziologie* as "the most
profound and stimulating book in sociology, in my opinion, that has
ever been written" (Duncan 1959, 116, n.25). Primarily, in this
context, Park should be remembered as the man who did more than
anyone else to secure a favorable hearing for Simmel among
generations of American sociologists. Even so, there is a real sense
in which Park's prefatory discussions in the Park and Burgess
Introduction stand as his de facto coming to terms with Simmel,
reflecting attitudes he would thereafter follow in deviating from a
strictly Simmelian approach. If Park relied on Simmel, it was in his
own irrepressibly eclectic fashion. If, thanks to Park, Simmel's
ideas were revivified by being translated into a more accessible
idiom, their potential use as a basis for a general analytic theory or

a distinctive methodology for social investigations was diluted and compromised. Park's disavowal of Simmel was no less real for being merely implicit.

Although the notion of social interaction was the root metaphor that tied Park with Simmel and formed the guiding idea of his own sociological work, he departed from Simmel both in the methodology for studying interaction and in his theoretic elaboration of the construct. On the methodological side, Park was a thoroughgoing empiricist. He prized direct contact with urban happenings and human types of many sorts, and encouraged students to follow his lead in observing street scenes and documenting personal life histories. "The first thing that students in sociology need to learn is to observe and record their observations. . . . Until students learn to deal with opinions as the biologists deal with organisms, that is, to dissect them—reduce them to their component elements, describe them, and define the situation (environment) to which they are a response—we must not expect very great progress in sociological science" (Park and Burgess 1921, v).[12] This was a methodological manifesto quite different from that of Simmel who ranged casually through his own luxuriant stock of knowledge to find the right anecdote or historical incident to illustrate some abstract point, and frankly accepted whatever odium might be incurred for advocating an intuitive grasp of the essence of forms as his basic methodological ploy.

Where Simmel was casual—in his acquisition of facts—Park was enthusiastically rigorous; where Simmel was rigorous—in his analysis of structural properties—Park was typically casual. Park's ambivalent response to Simmel appears in the way he alternately appropriates and rejects Simmel's conception of social interaction in the theoretical statements presented in the *Introduction*.

At times, Park seems to follow Simmel in equating society with human interaction, pure and simple—particularly when he suggests that the "four great types of social interaction" underlie the four main types of "social order": competition underlies economic equilibrium; conflict, political order; accommodation, social organization; and assimilation, "personality and the cultural heritage" (1921, 506–10). More characteristically, and especially in his later work, however, Park leaned toward the more conventional identi-

12. In this vein, Park later wrote: "A sociologist was to be a kind of super-reporter, like the men who write for *Fortune*. He was to report a little more accurately, and in a manner a little more detached than the average" (1950, ix).

fication of the social with the *moral* order, which he contrasted with the *ecological* order deriving from the mere pursuit of individual self-interest. "Society," Park asserts in this vein, "may be said to exist only so far as this independent activity is controlled in the interest of the group as a whole" (1921, 508). Social control, then, became for Park and Burgess "the central fact and the central problem of society"—not the normatively indifferent phenomena of human association, as with Simmel—and sociology "a point of view and a method for investigating the processes by which individuals are inducted into and induced to cooperate in some sort of permanent corporate existence which we call society" (1921, 42).

The bearers of moral or social order, moreover, are viewed by Park as organized collectivities. Again, following Simmel, Park sees collectivities not as substantive entities but as networks of interaction. Crowds are made up of persons interacting through milling, sects through the reciprocal stimulation of unrest, racial groups through the communication of shared grievances, publics through the circulation of news. Through these various processes of communication, collectivities attain some consensus regarding values and goals. *Concerted action* is thus the dynamic aspect of moral order and social control. Park's emphasis on concerted action as the primary referent of social interaction contrasts with Simmel's emphasis on *transaction* between parties, and Park's related definition of sociology as "the science of collective behavior" similarly contrasts with Simmel's definition of sociology as the science of forms of association of every sort.

These subtle shifts of emphasis and definition were not inconsequential. They steered the sociology practiced by Park and his students in a direction other than that followed by Simmel. Its empirical focus was on types of concrete collectivities rather than on the empirical referents of analytically abstracted types of social interaction.[13] It dealt no longer with the structural implications of different kinds of forms, as Park did in his dissertation on the crowd and the public, but with how these different kinds of collectivity emerge, persist, and change. Finally, by relegating competition and conflict to the sphere of the presocial, or subsocial, they promoted an identification of sociality with consensus, rather than a conception of all social facts as inherently based on dualistic tendencies.

13. In his contributions to human ecology, however, Park maintained an interest in such analytic abstractions when applying concepts like 'invasion,' 'succession,' and 'dominance.'

This casual method of dealing with Simmel's ideas is likewise illustrated in a number of particular areas where Park drew from Simmel. It is likely, as Coser has noted, that Park's "specific ideas such as those on social conflict, the marginal man, the characteristics of urban dwellers, and social distance were all stimulated by Simmel" (1977, 374). In each of these cases, however, Park's formulations differed from Simmel's without Park's showing any awareness that he was using those concepts in substantially different ways.[14]

One further divergence between the sociological orientations of Simmel and Park must be noted. Both strove, in their analyses of society, to maintain a truly detached perspective. They successfully combined an enormous empathic capacity with a quality of Olympian aloofness. For Simmel, however, this contemplative analysis of the human species and its social formations was worthwhile intrinsically; by implication, it was to serve purely aesthetic interests. For Park, on the other hand, the practical exigencies of modern urban society were always close at hand and always of interest. Park was particularly attuned to the problems of adjustment experienced by Negroes, Orientals, East European immigrants, and moral outcasts in a complex pluralistic society. His project of furthering empathic understanding was designed as an intellectual's contribution toward progressive social evolution. He viewed applied sociology less as an exercise in social engineering than as a form of indirect therapy through properly channeled information and increased public communication. He believed that "only to the extent that we are able to enter imaginatively into the lives and experience of others do we regard them as human like ourselves," and that the main task of sociology was to help members of alien groups become acquainted with one another intimately as persons (Matthews 1977, 177, 169, 192). It was thus natural for Park to sacrifice concern for the systematic analysis of social structures in favor of attention to the attitudes and sentiments of diverse groups in the urban public.

Durkheim, Weber, and Lukács sought to develop carefully reasoned, coherent conceptions of society and the forms of thought appropriate for its analysis. They were led to reject Simmel because of the contradictions between his ideas and their own systems. Park's case is the precise opposite: his project was chiefly to promote the dispassionate collection of facts, and theoretic con-

14. On Park's misrepresentations of Simmel's conceptions of the stranger and social distance, see Levine et al. (1976) as well as chapter 5.

structs were merely useful tools along the way. Time and again he
diverged from Simmel, without attempting to justify his different
formulations or even acknowledging the differences. In relation to
Simmel's work, which stands as an invitation to elaborate subtle
conceptual distinctions in the analysis of formal properties, such
carelessness must be viewed as a kind of neglect, if not repudiation.

Parsons

On the eve of the last decade in his long and productive life,
Talcott Parsons wrote that Simmel was probably "the most important single figure neglected in *The Structure of Social Action*
[hereafter, *Structure,*] and to an important degree in my subsequent
writings" (1968a, xiv, n.10). The remark is misleading insofar as it
implies that Parsons' response to Simmel was one of careless
inattention. The fact is that during the period when he was forging
the conceptual framework of his theory of action, Parsons experienced a serious and sustained engagement with some central ideas
of Simmel.

Parsons became acquainted with Simmel's work while studying at
Heidelberg in the mid-1920s. Although preoccupied with the writings of Sombart and Max Weber at the time, he became sufficiently
interested in Simmel to lecture on him regularly in his course on
social theory at Harvard in the early 1930s. He went on to draft a
substantial statement on Simmel for *Structure,* a statement that was
never published and was in fact mislaid and never again recovered
during his lifetime.

Like Durkheim, what Parsons found of greatest interest in Simmel
was his general approach to the study of social phenomena. In
contrast to Durkheim, it was not Simmel's stress on the specificity
of social facts as supraindividual phenomena that attracted him, but
rather Simmel's conception of the epistemological basis of sociology: his advice that sociology be constituted as an abstract analytic
discipline. To clarify this crucial point we must consider the set of
issues with which Parsons was grappling when he encountered and
then came to terms with Simmel.

The point of departure for Parsons' earliest theoretical work was
his perception of serious weaknesses in the explanatory power of
classical economics combined with his appreciation of its substantial
successes in certain respects. In dealing with this problem, his
rhetorical animus was directed against two views he believed to be
common at the time he was writing. One was the view of human

action, which he called "positivistic," that "tends to obscure the fact that man is essentially an active, creative, evaluating creature," and to suspect "any attempt to explain his behavior in terms of ends, purposes, ideals" as being a form of "teleology" (1935a, 282). The other was a view of the nature of economic science, which he called an "empiricist" view, that considers the task of economics to be one of "delivering a full and complete explanatory account of a given sector of concrete reality" (1935b, 420).

In the first work published beyond his doctoral research on Sombart and Weber, Parsons concentrated on the figure of Alfred Marshall. Parsons applauded Marshall for going beyond the "positivistic" views of action held by orthodox economists to stress the explanatory importance of "value" elements. However, Marshall maintained an empiricist view of economics, such that the boundaries of the discipline were widened to encompass normative as well as utilitarian elements. Parsons was dissatisfied with this move of Marshall's for two reasons. He argued, first, that Marshall's treatment of the value elements lacked the "perspective" which his treatment of the utility elements displayed; work on value elements within an economic frame of reference seemed to him scientifically inferior.

Second, the expansion of economics into an encyclopedic social science by Marshall and his followers was a form of "economic imperialism," which has the effect of "suppressing the 'rights' of neighboring sciences to an 'independent' existence in the society of the sciences" (1934, 522). Most particularly, of course, Parsons was interested in establishing a sphere of self-determination for his own fledgling discipline of sociology. He felt the need to do so acutely inasmuch as Harvard University had been the site of longstanding jurisdictional disputes between economics and sociology (Camic 1979, 542). In order to establish a rightful place for sociology he had to find a way to conceive sociology as a science with its own special domain. For that purpose he could accept the views neither of Durkheim nor of Weber. Durkheim held that sociology should be a comprehensive discipline, and that the various other social sciences should be regarded as particular branches of sociology and integrated into the latter through its establishment of general laws. Parsons found so diffuse a conception of the field wholly unacceptable.

Weber's view was that sociology should be a science of all social action. Although Weber thereby excluded from sociology what Durkheim would have called the morphological substratum (ecological and demographic factors), Parsons found Weber's conception still too diffuse. It would make sociology either a historical science or a synthetic science that subsumed the disciplines of economics and politics. In his earliest writing on the matter, Parsons rejected this "narrow encyclopedic" view of the field no less than he rejected the "broad encyclopedic" view commonly associated with Durkheim, Spencer, and Comte (1934, 528–29).

In contrast with these encyclopedic views of the field (which, he noted, offended other social scientists with their "irritating pretentiousness" [1935c, 666]), Parsons advocated a conception which "would give to sociology a subject matter essentially its own and not shared by any other systematic theoretical discipline." This "specific" view of the discipline, he wrote, had "heretofore . . . been held in methodological self-consciousness only by Simmel and his followers" (1934, 529). Moreover, to define that subject matter in terms of a particular set of concrete phenomena—as Durkheim had done when insisting that what sociology studies are concrete societies and real social facts—would be to commit the fallacy of empiricist reification. Such a definition would suit a branch of historical studies, one which legitimately focuses on some concrete period or area, but not a scientific discipline. For "the essence of science," Parsons held, "is theory and the essence of theory is analytical abstraction. Whatever its dangers, there is no other way" (1935c, 661). A genuine scientific specialty could only be established on the basis of adopting a particular analytic perspective. And it was Simmel, Parsons thought, who provided "the first serious attempt to gain a basis for sociology as, in this sense, a special science" ((1937, 772–73).[15]

If, then, as Parsons asserted, Simmel had pointed the way to conceiving sociology as a *special* science, one whose domain was to be constituted on the basis of certain analytic abstractions, could not Parsons proceed to follow Simmel's way of characterizing the angle of abstraction appropriate for sociology? For a while, it seems, he thought that he could. The very first time that Parsons attempted to define a specific sphere for sociology, he did so in perfectly Simmelian terms: "By sociology, I should mean a science which studies phenomena specifically social, those arising out of the *interaction* of human beings as such, which would hence not be

15. See also his statement two years earlier: "The nearest approach to . . . this conception of sociology as a systematic theoretical discipline . . . which enjoys recognized standing in the literature is that of the so-called 'formal' school, of which Georg Simmel is generally regarded as the founder" (1935c, 666, n.3).

reducible to the 'nature' of those human beings'' (1932, 338; emphasis in original). But to commit himself totally to Simmel's framework would be to regard *economics* in a manner Parsons found unacceptable. From Parsons' point of view, the problem with Simmel's formula—that sociology deals with the forms of social interaction abstracted from their contents—was that it left the study of the contents of social life—the various motives and purposes which lead actors to associate—to various disciplines (economics, politics, education, religion, and the like) residually classified on the basis of types of concrete ends pursued by actors. As he put it some years later:

> The main difficulty for Simmel was that the view he took of the other social sciences precluded relating his concept of sociology to other analytical social sciences on the same methodological level. To him sociology was the only abstract analytical science in the social field. (1937, 773)

In his search for an appropriate definition of the scope of sociology, however, Parsons sought not only to provide secure and defensible borders for his adopted discipline, but no less to guarantee the "rights" of the field from which he had migrated—he had been trained as an economist, and his first publications appeared in journals of economics—and for whose achievements he always maintained the highest respect. It was a cardinal assumption for Parsons that, whatever else happened in the organization of the sciences, the status of economics as an abstract analytic discipline had to be kept inviolate. Not long after completing his critique of Marshall, Parsons found a way to achieve both these objectives. He did so by yielding to economics the right to set the terms for organizing the whole universe of knowable social phenomena. What that meant was to enthrone "action" as the supreme category in social science, and to assign places to all specialized analyses of social phenomena, including those of sociology, in terms of a means-end schema. By assigning sociology to the "one so far unoccupied sector" of the means-end schema of analysis, it would be possible to "give to sociology a subject matter essentially its own and not shared by any other systematic theoretical discipline" (1934, 529).

Thus, from viewing sociology as a science which studies phenomena arising out of social interaction (1932), Parsons went on to proclaim that "a sociology which does not explicitly study the role of ultimate ends in human life is a poor thing indeed" (1934, 525).

The resulting charter for the society of social sciences can be represented schematically as follows:

Elements of Action	Corresponding Analytic Sciences
Ultimate means, or conditions of action:	
Physical environment	Geography
Organismic properties	Biology
Mental faculties	Psychology
Intermediate means-end sector:	
Means for attaining single ends	Technology
Allocation of scarce means for competing ends through production or exchange	Economics
Attainment of ends through the means of coercive power	Politics
Ultimate ends and the attitudes underlying them	Sociology

In the end, this would prove to be an unstable formulation, and Parsons would be moved to revise it radically two more times in the course of his career. In the 1930s, however, Parsons' chief concerns were to deal with the explanatory shortcomings of economics—its failure to deal with the ultimate ends of action—and to circumvent empiricist definitions of that field (and of sociology). Both problems were resolvable by insisting on the substantive importance of ultimate ends and by making sociology the special discipline to investigate them. This solution made it necessary for him finally to reject Simmel's formula.

Thanks to recently secured documentation on the matter, some of the stages of Parsons' ambivalent encounter with Simmel can now be charted with some precision. In 1932, we have seen, his own definition for sociology closely paralleled that of Simmel. During the next few years he began to work out the argument that appeared in *Structure*, one that entailed positing a highly significant convergence among the major figures of the sociological tradition. A footnote in a paper published in 1935 describes the project as follows:

> My own views have taken shape mainly in the course of a series of critical studies in European sociological theory. The important writers for my purposes may be divided into two groups—those starting from a positivistic and those from an

idealistic background. I should maintain the thesis that the two
groups have tended to converge on a conception somewhat like
that which I shall outline in the present essay. Of the writers
starting from a positivistic basis, two have been most important
to me—Vilfredo Pareto and Emile Durkheim. Of the other
group, the most important have been Max Weber, George [sic]
Simmel, and Ferdinand Toennies. (1935a, 283)

What is striking about this passage is the inclusion of Simmel
among the select group of authors whom Parsons identified as
personally important to him, and indeed his inclusion as one of those
who could be said to have been part of the grand convergence
between the "positivistic" and "idealistic" traditions.

Parsons' intentions in this matter are further revealed by the fact
that he proceeded to draft a section on Simmel for *Structure*. Not
long after the 1935 passage just cited appeared, however, two things
happened: the final form of the "convergence thesis" took shape,[16]
and Parsons made a decision to exclude the section on Simmel from
the published version of *Structure*. There can be no doubt that these
two events were connected, especially since we now have, from a
letter written a few months before his death, Parsons' direct
testimony: "The decision not to include the Simmel chapter had
various motives. . . . The space problem was by no means the whole
problem in relation to Simmel. *It is true that Simmel's program did
not fit my convergence thesis*" (1979, 3; emphasis mine).

Following the publication of *Structure*, Parsons never again
attempted to integrate Simmel's ideas into the body of his own
developing work. As was the case for Weber, the short piece in
which he sought to come to terms with Simmel was not published
during his lifetime; indeed, as noted earlier, he misplaced the draft
and, despite apparent efforts to locate it later, never succeeded in
recovering it. Only after his death did the piece surface.[17]

In the published version of *Structure*, what Parsons says about
Simmel is that he endorses Simmel's project to establish sociology
as an abstract analytic discipline, but rejects his formula for doing
this "for reasons that cannot be gone into here" (1937, 773). In the
unpublished pages on Simmel, Parsons reveals some of those
reasons. In a previous publication I have examined the main lines of

16. "I am pretty sure that the convergence thesis was pretty fully crystallized
before my long series of discussions with Henderson. I am not sure of the dating, but
I think it took place in the fall and winter of 1935–6" (1979, 3).

17. The long lost text was brought to my attention in 1980 thanks to the kind efforts
of Victor M. Lidz, one of the professional advisors to the Parsons estate.

his argument (1980, li-liv). The matter can be summarized here by observing that in this statement Parsons strongly commends Simmel's work for having contributed an important approach to sociological analysis, but also maintains that such an approach must be strictly subordinated to a sociology modeled on classical economics, that is, a sociology that follows the method of axiomatized deductive theory and conceives its subject matter in terms of a means-end schema. To have published that discussion, in *Structure* or elsewhere, would have committed Parsons publicly to legitimating a direction for sociological theory that clearly "cut across" his own approach to theory building and would to some extent have been competitive with it. That would have required him to tolerate a degree of ambiguity that is enormously difficult for a highly motivated scientist to sustain.

Years later, in *The Social System* (1951), when Parsons turned to a direct examination of the structural aspects of social systems, he would do so in terms of institutionalized norms and values rather than in terms of such variables as distance, position, size, valence, self-involvement, and symmetry—the key elements of what would be a general sociological theory along Simmelian lines (Levine 1981). His sociology would find it difficult to focus directly on relational phenomena such as exchange, conflict, communication, super- and subordination, and social networks because he had committed himself to defining sociology as a science of the evaluative elements of action *before* coming to the point (which Simmel reached four decades earlier) of insisting on the analytic distinction between the psychological, social, and cultural aspects of action. If his "social system" was spelled "interaction," it was pronounced "norms."

Parsons' decision to forget about Simmel was fateful for the remainder of his career as a social theorist and indeed for the course of American social theory in the twentieth century. Most of the "new" approaches in sociological theory that mushroomed in the 1960s—"conflict" theory, "exchange" theory, phenomenological sociology, and network analysis—had two things in common: a critical stance toward Parsonian theory, and a programmatic statement in which Simmel was hailed as a founding father.

Ambivalent Encounters

Georg Simmel is not dead, even though he was considered, rejected, and forgotten by five of the most influential shapers of contemporary sociology. His current prominence stems from an upsurge of translations and critical commentaries on his work within the last generation[18] as well as from attention paid him by proponents of the newer sociological approaches just mentioned. The renewed interest and reversal of judgment regarding his work is epitomized by Theodore Abel who, in 1929, faulted Simmel for propounding an approach that was at variance with his actual substantive analyses, which fault, Abel thought, "deprived him of making valuable contributions to sociology" (p. 48); but who then went on to proclaim, three decades later, that Simmel "could justifiably be regarded as the founder of modern sociology" and to suggest that it had taken many years of development in sociology since Simmel's death to enable the profession to appreciate his importance (1959, 474).

The point here, however, is not to hail Simmel's resurrection, but rather to ask what can be learned from our review of those five earlier encounters with his work. What does that experience tell us about the evolution of the sociological enterprise and what does it have to say about Simmel himself and the process of author-reader interaction?

The notion that to be truly "scientific" means to profess a discipline that embodies a single intellectual orientation or "paradigm" has led sociologists of the last generation to expend much too much energy arguing about the "right" orientation for their field. However insightful their accounts of the social phenomenon of divided labor, they have tended to forget, when regarding their own work, that if sociology is a single scientific field, it is so not by possessing a single ideology or common univocal language but by sustaining a general common enterprise to which different approaches make complementary contributions.

This is the case today; it has been true since the founding of the social sciences. Accordingly, any realistic history of sociology will posit, not a single line of scientific development, nor yet a plurality of traditions converging on a single line, but a perduring plurality of approaches, including their moments of convergence, divergence, or mutual stimulation—as well as long stretches of mutual ignorance.

Simmel lived during a time when the dominant theoretical orientations of modern social science were being codified. By the beginning of this century perhaps a dozen major research programs were well

18. See Levine et al. (1976, 819–22) and Frisby (1981, 187).

established. The most prominent of them embodied orientations that
may be called (1) atomic naturalism, (2) organismic naturalism, (3)
comparative interpretive studies, (4) radical evolutionism, and (5)
meliorist pragmatism. These orientations had antecedents in five
philosophical traditions that emerged in the eighteenth and nineteenth centuries: (1) the "utilitarian" tradition of British moral
philosophy, descending from Hobbes, Locke, and Hume through
Smith, J. S. Mill, and Marshall; (2) the "social realist" tradition of
French thought, descending from Montesquieu, Rousseau, and
Saint-Simon through Comte and Durkheim; (3) the hermeneutic and
historicist traditions of German thought, descending from Herder,
Savigny, and Schleiermacher through Dilthey and Max Weber; (4)
the socialist tradition, from Marx and Engels through Lenin and
Lukács; and (5) the American tradition from Peirce and James
through Thomas, Cooley, Mead, and Park (see Levine 1985).
Although all of these traditions encompass enormous internal variation, each of them can be shown to embrace a distinctive complex
of ideas and methods. The distinctive strengths and limitations of
these traditions become apparent when they are shown to have
addressed a common problem—interpreting the same event, like the
French Revolution; or a similar analytic topic, like the nature of
morality, political structure, or social evolution. In that process, the
complexities of the common subject become illuminated as well.

I would argue, then, that the outcomes of the engagements with
Simmel's thought exhibited in the five cases reviewed above constitute far more than biographical peculiarities: they represent what
logically might be expected to follow from the refraction of Simmel's
ideas by their encounter with the proponents of the traditions in
question.

Durkheim made himself spokesman for the tradition that may be
called "organismic naturalism." Its central notions, thoroughly
explicated by Comte, include the idea that societies constitute
emergent orders of natural phenomena, with properties that cannot
be derived from the properties of their constitutive elements; and
the belief that these phenomena are susceptible to the same kinds of
empirical examination that have been evolved for the study of less
complex phenomena in the natural sciences. Its research program
was to identify and classify the different types of supraindividual
human phenomena, and to explain them with reference to the
conditions that brought them into existence and the functions they
served.

At the time Durkheim encountered Simmel, he was campaigning actively to legitimate this orientation in the social sciences. That rhetoric informed his major publications of the mid-1890s, *The Rules of Sociological Method* and *Suicide*. He was attracted to Simmel, we have seen, by the prospect that Simmel's concern for the "specificity of social facts" might make him an ally in the project. Yet this affinity turned into rejection when it became clear that Simmel's sense of the "specifically social" was tied to a conception of social facts as analytic abstractions, not as concrete entities, and to a method that relied on the intuitive apprehension of forms, rather than inductive naturalistic observation. It seems that Durkheim appropriated Simmel's concept of social forms and turned it into his own concept of social morphology; he was able to do so, however, only by misconstruing Simmel's own project. Durkheim made two key mistakes in reading Simmel. He translated Simmel's distinction between contents and forms into a distinction between contents (*contenu*) and their "container" (*contenant*). This turns the distinction between intellectually separable aspects of concrete reality into two different kinds of concrete realities. Social morphology, for Durkheim, would then study the *contenant;* social physiology, the *contenu*. Durkheim then proceeded from what may be taken as an apt criticism of Simmel—from the point that the contents of social life are socially determined—to the questionable conclusion that the purely formal, structural aspects of social life are not isolable as phenomena that can be fruitfully grasped and examined sociologically. The ensuing rejection of Simmel's whole project then deprived Durkheim of valuable structural propositions that might have advanced his own research project appreciably.

Max Weber made himself spokesman for the hermeneutic and historicist tradition of German social thought. Their central notions, codified by Dilthey and Rickert, respectively, include the ideas that human phenomena are radically different from nonhuman natural phenomena in two respects: that human phenomena are constituted by the expression of intentions, such that to describe and explain them adequately requires an act of empathic understanding (*Verstehen*) of the subjective orientations of actors, and that historical phenomena are not reducible to the exemplification of general laws, but involve a unique constellation of elements embodied in concrete cases, the interest in which depends on some particular angle of relevance to the values of inquiring subjects. "Society," in this view, is not conceivable as another kind of natural organism, and indeed loses salience as an object of study altogether. Rather, the focus is on the shared orientations of strata and other associations of meaningfully oriented persons, and the interrelations of these types of associated actors in different times and places. The research program that eventuates may be designated "comparative interpretive studies," where the ultimate goal is to account for historical developments of special interest to us because of our values, and where systematic comparison of the degrees of elective affinity among diverse types of human formations serves to provide generalizations that support the explanatory understanding of those particular cases.

When Weber encountered Simmel, he was in the process of crystallizing the methodological views that informed this research program. He looked to Simmel for epistemological support of the program and found in Simmel's congenial neo-Kantian philosophy of history the most advanced delineation of a methodology of *Verstehen* then available. Although this served Weber's purpose as an interpretive historian, Simmel's departure from a historicist and hermeneutic stance in his approach to *sociology* diverged too radically from Weber's wish to make interpretive historical studies the fountainhead of comparative sociology. Similarly, Weber could appreciate Simmel's inspired portrait of the spirit of capitalism in his analysis of monetarized society, but had to reject its ahistorical, purely structural mode of presentation.

Even so, Weber's own substantive work contained a great deal of social structural analysis. By denying the appropriateness of Simmel's general conception, he deprived himself of certain programmatic formulations that might have integrated those analyses more adequately into a general sociological program.

In contrast to Durkheim and Weber, Lukács was at an earlier stage of his own intellectual development when he encountered Simmel. He became spokesman for a major intellectual tradition, that of Marxism, only after he had spent many years working within a largely Simmelian framework. It was the experience of alienation in capitalist society that aroused him to begin with, and he found in Simmel a philosophy of culture and an interpretation of modernity that helped him make sense of that experience and of the countervailing experience of aesthetic creativity as well. He appropriated from Simmel the basic concept of the "tragedy of culture," only to translate that conception, under the later sway of Marxian theory, into a form of false consciousness. Like any representative of Marxism, Lukács after 1918 would have had to reject Simmel's conception: as an illegitimate abstraction from concrete historical realities, as lacking a more inclusive synthesizing conception of human evolution—and hence without ideological grounding in the class struggle—and as an expression of a historically retrogressive position of bourgeois individualism. So complete a negation of Simmel's position precluded the appreciation of the "critical" potential of Simmel's philosophy of life and social forms, that is, its implicit notion that forms are indeed susceptible to critical assessment with respect to internal flaws and adaptive inappropriateness.

Robert Park made himself spokesman for a sociology oriented to the direct observation of human events. Although not himself philosophically articulate, he followed his master John Dewey in affirming several elements of a pragmatist outlook including the rejection of intellectual formalism, the contemporary importance of objective accounts of current social conditions, and the role of such accounts in raising the quality of communication and deliberation in modern publics.

When Park encountered Simmel, he was searching for a general conception of society to use in orienting his analysis of the role of the news media in the creation of modern public opinion. Simmel's notion of social interaction was congenial to him both because it avoided the abstract formalism of atomic and organismic theories, and because its stress on reciprocity paralleled the pragmatists' emphasis on reflexivity. But Simmel's approach entailed a kind of "formalism" of its own, an intellectual emphasis on the abstraction of forms that was tied neither to direct observational inquiries nor to the practical problems of modern life. Park's return to the world of journalistic and philanthropic activity following his doctoral work in Germany confirmed this orientation. When he came to elaborate his own sociological outlook, in the textbook with Burgess, he adapted Simmel's ideas eclectically but abandoned his general sociological project. His preoccupation with community, communication, and consensus shifted his analytic focus from transactions to concerted action, and his pragmatic emphasis on the solution of presenting social problems led him to neglect the theoretical potential of Simmel's work.

Some such reactions were, in retrospect, quite expectable from proponents of the traditions of organismic naturalism, hermeneutic historicism, radical evolutionism, and pragmatic meliorism, respectively. The case of Parsons, as a comparable representative of one of the major intellectual traditions, is complicated by the fact that

Parsons himself emerged as a forceful critic of the very tradition I believe he may be said to represent when he encountered Simmel.

The research program of "atomic naturalism," initiated by Hobbes in the 1640s, has informed a major tradition of work in the social sciences for three centuries. Here are its formal properties. It starts with the conception of a *propensity for action* that is (1) located with individuals, (2) naturally grounded, (3) universally distributed, and (4) intentionally and deliberately acted upon. From there it moves to a conception of a *social field* constituted by the typical kinds of interactions produced by individuals so disposed. It culminates with a conception of a relatively stable order, analogous to that of *mechanical equilibrium,* produced by the aggregation of those social interactions. In method, this research program is oriented to representing the atomic motions of actors in mathematical language, and to representing the relationships among the components of the theoretical system in logical-deductive fashion.

A century ago, this tradition achieved its prevailing contemporary form with the elaboration of marginal-utility economics as codified by Marshall. Accepting the validity of Marshallian economics was the starting point of Parsons' earliest work. Parsons believed that Marshall's correction of the previously prevailing conception of *homo economicus* was sound. He affirmed Marshall's attention to the normative and ideal components of action in addition to the utilitarian propensities previously considered exclusively by Anglo-Saxon economists. His chief critique of Marshall was that consideration of the nonutilitarian aspects of action could not properly be encompassed within the discipline of economics; that a more differentiated—and "abstract analytic"—conception of the intellectual disciplines was required.

A few months before he died, Parsons expressed the following lament: "To me one of the most distressing things about the elaborate secondary discussion of my work is the extent to which there is failure to appreciate the importance of economics in the whole picture. . . . This problem was completely central to the design of *The Structure of Social Action*" (1979, 2). The complaint was more than justified, in view of what nearly all previous commentators have written. The examination of Parsons' ambivalent response to Simmel, however, cannot proceed very far without taking that preoccupation into account.

In his search for a way to restrict economics to the analysis of the instrumental dimension of action, Parsons invoked the example of Simmel as one who had arrived at the appropriate notion of founding the scientific disciplines on the perspective of analytic abstractions. His commitment to economics as the paradigmatic case of this, however, forced him to define sociology as concerned with the nonutilitarian components of action, and thus to reject the substance of Simmel's program outright. Had he not been constrained to reject Simmel so thoroughly because of these disciplinary considerations, he would have found far more substantive support in Simmel's writings for the conception of action as inherently multidimensional—not least in Simmel's precocious discussion of the formation of conscience in his chapter on super- and subordination (and not to mention, in view of Parsons' later work, Simmel's discussion of money as a generalized medium of exchange). But that rejection was expectable, given *any* form of commitment to a program of atomic naturalism starting with some principle regarding propensities for action, a commitment that Parsons retained in *Structure* despite his enormously creative work in fusing it with aspects of the traditions of organismic naturalism and comparative interpretive studies as well.

The foregoing discussion by no means implies that the authors in question were ill-advised to respond to Simmel in a highly critical fashion. Given the intellectual orientations they espoused, they were of course correct to reject the contradictory aspects of Simmel's teaching. In the process, they produced a number of trenchant and lasting critiques of Simmel's work. In dealing with the ambivalence aroused by their encounters with Simmel, however, they apparently felt some compulsion to identify wholly with the negative side of their evaluation. With the partial exception of Park, none of them was able to sustain the ambiguity involved in seeing that even though Simmel's principles and methods were on some important points at variance with their own, they could continue to draw on his ideas in selective ways that might have enabled them to pursue their own agendas more completely. Nor were they able to appreciate that, in so doing, they would have been making precisely the sort of use of Simmel's work that he himself considered appropriate.

Simmel

Although traditions represented by Durkheim, Weber, Lukács, Park, and Parsons were among the many circulating in the milieu in which Simmel labored, he himself preferred to be independent of all of them. As Karl Hampe, dean at Heidelberg, wrote in 1908: "One can categorize Simmel in none of the general intellectual currents of the time; he has always gone his own way" (Gassen and Landmann 1958, 25). And in his own way, Simmel produced several kinds of work that appealed variously to his contemporaries who sought to advance the social science enterprise: a way to demarcate the field of sociology; a neo-Kantian philosophy of history; numerous essays on social forms; a philosophy of culture; and analyses of modern society and culture.

What, then, was Simmel's own way? For generations, readers sympathetic to Simmel have been haunted by the challenge of trying to do justice to that perplexing figure, to provide that penetrating grasp of his deepest intentions that Simmel considered the due of outstanding creative personalities, and which he provided so memorably for Kant, Goethe, Schopenhauer, Nietzsche, Michelangelo, and Rembrandt.[19] I have tried my hand at the task on five different occasions during the last quarter century (1957, 1959, 1971, 1976, 1981), yet never, surely, with any sense that I had begun to exhaust the subject.

Indeed, to speak of "exhausting the subject" is a contradiction in terms when referring to any of the authors whom we choose to regard as classics, not to mention one whom critics as disparate as Ernst Bloch and George Santayana described as having the finest mind of all the European thinkers of his day, and whom Siegfried Kracauer once characterized as "the philosopher of West European civilization in the period of its highest maturity" (Frisby 1981, 133). The attempt to define an author's core creative intentions is all the more embarrassing in the case of Georg Simmel who, after all, presents us with both a regulative idea that defies the notion of exhaustive treatment in principle, and a persona that is profoundly, inescapably, essentially ambiguous.

Rather than rehearse yet again that set of guiding principles and methods I have previously formulated, with varying nuances, as constitutive of Simmel's own sociological outlook, I propose to focus on that very quality of ambiguity that makes interpretations of

19. Charles Hauter vividly depicted Simmel's manner of doing this: "Simmel's manner of reading was strongly intuitive. He located the essential passages of a work with a confident glance. . . . More significant was the way Simmel used an inner eye to penetrate to the deeper intentions of an author. This was less a matter of what is commonly called *Verstehen* than the discovery and observation of a philosophic and intellectual current rolling through the mind of an author, a current that so to speak went through his mind like an objective flow after it had somehow emptied into it" (Gassen and Landmann 1958, 253).

Simmel so difficult. Of some relevance, I may note, are my earlier emphases on Simmel's penchant for paradoxes and antinomies (1959, 29–30), and on his tendency to shift meanings of key terms, like form and content, according to context (1957, 14; 1981, 65). Although this aspect of Simmel's style has rarely been accorded sustained attention in the literature, it has by no means gone unnoticed. So Kracauer, himself among the first to have essayed to grasp the inner principles of Simmelian thought, has written (in the pages of his still largely unpublished manuscript on Simmel):

> Simmel unceasingly changes perspectives and constant meaning attached to concepts is almost never to be found in his work.
> . . . Where previously hard boundaries were drawn, there now emerge crossings, here one thing flows into another. Not for nothing is 'nuance' a catchword of the time. Everything shimmers, everything flows, everything is ambiguous, everything converges in a shifting form. (Frisby 1981, 71, 98)

In the comments of those who have reacted to this quality of Simmel's thought, two sorts of responses predominate. What one might term a "positivist" response appears in those who find this quality a symptom of Simmel's scientific immaturity. Durkheim, we have seen, faulted Simmel for using excessively elastic concepts and for the extreme indeterminacy of his work generally. Weber objected to the indeterminacy of Simmel's notion of interaction and his excessive reliance on analogies. Abel based his rejection of Simmel in 1929 in good part on the ambiguity of Simmel's treatment of social forms, and Parsons criticized Simmel later on for not having been a systematic theorist.

A second response to the ambiguous quality of Simmel's thought is to judge it not as flawed in the light of scientific or logical standards, but as a deliberate expression of Simmel's antiscientific, "aesthetic" attitude. The label of aestheticism has been attached to Simmel by dozens of commentators. While a few have found his "aesthete's sociology . . . for the literary salon," as von Wiese described it in 1910, to possess genuine entertainment value, the dominant tendency has been to make a somewhat negative, "social critical" response when regarding Simmel's work in this light, a response based on the judgment that Simmel's aestheticism masks a lack of serious commitment to social goals and ideological positions. Kracauer took note of Simmel's great gifts for seeing meaningful connections among the most diverse objects—"an unlimited capacity for combination allows him to set out in any direction from any

single point"—but went on to note the "reverse side" of the fact
that his essays were so immensely interesting:

> They *only* arouse interest. One does not feel pressured by them
> in a specific direction, they indicate no course in which our life
> should flow. . . . He never engages his soul and he foregoes
> ultimate decisions. (Frisby 1981, 7, 79)

Lukács particularized the judgment of aestheticism by portraying
Simmel as an impressionist:

> He is the true philosopher of impressionism. This is not to say
> that he merely gave conceptual articulation to what the
> impressionist developments in music, the visual arts, and poetry
> had expressed; his work is to be viewed much more as a
> conceptual formulation of the impressionist world view. (1958,
> 172)

For Lukács, however, impressionism represented a principled rejection of commitments to "fateful and fate-creating ultimate formations"; and Simmel, too, had to be seen as a mere transitional
phenomenon, lacking a center of firm commitments and subsequently, of course, as objectively counterrevolutionary.

Much recent German commentary on Simmel has been taken up
with this theme of aestheticism in Simmel, and typically with the
stance that such an approach is morally suspect. Thus, Hübner-
Funk concludes her discussion of aestheticism and sociology in
Simmel by asserting: "A sociology understood as an end in itself
will always—sooner or later—end up in the dangerous waters of
aestheticism" (1976, 58). Most recently, David Frisby has extended
the Lukácsian line of interpretation in a book on Simmel, *Sociological Impressionism,* which argues that Simmel's theory of cultural
alienation, his aestheticization of social reality, and his shifting
perspectives together reflect a basic pattern of distancing himself
from social reality: "The inward retreat becomes his final political
perspective" (1981, 156).

It is possible, however, that the prevailing responses to Simmel's
penchant for ambiguity have not yet "exhausted the subject." It is
possible that there is more to Simmel's refusal to flee from ambiguity
than scientific deficiency, aesthetic titillation, or social withdrawal.
That is a possibility that should be explored.

Germane to such an exploration, if not conclusive, might be
Simmel's own statement about what his inner intentions actually
were. Far from rejecting a scientifically respectable approach to

inquiry, Simmel sought—in his 1896 paper on the methods of the social sciences, for example—to establish a rigorous basis for the disciplines of psychology and sociology. Far from inviting us to bask in a shimmering world of impressions, he prefaces his *Soziologie* in 1908 with the advice that his enterprise is one that aims to give "to the hitherto nebulous concept of sociology a univocal content, one governed by a methodically determinate problematic." That he may not have been fully successful in this—F. H. Tenbruck (1959, 63–64) was surely right to say—is due to the fact that, when he was writing, the social sciences did not have available the conceptual tools which Simmel needed to articulate this conception adequately.

What is more, Simmel was forthright in rejecting a position of total subjectivism and intellectual lability. He expressly intended his view of things to *combat* such a position. He could scarcely have been clearer on this matter than in the following statement from his autobiographical fragment:

> The tendency of our times was to decompose everything that is substantial, absolute, and eternal into the flux of things, into historical changeability, into a purely psychological reality. It seemed to me that one could keep this tendency from issuing in an unprincipled subjectivism and skepticism only if one substituted, in place of those substantive fixed values, the dynamic interactions *[Wechselwirksamkeit]* of elements. . . . The core concepts of truth, value, objectivity, etc., gave way, in my thinking (in the *Philosophy of Money,*) to a notion of reciprocal relationships—a view of them as products of a kind of relativism that signified no longer the dissolution of all certainties, but precisely their *guarantee by means of a new conception of certainty.* (Gassen and Landmann 1958, 9; emphasis mine)

On the evidence of this and comparable assertions elsewhere,[20] I would say that it was not the aimless wandering of a "man without qualities," as Frisby and others have portrayed him, but a Kantian quest for certainty—to determine what one can securely know by

20. Compare the passage in his 1896 essay, "Zur Methodik der Sozialwissenschaft": "Das ist so wenig Skeptizismus, dass vielmehr umgekehrt das Festhalten an einem allgemein gültigen, absolut einheitlichen Ideale für Erkenntnis, Sittlichkeit und Gesellschaft zu skeptischer Verzweiflung führen muss, wenn wir uns dem gegenüber in nie gelöste Zwistigkeiten, Unsicherheiten, Unzulänglichkeiten verstrickt sehen. Dagegen gewinnen wir eine feste—im Unterschied von einer starren—Position, sobald wir das Objektive, im Erkennen wie im Handeln, für einen *Verhältnisbegriff* Vorstellungen und Tendenzen zu den schwächeren oder vorübergehenden oder individuelleren ausdrückt" (235).

first examining the limits of our constructions of reality—that animated Simmel's lifelong philosophical journey. For what Simmel consistently affirmed is that historical as well as natural phenomena can become objects of experience only through the imposition of one or another form that makes them determinate and gives them identity—a position now widely accepted in the philosophy of science. To that expanded Kantian notion he early on added the affirmation that persons can become objects in social interaction only through the attribution to them of subjectively constructed personal identities—a position increasingly prominent in contemporary social psychology. Common to both these theorems is the rather Hegelian notion that substances, events, and personalities do not possess fixed characters and univocally determinable essences, but rather that the real properties of things emerge from a process of interaction between form-giving subjects and form-created objects.

In the process of reading, the philosophic and the social-psychological dimensions of this outlook are conjoined. The author, we may say, is perceived as a particular type of person with whom one interacts, and the subject matter is conceived in terms of the cultural frame the reader brings to the work. Just as the performance of a theatrical role, discussed in Simmel's essay on the dramatic actor (1920–21), represents an interaction between the playwright's construct and the actor's distinct personality, so the act of reading entails a reciprocal relationship: it makes a statement both about the reader and about the author. Ever mindful of this truth, Simmel was honest enough to note that the publication of his Kant lectures was "not only a book by Simmel about Kant, but also by Kant about Simmel" (Gassen and Landmann 1958, 251). And he was sufficiently consistent to foresee, in the famous testamentary passage from his diary, that he would die without intellectual heirs—

> and that is as it should be. My legacy will be like cash, distributed to many heirs, each transforming his part into use according to *his* nature.[21] (1919, 121)

The Simmelian conception of the process of intellectual appropriation as a form of interaction parallels a recent psychoanalytic exposition on the psychology of reading by George Moraitis.

21. The passage concludes: "a use which will no longer reveal its indebtedness to this heritage." Clairvoyant. Many years later, Erich Pryzara would reckon Simmel among those few "great and forgotten" figures who "today are wells from which people secretly draw water, without running the danger that anyone else will discover these wells" (Gassen and Landmann 1958, 224).

Moraitis designates the phenomenon as "editing," which he defines as "the process by which the ideas of the author and those of the reader are synthesized into some form of coherent entity." Such a process, Moraitis argues,

> inevitably involves omissions, additions, and several other alterations of the original text that will facilitate the desired synthesis. Part of this editing is conscious and deliberate, and part is unconscious, with the author or reader being unaware of the meaning and intent behind it. . . .
> Totally unedited thought processes are an abstraction that in reality does not exist. In a topographic sense, the editorial work can be conceptualized along three horizontal levels. The first level correlates to the repression barrier that separates conscious thinking from the unconscious thought process. The second level pertains to the boundary between verbalized and unverbalized thought processes. The third pertains to the boundary that separates verbal thought from written productions. (1981, 241, 244)

Although written from the viewpoint of individual psychology, these formulations adumbrate a model of the experience of reading as an interactive process. To complete that model, we need to supplement representations of the psychic processes of the author with those of the cultural materials being communicated. The degrees and types of selectivity involved in reading depend not only on the openness and flexibility of the reader and the openness and clarity of the author, but also, to an important extent, on the types of culturally constituted frames they bring to bear. With respect to the materials communicated by an author, there is a continuum having to do with the degree of constraint exerted by the kinds of materials represented. Maximum constraint is exerted by materials which involve precise definitions and mathematical formulations. Minimal constraint is exerted by materials that are qualitative in character and involve what W. B. Gallie has referred to as "essentially contested concepts." The literature of the social sciences, of course, is peculiarly susceptible to ambiguity in the materials presented, with the result that time and again readers of such literature not only are highly selective in their appropriation of those materials but frequently tend to produce patent misconstructions or creative misinterpretations.[22]

22. For an earlier discussion of a comparable continuum of "stringencies"—the constraints on the scope of legitimate modes for dealing with problems in various cultural genres—see Kaplan and Kris (1948, 423–30). For a survey of some of the

For such a conception of the process of reading, Simmel provided the first and perhaps still the only foundation that rests both on philosophical and social-psychological argument. His penchant for paradox and antinomies, his shifting use of terms, and his notion of plural worlds or cultural perspectives may accordingly be seen as expressions of his basic intention to secure certainty by repudiating rigidity. Simmel freely presented himself to his own audiences as one committed to working on the side of the continuum of cultural expressions that entails fewer constraints on readers and listeners.

What, then, of the ambivalent reception of his work by the readers reviewed earlier in this chapter? For understanding the pattern of their experience of Simmel, Moraitis' account of the editing process is again apt:

> Readers, by and large, at first identify what is familiar and has a place in their own perception of themselves and the universe. When confronted with a great quantity of novelty, however, they may simply ignore it, or register it without making an immediate attempt to bring it under the influence of the rigorous editing process. The existence of such input is bound to create internal tension, the tolerance of which is directly related to an individual's capacity to tolerate ambiguity and contradictions. (1981, 245)

When discussing in psychodynamic terms instances of highly motivated inattention of the sort Moraitis alludes to here, one is wont to invoke the notion of repression. What appears to be at work in these cases, however, is really quite different. It is a dynamic that Freud delineated in the late 1920s but which remained rather obscure until recently—the mechanism of disavowal (*Verleugnen*). In the skillful recovery of Freud's argument by Michael Basch (1983), disavowal appears as a defense against anxiety that differs from repression in that it wards off an environmental reality, not an internal impulse. It is further distinguished from perceptual mechanisms, like psychotic distortions and hysterical blindness, that actually block the recognition of signals from the environment. Instead, disavowal denotes a response in which one acknowledges the external or historical reality but where the self repudiates its existence as emotionally significant.

None of the readers discussed above came to deny Simmel's standing as a prominent sociologist, but each was moved to disavow

---

misconstructions and creative misinterpretations apparent in traditions of research related to Simmel, see Levine et al. (1976).

him: to repudiate a personal significance that Simmel had for the direction of his work. This is because each strove to establish a single, determinate way to look at society and to promote the enterprise of sociological analysis.

Given his single-minded devotion to a positive science of naturalistically conceived and described societal facts, Durkheim first identified with Simmel's familiar notion of supraindividual social phenomena, but then could not tolerate the idea of another way of delimiting sociology or yet a methodology that did not orient itself toward unambiguous definitions and observational procedures. His self-conception as a producer of univocal social science was so strong that he was unable to appreciate the multiple ambiguities surrounding his own usage of such central terms as 'society' and 'anomie,' as we have seen in an earlier chapter.

Lukács, we have seen, identified with the congenial critique of capitalist society implicit in Simmel's *Philosophy of Money*. Yet his quest for a firm and unambiguous ideological center led him eventually to repudiate, with some vehemence, a position that offered him no absolute verity, a disavowal he could easily effect by labeling Simmel an "impressionist" and thereby denying him both intellectual substance and ideological firmness.

Parsons, driven to delineate "the *core* line of development in sociological theory" (1968a, xiv), identified with the congenial Simmelian appeal to constitute sociology as an abstract analytic discipline, but could not tolerate the ambiguity entailed in legitimating Simmel's approach as an alternative way to construct sociological theory, and so negated him through neglect—since "Simmel's program did not fit my convergence hypothesis."

Park and Weber were somewhat less rigid than these three other readers of Simmel. Park found congenial in Simmel the notion of society as constituted by processes of interaction. He did not need to repudiate Simmel overtly because conceptually he was eclectic. Even so, he never quite acknowledged the fact of the divergence of Simmel's sociology both from a number of his conceptual formulations and from the strictly observational type of sociology he promoted among his students.

Philosophically, Weber was closer to Simmel than any of the others. He identified with Simmel's helpful ideas on *Verstehen* and on certain other methodological issues. He was also clear about how his orientation diverged from Simmel's, and sufficiently tolerant of ambiguity to write that even when Simmel's expositions were perhaps "ultimately not tenable," they contain a wealth of stimulation for one's own further thought, and that Simmel's mode of exposition "attains results that are intrinsic to it and not to be attained by any imitator." In the final analysis, however, Weber would have to discount aspects of Simmel's methodology as "unacceptable," and many of his substantive formulations as having to be "rejected outright," without appreciating the possibility that they might represent a valid alternative approach and one, indeed, that came closer to describing much of what Weber was doing than did his own programmatic statements.[23]

Simmel differed from all these authors, then, not only in his advocacy of different principles and methods for the science of sociology and his espousal of different interpretations of modern society and culture. He differed also in his attitude toward the intellectual enterprise generally. In that perspective, Durkheim, Weber, Lukács, Park, and Parsons are alike in their exclusive pursuit of the univocal—be it in conceptual definitions, empirical observations, substantive hypotheses, or ideological interpretations.

It is true that Simmel, too, made the effort to give sociology a "univocal content": to specify it as a discipline responsible for determining the forms of social interaction, and to conceptualize those forms primarily in terms of what I have called the variables of distance, position, size, valence, self-involvement, and symmetry (1981, 69–70). He did not reach the point—largely because sociology had not yet become sufficiently differentiated internally—of seeing the possibilities of extending to sociology itself that pluralistic, relational epistemology that he had worked out for the diverse worlds of culture at the highest level of generality. That kind of extension, however, is clearly implicated by his philosophic outlook. If Simmel could insist that "religious" phenomena, say, have one set of meanings when viewed sociologically, another set when viewed philosophically, yet another psychologically, and still another when viewed within the world of religion itself, he could not but acknowledge the appropriateness of seeing the sociological facts of religion as differently constituted depending on whether one views social facts as did Durkheim, Weber, Lukács, Park, Parsons, or others. In this vein, we must say that Simmel's tolerance of ambiguity—nay, his belief that all propositions are potentially ambiguous, since all ideas are radically relational—was very far indeed from being a symptom of logical debility or an expression of

23. For a more extended discussion of this point, see Tenbruck (1959).

an ultimately unserious, aestheticist orientation. We may regard it, rather, as pointing the way toward a more capacious foundation for the social sciences of the future, where deviation from one's univocal track leads not to disavowal but to the exploration of novelty and the mature encounter with otherness.

7

Rationality and Freedom, Inveterate Multivocals

Countless denizens of the modern era have been shamed away from policies they favored when told that such courses of action were not 'rational.' Even more have made a greater turn—the sacrifice of their lives—when summoned to struggle on behalf of the ideal of 'freedom.' The demonstrable power of the ideals of rationality and freedom to structure motivations documents at once the barrenness of theories that ignore symbolic forces in human action and the soundness of Edelman's analysis of hortatory language. For the hortatory use of rationality and freedom over the past two centuries has indeed persuaded many publics to commit themselves to clear lines of action in spite of the almost total ambiguity of the terms themselves.

For those who would understand the complexities to which the notions of rationality and freedom allude, the work of Max Weber can be commended above all others. Although Weber did not of course utter the first words on the problem of rationality and freedom in modern life (nor has he had the last word), he did recast the entire discussion of the subject—in terms which have by no means lost pertinence for analyzing a world increasingly shaped by scientists, industrialists, and bureaucrats.

Before reaching the mind of Weber, this problem was presented grandly by a number of eighteenth-century writers who subscribed to a general formulation which subsequently underwent a series of critical transformations. The philosophers of the Enlightenment, writes Ernst Cassirer, were suffused by the sense that a new force was at work in their time, a formative power that manifested itself in a great variety of energies and shapes. The name given to this essentially homogeneous formative power was 'reason.' "'Reason,'" he observes, "becomes the unifying and central point of this century, expressing all that it longs and strives for, and all that it achieves" (1951, 5).

Not the least appreciated attribute of this force of reason was its assumed capacity to promote human freedom. For Voltaire, reason served to liberate men from superstition, bigotry, and intolerance. For Montesquieu, reason applied to the study of political forms could enable men to devise a constitution that realized the greatest possible freedom. For Diderot, to follow the laws of reason was to shake off the yoke of authority and tradition.

This conjoint celebration of reason and freedom by eighteenth-century thinkers had some well-known repercussions in modern history. It animated the framers of the American Declaration of Independence. It was used and abused by the makers of the French Revolution. It initiated a great tradition of German social thought: as Hegel wrote to Schelling in 1793, despite the excesses of the French Revolution "reason and freedom remain our principles" (Marcuse 1941, 11).

Pre-Weberian Formulations: Kant and Hegel

It was Immanuel Kant who first transformed the philosophes' rather diffuse praise of reason and freedom into a differentiated schema of precise philosophical argument. If rationality and freedom remain preeminent linked ideals for Kant, it is not true that for him all forms of rationality promote freedom or that all kinds of freedom represent ideal states. Rather, Kant takes pains to distinguish and assess different forms both of rationality and freedom.

For Kant, rationality is a property of human subjects that appears when their mental powers are developed to the point of achieving cognition according to principles. Kant identifies three such higher faculties of cognition: understanding (*Verstand,*) judgment (*Urteil,*) and reason (*Vernunft*). Understanding serves to ascertain the deterministic laws of natural phenomena, and judgment serves to produce aesthetic and teleological assessments; neither of these cognitive activities, however, is directly constitutive of human freedom. Only *Vernunft,* the faculty responsible for producing morality, is related to the attainment of freedom.

Kant also distinguishes three kinds of freedom: freedom of choice, or free will; freedom as self-regulation, or autonomy; and freedom as civil liberty. *Freedom of choice* is a natural property of all human beings, and refers to the fact that human conduct is not wholly determined by animal impulses. *Autonomy* is the capacity of a subject to legislate and abide by ethical imperatives of his own making. *Civil liberty* refers to a condition in which men are protected by the rule of law against constraints on their actions emanating from the arbitrary wills of other actors.

To the first kind of freedom reason relates only indirectly, simply in the sense that by virtue of being an animal with the *potential* for reason, man possesses an innate capacity to determine for himself what he will do. This capacity is not itself rational, however; free choice stems from the elective will, *Willkür*, which is a faculty of desire, not of cognition. Freedom of choice simply represents a factor of organismic indeterminacy in the constitution of man; as such, Kant considers it neither morally valuable nor dependent on the actual exercise of rational powers.

The two other kinds of freedom, by contrast, do constitute ideal conditions for Kant, and both are closely tied to the use of reason. First and foremost, reason gives man freedom by enabling him to legislate ethical imperatives for himself, to experience autonomy through the exercise of a purely rational will (*Wille*, as contrasted with *Willkür*). Moreover, practical reason dictates the propriety of joining with others in a civil society and, through that collaboration of rational wills, establishing a juridical condition that guarantees to everyone independence from the constraint of another's will so far as this is compatible with the freedom of everyone else in accord with a universal law. Kant's summary position, then, would be that rationality in the form of practical reason (a kind of subjective rationality) promotes both human autonomy (a kind of subjective freedom) and civil liberty (a kind of external or objective freedom).

Although these and other formulations of Kant were absorbed in various ways into the complex of intellectual resources from which Weber was to draw heavily, there is one particularly important respect in which Kant anticipates and orients the thinking of nineteenth-century writers whom Weber confronted. This is his turn from treating reason and freedom exclusively in the framework of a static metaphysic of morals and its related view of human nature to their examination in a historical perspective as well. In his later reflections, Kant maintained that a purpose could be discerned in the natural unfolding of the history of humanity—and this purpose was in fact to perfect the use of human reason and to establish societies that guarantee freedom under external laws (Kant [1784] 1963; Galston 1975).

It is this historicizing afterthought of Kant which Hegel seized to make the entire ground of his conception. Although freedom and reason (*Vernunft,* which following Kant is contrasted with *Verstand,* mere scientific understanding) continue to signify pre-eminent ideals for Hegel, he sees them not as states attainable by every person simply by virtue of being human, but as species objectives to be attained through a long and arduous evolutionary struggle. It is this very struggle that constitutes history as Hegel prefers to define it.

Hegel defines history, however, in two distinct senses: in an objective sense, as the actual sequence of human events, and in a subjective sense, as the narration of such events. The development of rationality and freedom, accordingly, follows two distinct paths. On the one hand, history is the sequence of struggles by which political communities successively emerge to negate and transcend the cultural values of their predecessors; objective reason is the progressive embodiment of that struggle in the form of increasingly perfected systems of morality represented by the state and its laws; and objective freedom is maximally obtained when all the constituent units of society submit their wills to the laws and regulations of the state. On the other hand, history is the reconstruction of that progressive record of events by human subjects; subjective reason is the active self-consciousness of the subjectivity of oneself and others and the growth of Mind in articulating that self-consciousness through the creative work of art, religion, and philosophy; and subjective freedom is the transcendence of passions and impulses by the achievement of ultimate self-knowledge through philosophical speculation.

The two dimensions are closely related. Subjective reason and freedom are possible only because what history comprises are the manifestations of universal ideas of reason and freedom in concrete communities; objective rationality and freedom are possible only because the subjects it considers are rational subjects in pursuit of freedom. Both types of freedom entail the subordination of impulse to the constraints of reason, and both represent freedom in the sense of self-perfection.

Hegel's conception of rationality and freedom thus differs radically from that of Kant. Not a guaranteed sphere within which actors can do what they wish without interference from others but a regime of duties stipulated by and enforced by political institutions constitutes the domain of objective freedom; not moral laws of the autonomous individual's own making but recognition of the rationality of the state's demands is the locus of subjective freedom. For Hegel "it is not the particular members of the society that constitute an individual, free, self-integrated, and self-conscious entity; it is the society as the resolution of the partial freedom and self-consciousness of the members" (O'Brien 1975, 161).

Pre-Weberian Formulations:
Toennies and Simmel

This shift toward the representation of increased rationality and freedom at the level of large-scale societal processes was perhaps the aspect of Hegel's treatment of the problem that had the most lasting repercussions in German social thought. In the next major reformulation of the problem, Ferdinand Toennies would hail Hegel's achievement in demonstrating the historical necessity of the rational modern social structures—civil society and the state— thereby deflating the movement by romantic writers, legal historians, and reactionary thinkers to reject them as theoretical errors. At the same time Toennies faulted Hegel for presenting a vague and obfuscating view of social life and for propounding the idea of a unilineal development toward perfection. In seeking to correct these shortcomings Toennies attempted to bring persons back into the picture, to uncover "the real relationship between individual will and social groups" which Hegel had "blotted out" ([1912] 1971, 27), and to replace the notion of *Vernunft* as a transcendent teleological ideal with a variety of relatively neutral analytic concepts. In so doing, he laid the groundwork for the modern sociological treatment of rationality and freedom.

It was a constant feature of Toennies' sociological vision, in his own later words, to "see in the entire historical development since the Middle Ages the gradual setting free of rationalism and its increasing dominance as inherently necessary processes, and especially as processes of human mind as will" ([1932] 1971, 6). To conceptualize this vision he constructed a pair of ideal types to represent fundamentally contrasting kinds of human volition, *Wesenswille* and *Kürwille*.[1] Both *Wesenswille* and *Kürwille* involve

---

1. The terms are scarcely translatable, but Loomis' translation of *Kürwille* as "rational will" is especially unsatisfactory, for two reasons. "Rational will" is often identified with Kant's *Wille*, which for Kant was identical with pure practical reason. The term Toennies used in the first two editions of *Gemeinschaft und Gesellschaft* was *Willkür*, precisely Kant's term for the elective will as opposed to rational will. Toennies' *Willkür* or *Kürwille*, then, is more accurately rendered as elective will, or

rational activity, and both manifest freedom since, as Toennies defines it, freedom denotes the psychic energy that comprises both kinds of human volition ([1887] 1957, 136). Moreover, the distinctive types of social formations which they respectively generate, *Gemeinschaft* and *Gesellschaft,* community and society, both manifest freedom. This is so, first, because both kinds of formation involve volitional affirmation, and second, because both have some kinds of laws that guarantee certain kinds of freedom ([1926] 1974, 174). Accordingly, the transition from *Gemeinschaft* to *Gesellschaft* is not a movement from nonrationality and unfreedom to rationality and freedom; but from one mode of volition and social organization in which rationality and freedom are defined and circumscribed by the immersion of selves in an organic community bound by shared sentiments and mutual understanding, to another in which rationality and freedom are exhibited in the deliberative processes by which persons associate on the basis of instrumental considerations and contractual arrangements.

Why, then, does Toennies repeatedly maintain that the development of *Gesellschaft* entails the development of rationalism? The point is this: in *Wesenswille* thought is subordinated to volition. That is, rational activity occurs in order to realize desires derived from genetic inheritance, habit, group sentiments, custom, and religion. In *Kürwille,* by contrast, volition is subordinate to thought. In *Kürwille,* rational activity attains a kind of independence such that it can conceive novel ends, project alternative futures, and calculate a variety of means. It is this autonomous status of rational activity that Toennies has in mind when ascribing an expanded role to rationality in *Gesellschaft.*

Viewed as a critical extension of Hegel, this formulation of Toennies not only purports to be a secular empirical analysis, but further modifies Hegel's treatment of reason in history by stressing the distinction between two levels of historical phenomena: an objective, social level and a subjective, individual level. Hegel had, as Toennies put it, defined the objective mind as the system of social life, and for Hegel "the state was to emerge as social rationality in all its purity" ([1894] 1974, 66). Toennies insisted on supplementing this level of analysis with one focused on variations in the quality of individual intentionality, on different modes of rational volition.

---

arbitrary will, as Cahnman and Heberle have done. (*Wesenswille* might best be translated as primordial will.) A second reason for objecting to *Kürwille* as rational will is the implication that *Wesenswille* is devoid of rationality, which as the text indicates was not the way Toennies conceived it.

Thus, for Toennies to treat the development of rationalism as a social phenomenon means to identify "a development in *both individual and social reason [Entwicklung der individuellen und der sozialen Vernunft]*" (1926, 98; 1974, 174; emphasis mine): in his own analytic terms, a development both of the capacity for *Kürwille* and of the enactments of *Gesellschaft*.

Enhanced freedom is a major consequence of this development in individual and social reason. Gradually, Toennies states, the activity of persons oriented by *Kürwille* and the institutions of *Gesellschaft* dissolve the unifying social bonds based on time-honored custom and belief, bonds that restrict the individual's freedom of movement and conception. They produce persons who are free, self-determining agents, free to subjugate one another or free to conclude agreements, free to establish contracts, and free to adapt their attitudes to the findings of science ([1887] 1957, 224, 234).

Kindred themes are broached in the work with which, as Toennies put it, nineteenth-century sociology "reached an impressive finale" ([1926] 1974, 182), Simmel's *Philosophie des Geldes*. In his first sociological monograph (1890), Simmel had outlined a number of developmental patterns that together portrayed modern society as a highly differentiated social world wherein individuals are liberated from a variety of jural and customary constraints in ways that enormously expand their freedom of action. In the long treatise on money published years later, Simmel developed a more original and profound set of interpretations. There Simmel depicted a new mode of rational activity manifest in the pervasive utilization of money as a generalized medium of exchange. Money, Simmel writes, favors the ascendance of intellectuality over emotional responses. Being a quantitative measure, the repeated use of money required the development of calculative skills and habits. Being a strictly instrumental possession—money is the absolute tool, the means flexible enough to serve any end whatsoever—its habitual use requires that considerable energy be devoted to the rational analysis of costs and benefits, means and ends.

In pursuing this analysis, Simmel does not consistently adhere to the kind of distinction urged by Toennies, between subjective and objective rationality. Although Simmel does make, and use to very good effect indeed, a distinction between what he calls subjective and objective culture, when treating the rationalism of modern social relations based on the circulation of money he tends to confuse the objective significance of money as a social phenomenon and the subjective orientations of those who use it (a confusion for which he would later be criticized by Weber[2]). On the other hand, he goes well beyond Toennies and other writers of the time in making and using clear distinctions among different kinds of freedom.

Of the many kinds of freedom which Simmel mentions at different points in his work, three are of recurring and central importance. We may gloss these in terms of the already mentioned distinction between subjective and objective freedom. Simmel distinguishes two kinds of objective freedom, kinds of freedom that refer to an actor's position in a nexus of relations with objects: a "negative" freedom of liberation from external constraints and obligations, and a "positive" freedom to obtain satisfactions through the control of resources. In addition, Simmel develops a notion of subjective freedom in the sense of individuality, freedom as the development of one's personality according to the dispositions of one's own nature.

What Simmel goes on to argue in *Philosophie des Geldes* is that all three kinds of freedom are promoted by the use of money and its related rational mental habits. Money promotes freedom in the sense of liberation from external constraints: by enabling values to be assigned precisely and impersonally, money makes it possible for individuals to be connected to other persons only insofar as they need or wish to be so connected, and to be freed from the ancillary constraints and obligations that encumber relations to patrons, suppliers, clients, and customers in societies that lack monetized media of exchange. Money promotes freedom in the sense of ability to realize one's goals in a number of respects. Of all objects, money offers the least resistance to an agent. It is the most possessable of all things, hence completely submissive to the will of an ego. It can be acquired in countless ways. There are no limits to the amount of it that one can possess. As the absolutely general instrumentality, money maximizes the options available to anyone having a finite amount of resources.

Finally, money promotes freedom in the sense of individualized self-development, by providing an effective means of differentiating between the subjective center and the objective achievements of a person. Individuals' performances may be paid for with money while their persons remain outside the transaction. Conversely, individual persons can be supported as such by monetary contributions from anonymous others, while their specific performances

2. "[Subjectively] *intended* and objectively *valid* 'meanings' are two different things which Simmel not only fails to distinguish but often mixes up with one another" ([1921 (1976)] 1968, 4 [1]; translation altered).

remain free of financial considerations. Further in this vein Simmel argues that the separation of workers from their means of production (for which "a money economy paved the way"), while viewed by some as the focal point of social misery, may rather be viewed "as a salvation" insofar as it provides conditions for the liberation of the worker as a human subject from the objectified technical apparatus of productivity ([1907] 1978, 337).[3]

Enter Weber

The formulations of Kant, Hegel, Toennies, and Simmel provided some of the ideas from which Weber drew selectively in developing his own sociology of rationalism. Although Weber's work was arguably stimulated by their formulations in certain ways,[4] what is perhaps more notable is that Weber's treatment of the topic of rationality differs dramatically from those of all of his predecessors in three respects.

First, the conceptual apparatus Weber developed to represent the forms and processes of rationalization is much more differentiated than that employed in any of the earlier analyses. Second, through his comparative studies of efforts to rationalize culture in classical antiquity, the Near East, China, and India, Weber decisively transcended the Europocentric notion that the development of rationalism is a uniquely Western phenomenon. Indeed, he can be viewed as crediting the Orient for having developed heights of rationality in some respects superior to those reached in the Occident.[5]

3. Simmel's complex argument on this subject also includes lines of thought which treat the negative consequences both of excessive freedom and of rationalization as a source of alienation. For a more extended exposition, see Levine (1981).

4. For example, Kant's formulation of the categorical imperative was for Weber an archetypical example of what he came to call value rationality; Hegel's treatment of the course of rationalization in world history set up the project which Weber strove to recast (on Weber's silent homage to and acute consciousness of Hegel as his major intellectual antagonist, see Bruun 1972, 39); Toennies' treatment of *Gemeinschaft* and *Gesellschaft* as social forms based on differing degrees of rational volition became the paradigm for Weber's first sketch of a *verstehende* sociology in his 1913 *Logos* essay; and Simmel's last chapter of *Philosophie des Geldes* was cited as a "brilliant portrayal" (*glänzenden Bilder*) of the spirit of capitalism in the Protestant Ethic essay ([1920] 1958, 193 [33]).

5. See, for example, Weber's assertion that "in the area of thought concerning the 'significance' of the world and of life there is nothing whatsoever which has not already been conceived in Asia in *some* form" ([1923] 1958b, 331 [365]; emphasis in original; translation altered).

Regarding developments in Western Europe, finally, Weber's position concerning the effects of rationality on freedom challenges the formula with which all the previously mentioned thinkers, in spite of their numerous substantive differences, were in agreement. Far from viewing the advance of rationality as a prime source of freedom in the modern West, Weber frequently decried it as a serious threat to freedom. Prevailing interpretations of Weber typically focus on this aspect of his position: thus, "when it came to [analyzing] the trends toward rationalization . . . of modern society, Weber tended . . . to assert that the chances were very great indeed that mankind would in the future be imprisoned in an iron cage of its own making" (Coser 1977, 233); for Weber after 1903, "the *Leitmotiv* of Western history has changed from progress through self-liberation to enslavement through rationalization" (Mitzman 1970, 168); "Weber's sympathy, or rather his grim anxiety, is on the side of personality *against rationality*" (Cahnman 1978, 191; emphasis mine).[6]

To advance beyond Weber in the understanding of these issues, I contend, requires two efforts. The first is to recover what Weber actually said concerning the forms and processes of rationalization. Weber's penetration of these issues was not only unprecedented, it remains unsurpassed. No subsequent discussion of rationalization with which I am familiar has mastered the levels of complexity and insight that Weber reached. To do this we must bring more order to Weber's formulations than he himself produced.

Second, we must subject the formula that modern rationalization produces unfreedom to a searching critique. I shall argue that any global assertion that rationalization curtails freedom must be fundamentally flawed, in good part because of its failure to take into account the full scope of Weber's argument on the problem and beyond that its failure to apply the gamut of Weber's rich array of distinctions regarding rationality to the question of freedom in the modern world.

---

6. This is not, of course, to say that Weber was the first to sound the alarms about certain negative tendencies in modern society. Apart from the varied antimodernist currents in nineteenth-century culture, notable critical diagnoses were made by Marx, Nietzsche, and Simmel, all of whom had serious impact on Weber. Still, it was Weber who first thematized the intimate association between historical processes of rationalization and the curtailment of freedom.

The Weberian Conception of Rationality

Few sources indeed are informed by a sustained appreciation of
the fact that for Weber the concept of rationality was multiply
ambiguous.[7] This is no less than astonishing in view of Weber's own
declaration, in a footnote to his most famous work, *The Protestant
Ethic and the Spirit of Capitalism:* "If this essay makes any
contribution at all, may it be to bring out the complexity
(*Vielseitigkeit*) of the only superficially simple concept of the 'rational'" ([1920] 1958b, 194 [35]). Within the text itself, moreover,
Weber makes the point that "one may rationalize life from fundamentally different points of view and in very different directions.
'Rationalism' is a historical concept that contains a world of
contradictions in itself"—a point given added emphasis in the
revised edition of 1920, where Weber observed, "This simple
proposition, which is often forgotten, should be placed at the
beginning of every study which essays to deal with rationalism"
([1920] 1958b, 77–78 [62]).[8]

The problem of securing an adequate grasp of the *Vielseitigkeit* of
Weber's conceptualization of rationality is complicated by the fact
that Weber himself did not use the relevant distinctions in a clearcut
and consistent manner, nor did he ever produce the theoretical
clarification of the *"many possible meanings* of the concept
of 'rationalization'" (Vieldeutigkeit *des Begriffs der 'Rationalisierung'*; emphasis in original) which he promised in introducing
the later part of *Economy and Society* ([1921 (1976)] 1968, 30 [16]).
Even for those who are aware of the serious need for such
conceptual clarification, then, the matter remains vexed.

Although Weber's failure to provide a definitive analysis of the
meanings of rationality arguably reflected a lack of time, it can also
be seen as expressing his considered ambivalence toward any effort
to create systematic conceptual inventories. While Weber considered it worthwhile to secure univocal meanings in particular exposi-
tory contexts, he also believed that the meaning of terms might
legitimately shift from one context to another, and he appreciated
the expressive value of ambiguity in scholarly writing—in practice
as in principle, for he was a master of irony. On this matter his

7. The few significant exceptions include Bendix (1965), Schluchter ([1976] 1979b),
and Kalberg (1980).
8. "Rationality" and "rationalism" are used interchangeably by Weber to denote
a property of action or symbolic products. "Rationalization" refers to a historical
process of making action or symbolic products more rational.

position opposed that of Durkheim, who felt that we should clarify terms in order to represent the true nature of things. Well, Weber asked, is there any way to arrive at unambiguously defined concepts on the basis of a "'presuppositionless' description of some concrete phenomenon or through the abstract synthesis of those traits which are common to numerous concrete phenomena?" ([1922] 1949, 92 [193]). For Weber, the constructing of univocal definitions contained an irreducibly arbitrary element, and its point was simply to facilitate accurate communication.

Even though it may be impossible, then, to reduce the full complexity of Weber's analysis of rationality to the confines of a single analytic scheme, it may be helpful in securing a purchase on the richness of his analysis to render it more deliberately systematic. As a contribution toward sorting out some of this complexity, I propose as a preliminary step to make use of the distinction between subjective and objective manifestations of rationality which surfaced in reviewing the earlier authors. This is a commonplace distinction and each term refers to a wide variety of phenomena. The locus of subjective rationality is the *mental processes* of actors. Such notions as Kant's practical reason, Hegel's self-consciousness, Toennies' rational volition, and Simmel's calculating habits of mind refer to various aspects of kinds of subjective rationality. Other contemporary notions include Pareto's concept of subjective logicality and, more generally, the economists' notion of utility-maximizing orientations.

The locus of objective rationality is courses of action and symbolic products assessed in terms of *institutionalized norms*. Hegel's notion of reason embodied in laws and political institutions, Toennies' notion of the constitution and judicial agencies of *Gesellschaft* as embodying "naked social reason," Simmel's conception of social relations based on precise, impersonal calculation, and Pareto's concept of objective logicality are illustrative.

Although Weber did not consistently make use of the distinction when analyzing the phenomena of rationality and rationalization, I believe that without clearly distinguishing subjective and objective rationality it is impossible to do justice to his complex of observations on this subject. There are several warrants for this claim. For one thing, there are passages in his methodological writing where Weber does articulate a distinction between subjective and objective rationality. Both "On Some Categories of Interpretive Sociology" ([1913] 1981) and "The Meaning of 'Ethical Neutrality' in Sociology and Economics" ([1917] 1949) include discussions of the importance of distinguishing these two dimensions of social action. Subjective rationality is taken to refer to action that is conscious and deliberate (contrasted with action undertaken for motives that are unconscious or disavowed) and/or action that is oriented to means that are *regarded* as correct for a given end. Objectively rational action, by contrast, is taken to refer to action that uses technically correct means in accord with scientific knowledge and/or has been subjected to some process of external systematization (1922, 408–11; [1922] 1949, 34 [488]). Weber goes on to insist that a "progressive subjective rationalization" (*fortschreitende subjektive Rational-isierung*) of conduct is not necessarily the same as an advance in the direction of objectively rational conduct; and that what appear as objectively rational human adaptations have been brought into being in numerous historical instances through completely irrational motives.

Beyond this, there are other passages where this distinction is clearly implicit in Weber's discussion. Most notable, perhaps, is the contrast, in sections 6 and 7 of chapter 1 of *Economy and Society,* between the various ways in which actors can be *oriented* to uphold the norms of a social order, and the grounds on which legitimacy can be *ascribed* to a social order. Viewed together with Weber's other discussions of legitimacy, the latter must be viewed as a typology of institutionalized forms, involving beliefs and related sanctions to which the representatives of an order have recourse in the exercise of their legitimate authority. The former typology is one of the subjective intentions of actors as they comply with or deviate from that order. Thus an order which rests on objectively rational grounds (e.g., on the basis of a consensually validated legal constitution) may be adhered to because of the nonrational dispositions of the subjects (e.g., their emotional need to comply with authority figures).

Finally, I would argue that although Weber signaled his intention, in the prefatory note to *Economy and Society,* to distinguish subjectively intended meanings from objectively valid meanings as sharply as possible ("tunlichste Scheidung der *gemeinten* von dem objektiv *gültigen* 'Sinn'"), his general failure to articulate the distinction between subjective and objective rationality more forcefully and consistently appears plausible if two considerations are kept in mind: Weber's tendency to avoid using the category of "objective validity" because of its connection with normative approaches in social studies, such as jurisprudence, from which he was aggressively trying to dissociate his empirical sociology; and his lack of a viable theory of institutionalization, such that he did not have at his disposal a ready and precise way of distinguishing the term 'objective' in the sense of *valid* from 'objective' in the Durkheimian sense of supraindividual or *institutionalized*. To avoid this ambiguity and remain mindful of Weber's sensitivity on this point, I propose hereafter to use in the latter sense the term 'objectified' in place of 'objective.'

Since it appears, then, that there are ample justifications for doing so, let us proceed to organize Weber's manifold references to rationality in the terms just suggested.

Subjective and Objectified Forms of Rationality

Weber discusses rationality as a quality of subjective mental processes in two contexts. These correspond, very broadly, to Kant's distinction between *Verstand* and *Vernunft,* the capacity for rational understanding of phenomena, and the capacity to use reason as a source of directives for willed action. Weber has little to say about the operation of mind in its understanding of natural phenomena, but focuses his attention on mental operations involved in understanding human conduct. He presents, with little elaboration, a straightforward dichotomy, between (1) rational understanding, itself further divisible into mathematical and logical understanding, and (2) empathic understanding. Rational understanding entails an intellectual grasp of the coherence of the elements of action in the actor's situation. In empathic understanding, the observer draws on his personal fund of emotional self-knowledge to experience imaginatively the emotional context of that situation (1968, 5). It is empathic understanding if, attending to a student's rapid breathing and staccato talk, I intuit that he has come early to an appointment because he is anxious; it is rational understanding if I have knowledge of his schedule and calculate that he has an important class soon after for which he does not want to be late.

Weber's other discussion of subjective rationality appears in his classification of the types of social action (1968, 24–26). Social action can be conceptualized in terms of four ideal types, two of which are rational, two nonrational. A person's action is rationally oriented, for example, if he greets another person because of a consciously held belief that it is a moral duty to show respect for all human beings (value-rational *[wertrational]* action); or because he has reasoned that the costs of appearing rude or indifferent outweigh the advantages of remaining self-absorbed (means/end-rational *[zweckrational]* action). A person is nonrationally oriented when greeting someone because of long-established custom (traditional action) or a momentary burst of good feelings about that person (affectual action).[9]

There are two principal places in his oeuvre where Weber sets forth considerations that enable us to discriminate the variety of manifestations of objectified rationality. When discussing the point that "there have been rationalizations of the most varied sort within various spheres of life in all civilizations" (1958b, 26; translation altered[10]), Weber asserts that to characterize these different rationalizations one must determine (1) what spheres of life are being rationalized, and (2) with respect to what ultimate points of view and in what directions (*letzten Gesichtspunkten und Zielrichtungen*) they are rationalized. Furthermore, in another passage (to be discussed below), Weber sets forth still another set of distinctions concerning (3) the different forms which rationality may take.

By "spheres of life" Weber meant what sociologists today often refer to as institutional orders. Weber himself treated, at varying length, the phenomena of rationalization in at least a dozen distinct institutional spheres: economic organization; political order; military organization; legal systems; social stratification; education; religion; ethics; science; music; art; and erotic life.

By "ultimate points of view" Weber was referring to the particular ends on behalf of which the rationalization of some sphere of life has been carried out. Thus, the law could be rationalized in order to solidify caste or class distinctions, or in order to ensure equality of treatment for all members of the community. Science could be rationalized in order to understand better the working of divine

9. This typology is well known and requires no elucidation at this point beyond some comment on the category of *Zweckrationalität*. Many writers have understood this to refer to action in which consideration is given only to questions of technical expediency. Admittedly there are passages in Weber's writings which permit a narrow construction of this sort. However, in his chief discursive exposition of the category, Weber presents a broader definition: action is *zweckrational,* he writes, "when the end, the means, and the secondary results are all rationally taken into account and weighed. This involves rational consideration of alternative means to an end, of the relations of the end to the secondary consequences, and finally of the relative importance of different possible ends" (1968, 26). I shall adhere to Weber's explicit statement on the matter and regard means/end rational action in this more inclusive sense, one that includes what he elsewhere calls rational *economic* as well as technically oriented action.

10. "Rationalisierungen hat es daher auf den verschiedenen Lebensgebieten in höchst verschiedener Art in allen Kulturkreisen gegeben" (1920, 12).

providence and to glorify the Creator, or to provide knowledge that may be used to improve living conditions. Religious beliefs and practices could be rationalized in accord with ascetic or mystical ideals. In other Weberian language, modes of rationalization differ according to the "irrational presuppositions" which ground and direct the various ways of leading a rationalized style of life.

What I am glossing as the diverse "forms" of rationalization represents the dimension of variation which Weber delineated briefly in his introduction to *The Economic Ethics of the World Religions,* when he enumerated some of the "very different things" that "rationalism" may mean. (The full text is provided in the Appendix.) Although Weber does not intend here to present an exhaustive or systematically developed typology, he does clearly differentiate four emphatically distinct conceptions of what it might mean to describe a cultural phenomenon as rational.

One meaning of rationality, in Weber's words, is the "methodical attainment of a particular given practical end through the increasingly precise calculation of adequate means." Although exhibited in its most developed form by such strata as peasants, merchants, and artisans, this type of rational action is to some extent universal. It is informed by a general human tendency to attain worldly goals by adapting to the exigencies of everyday life. Weber notes that the most elementary forms of magical and religious behavior exhibit a degree of rationality of this sort (1968, 400), a point akin to Malinowski's (otherwise somewhat different) observations from Trobriand culture in refuting the notion that the thought of primitive peoples is fundamentally prelogical. I shall refer to this as "instrumental rationality."

A second meaning of rationality, Weber writes, is "increasing theoretical mastery of reality by means of increasingly precise and abstract concepts." Rationalization of this kind is designed to produce a coherent, meaningful picture of the world, and is preeminently the achievement of religious or secular intellectuals. It involves the basic cognitive processes of generalization and logical systematization. It may be referred to as "conceptual rationality."

The next meaning of rational mentioned by Weber is one that relates to evaluative standards. This kind of rationalization is conceived as a process of establishing valid canons against which that which is empirically given can be assessed, canons not derived from traditional or mystical sources. Weber's example of this type of rationality in the passage is the aesthetic canons of Renaissance humanism. Primarily, however, in the comparative studies he treats this form of rationality in the context of considering ethical ideals which have a transformative effect on everyday life, ideals such as justice, equality, piety, or nirvana. Religious and secular prophetic figures are viewed as the typical sources of such ideals. More generally, this form of rationality can be identified with what Weber refers to in the economic and legal spheres as "substantive *[materielle]* rationality," a rationality which accords predominance to ethical imperatives, utilitarian rules, or political maxims (1968, 85, 657).

Finally, rationality may take the form of what Weber calls *Planmässigkeit,* a methodical ordering of activities through the establishment of fixed rules and routines. This kind of rationalization is designed to maximize the predictability of activities and norms in a particular sphere of action and to minimize the influence of personal ties and social sentiments. Weber tended to refer to this as "methodical rationality" in the sphere of religion (1958b, 197), and as "formal rationality" in spheres of law and economic action (1968, 85, 657). I shall use the latter term here.[11]

11. This typology quite parallels the fourfold classification of Weber's forms of rationalization independently developed by Kalberg (1980). For two of the four categories, other terminology seems to me preferable. I have used "instrumental" rather than "practical," inasmuch as the latter term generally has reference to praxis or action, and "substantive" and "formal" types of rationalization refer to practical rationality in this commonplace sense no less than does instrumental. I have used "conceptual" rather than "theoretical," inasmuch as this mode of rationalization applies to spheres like law, music, and religion where the interest is other than what is commonly considered theoretical. "Methodical" is perhaps a more descriptive term than "formal," but I have decided to follow Kalberg's usage in this case in order to minimize the appearance of differences between what are essentially identical interpretations of Weber's schema.

Although many other observations made by Kalberg in this paper seem persuasive, I do take issue with some features of his application of the schema. It seems to me (a) a contradiction in terms to say that formal rationality cannot be associated with a methodical way of life (1169); (b) confusing to say that bureaucracy calculates "the most precise and efficient means for the resolution of problems by ordering them under universal and abstract regulations" (1158), since this blurs the distinction between the principles of instrumental and formal rationality; (c) important to stress the independent variability of subjective and objectified forms of rationality; (d) puzzling to read that for Weber the origin of substantive ethical rationalities was "largely a result of economic factors" (1171); and (e) misleading to suggest that only value-rational action possesses the potential to rupture traditional ways of life (1171), for Weber argues that "ratio" can also be a revolutionary force by working from "without" in ways that transform men's living conditions and "finally," in consequence, men's attitudes ([1921 (1976)] 1968, 245 [142])—as the introduction of technological change into so many "traditional societies" in the last half-century dramatically indicates.

Some effort is required to keep these distinctions clearly in mind, especially since Weber's own usage is at times confusing. Conceptual rationality is a predicate of symbolic systems, not of social action; its relation to action is significant, but indirect, as Kalberg has pointed out. Conceptual rationality is manifest to the extent that symbolic representations are governed by norms of precision, inclusiveness, and coherence; conceptual rationalization is a response to the human desire for *meaning and understanding* of the world.

The three other forms of objectified rationality have reference to socially sanctioned courses of action. Instrumental rationality is manifest to the extent that the operative norms are those of technical efficiency; it reflects the wish to use maximally *adequate means* in attaining given ends. Substantive rationality is manifest to the extent that the operative norms are subordinated to some overarching value; it reflects the desire to achieve *motivational integrity*. Formal rationality is manifest to the extent that the operative norms channel action according to clearly stipulated procedures; it reflects the wish to act within a *calculable order* of activities and relationships.

For three of the institutional spheres which Weber treated most extensively, possible examples of objectified rationality are illustrated in figure 4.

Speculating for a moment beyond Weber, I wish to make two further comments on this typology. One is to suggest that there are probably significantly different affinities between the several institutional spheres and the various forms of rationality. Thus science, as the sphere primarily concerned with understanding the world, would have a special affinity for conceptual rationality, and law, as the sphere most concerned with regulating relations among actors, would have a special affinity for formal rationality.

The other is to suggest that the four forms of objectified rationality have approximate counterparts in the forms of subjective rationality. For three of these, the previously mentioned Weberian terms are indicative: rational understanding is the subjective counterpart to conceptual rationality; the means/end-rational orientation corresponds to instrumental rationality; the value-rational orientation to substantive rationality. Although Weber did not provide a term to designate the subjective orientation which parallels formal rationality, he frequently described a psychic tendency for actors to secure order by enacting regulative norms, a tendency he glosses as "one of the factors motivating social action" (1968, 333). It should be remembered, however, that the empirical connection between sub-

Figure 4
Objectified Rationality in Three Institutional Spheres

Form of Objectified Rationality	Institutional Spheres		
	Religion	Economy	Law
Conceptual	Systematic theodicy	Science of economics	Clear and consistent codification of legal propositions
Instrumental	Use of prayers successful in exorcising noxious spirits	Use of efficient production or marketing techniques	Use of skilled diviner to establish a defendant's guilt or innocence
Substantive	Pursuit of nirvana as ultimate soteriological ideal	Allocation of resources according to a standard of fairness	Subordination of legal decisions to an articulated ideal of justice
Formal	Monastic devotional routines	Capital accounting	Reliance on abstract procedural rules

jectively rational orientation and objectively rational action is variable: actors may observe the norms of objectified rationality of a given sort for a variety of rational *or* nonrational reasons.

The full set of distinctions outlined above is presented schematically in figure 5. Only with a schema of this order of complexity can we begin to appropriate all that Weber has to say on the subject of rationality. The schema alerts us to one of the hallmarks of Weber's interpretive genius: his revelation that there are historically consequential affinities and conflicts among independently varying manifestations of rationalization.

A few references may remind us of some of the complex relationships among different forms of rationality which Weber illuminated.

Between forms of subjective rationality, there is an inherent tension between value-rational and means/end-rational orientations: the latter regards the former as irrational and always increases at the expense of the former (1968, 26, 30).

In the relation *between subjective and objectified rationality,* there are moments of affinity between value-rational orientations and substantive rationality, since the prophets or lawgivers who establish substantively rational codes would have to be oriented in a

Figure 5
The Various Meanings of Rationality in Weber's Work

I. Forms of Subjective Rationality and Nonrationality

Mental Quality	Orientational Spheres	
	Cognitive Processes	Conative Processes
Rational	Rational understanding (*rationales Verstehen*) 1. mathematical 2. logical	1. Means/end-rational orientation (*Zweckrationalität*) 2. Value-rational orientation (*Wertrationalität*)
Nonrational: emotional	Empathic understanding (*einfühlend nacherlebenes Verstehen*)	3. Affectual orientation
habitual		4. Traditional orientation

II. Forms of Objectified Rationality

Forms of Rationalization	Institutional Spheres
	Economy, Polity, Law, Military, Religion, Ethics, Science, Art, etc.
Conceptual	Within each of the institutional spheres—but to different degrees according to presumptive differentials in elective affinity between type of sphere and form of rationality—the different forms of rationality have been and can be pursued in different directions on the basis of orientations to diverse ends or "nonrational presuppositions."
Instrumental	
Substantive	
Formal	

III. Correspondences between Subjective and Objectified Forms of Rationality

Objective Forms	Subjective Counterpart
Conceptual rationality	Rational understanding
Instrumental rationality	Means/end-rational orientation
Substantive rationality	Value-rational orientation
Formal rationality	Disposition toward calculable regulation

value-rational way; however, that subjective and objectified forms of rationality often vary inversely has been shown above.

The relations *among different forms of objectified rationality within the same institutional sphere* admit of many possibilities: the formal rationalization of religious practice has favored the conceptual rationalization of religious beliefs (1968, 417); conceptual rationalization of religious knowledge as in Brahmanic contemplation stands in contrast with the formal type of rationalization of religious technique as in classical yoga ([1923] 1958b, 165); and the formal rationalization of law exists in chronic tension with substantive rationality in the legal sphere (1968, 811–13).

Regarding the relations among different courses of *rationalization within different institutional spheres,* Weber writes, for example, that the conceptual rationalization of religious doctrine has occurred at the expense of instrumental rationality in the economic sphere (1968, 424) and has inhibited the formal rationalization of law (1968, 577), but also that substantive rationality in a this-worldly ascetic direction was a key factor in promoting the formal rationalization of economic action in early modern capitalism.

Finally, it should be noted that even when Weber was concerned to show affinities among different types of rationalization in different institutional spheres in Western history, he stressed repeatedly that those different rationalization processes took place at different times and in different places (1958b, 77; 1968, 1400).

To my mind, the foregoing considerations establish beyond doubt that it is untenable to attribute to Weber the belief that rationalization refers to a univocal unilineal historical process.

Rationalization and Situational Freedom

Enough has been said, now, to equip us for confronting the difficult problem to which this chapter is finally addressed: What is Weber's argument regarding the relationship between rationality and freedom, and how adequate is this argument?

In contrast to the discussions of rationality which permeate Weber's oeuvre, his comments on freedom are few and far between. Albeit conspicuously devoted to the ideal of freedom, and indeed hailed as "the last great liberal of modern times" even by an outspoken critic of the authoritarian implications of some of his political ideas (Mommsen, in *Stammer,* 1971, 183), Weber rarely made the subject of freedom thematic in his scholarly studies nor, despite his expressed awareness of the multivocality of the concept, did he at any point articulate a typology of different kinds of freedom. An especially circumspect interpretive effort is thus mandated by the fact that Weber's best-known statements appear only as rhetorical footnotes to his scholarly analyses.

As has already been suggested, the position most commonly associated with Weber is one which contradicts the Enlightenment equation of rationality and freedom and the nineteenth-century sociological consensus regarding the close link between the growth of rationalism and the rise of individualism. Although Weber carries forward certain lines of interpretation pursued by Toennies, Simmel, Sombart, and others so as to describe modern capitalist society (and, he prognosticates, modern socialist society a fortiori) as pervaded by a thoroughgoing rationalization of world view and life conduct, he is generally thought to associate that condition with a radical and perhaps fatal curtailment of human freedom. Such an interpretation, I feel, is simplified to the point of distortion. To reach a more adequate understanding of Weber on this complex question I propose, first, to look at the specific formulations wherein Weber connects rationalization with repressiveness; second, to examine other portions of his work which express a contrary argument; and third, to present some considerations which bear on a general assessment of Weber's position.

The passages where Weber actually conveys the observation that rationalization curtails freedom appear in two contexts—where he is commenting on conditions within the two institutional spheres of economic production and political authority. Regarding the economic system of modern industrial capitalism Weber observes that "the technical and economic conditions of machine production . . . today determine the lives of all the individuals who are born into this mechanism . . . with irresistible force" (1958b, 181). The exigencies of mechanization and the need for discipline in factories and modern commercial establishments repress the natural rhythms of the individual human organism and promote relentless authoritarian coercion (1968, 1156, 731). The capitalistic interest in standardizing the production of commodities promotes a powerful tendency toward the uniformity of life-styles (1920, 187).[12] For such reasons, Weber concludes that "all *economic* weathervanes point in the direction of increasing 'unfreedom.'" It is most ridiculous to think that present-day advanced capitalism, as it is currently being imported into Russia and now exists in America—this 'unavoidability'

12. The English translation of the passage in question (1958, 169) is inaccurate. A more faithful rendering would be: "That powerful tendency to make life-styles uniform, which today is so immensely aided by the capitalistic interest in the 'standardization' of production . . . " ("Jene mächtige Tendenz zur Uniformierung des Lebensstils, welcher heute das kapitalistische Interesse an der 'standardization' der Produktion zur Seite steht . . . " [1920, 187]).

of our economic development—has some elective affinity with 'democracy' or even with 'freedom' (in *any* sense of the word)" ([1906] 1958a, 60–61; emphasis in original.)

Whereas Weber speaks of the curtailment of freedom under the factory system of production as a kind of bondage to inanimate machines, he describes the repression due to bureaucracy as bondage to an "animated machine." In contrast to earlier, irrational forms of bureaucracy, modern rational bureaucracy because of its specialized personnel and codified routines is "escape-proof." It is fabricating a cage which men will perhaps be forced to inhabit someday in a condition as powerless as that of the fellahs of ancient Egypt (1968, 1401–2).

Summarizing this double threat to freedom, Weber writes, in his chapter entitled "Discipline": "This whole process of rationalization, in the factory and especially in the bureaucratic state machine, [is a] universal phenomenon [which] more and more restricts the importance of . . . individually differentiated conduct" (1968, 1156). And commenting on the prognosis in his discourse "Parliament and Government in Germany," Weber asks plaintively, "Given the basic fact of the irresistible advance of bureaucratization, the question about the future forms of political organization can only be asked in the following way: How can one possibly save any remnants of 'individualistic' freedom in any sense?" (1968, 1403).

These are strong statements. Their force may be somewhat attenuated, however, by three considerations. First, although Weber does stress the pervasive character both of economic activity and of bureaucratic authority in modern society—noting that capitalism is "the most fateful force in our modern life" (1958b, 17) and that bureaucratic organization has been tending to permeate many kinds of private association as well as public administration—the fact remains that these are but two of the spheres in which modern life has been rationalized, and that Weber may be shown to argue that rationalization *within other spheres* enhances freedom.

Second, Weber's statements about the repressive effects of rationalization within those two spheres have reference almost exclusively to the methodical or formal type of rationality, whereas his treatment of *other kinds of rationality* (and relations among different forms of rationality) within those spheres may be shown to indicate ways in which rationalization enhances freedom.

Third, the curtailment of freedom described in those statements has reference only to certain kinds of freedom, whereas Weber's treatment of freedom in other contexts may be shown to make *freedom in a different sense of the term* dependent on increased rationality.

This last point indicates a need to clarify the semantics of 'freedom' as we proceed. Although Weber himself failed to distinguish different senses of the term, he does use the concept of freedom in varying senses at different points in his work. The major shift in his usage is between an objective notion of *situational freedom*, referring to the scope of external constraints on the movements of actors, and freedom in the subjective sense of *autonomy*, the condition in which individual actors choose their own ends of action.

In the passages just cited, Weber's reference is clearly to situational unfreedom: the curtailment of opportunities for alternative courses of action on the part of individuals employed within capitalist industrial enterprises and subjected to bureaucratic regulation. His best-known position can thus be formulated more precisely as follows: the establishment of formal rationalities in the spheres of capitalist economic activity and bureaucratic domination restricts freedom in the sense of imposing more situational constraints on action.

Indeed, it is never rationality in general, but only the formal or methodical type of objectified rationalization which Weber has in mind when he permits himself those rhetorical flourishes for which he is so renowned. There is simply no place in his writings where either subjective rationality or objectified rationality in its conceptual, instrumental, or substantive forms is associated with a threat to freedom. Insofar as Weber indicts the rationalization process, it is only when it takes the form of the impersonal regulation of human activities according to fixed rules and routines. Yet the critique of this type of rationalization in modern life is limited to the spheres of economic and political action. In a different sphere, that of law, formal rationalization was seen by Weber to be a major world historical source of situational freedom.

A system of formally rational law exists when what are acknowledged as legally relevant facts are so identified on the basis of abstract generic characteristics. In its most fully rationalized form, such characteristics are disclosed through the logical analysis of meaning and are juridically interpreted through the application of determinate legal concepts which derive from highly abstract rules. In Weber's view the operation of a formally rational juridical system enhances the possibilities of situational freedom. It does this by stipulating certain privileges (*Freiheitsrechte*). One set of these privileges consists of guarantees that a person may engage or fail to engage in certain kinds of conduct without interference from third parties, especially state officials. Instances of this include "freedom of movement, freedom of conscience, and freedom of disposition over property." Another type of privilege is that which grants to an individual the right to regulate his relations with others through his own transactions. This constitutes the "freedom of contract" (1968, 667–69).

Weber was too realistic not to note that authoritative powers have at times had resort to "technical devices" to circumvent the protection of individual rights by the judiciary, and he laid stress on the possibility of repressive outcomes of a formally rational legal system in situations where powerful property holders operate in a formally free market to exert considerable de facto coercion upon the poor (1968, 876, 731). Such coercion, however, was shown to follow from inequalities of wealth and power, not from the rationalization of law as such. Regarding the latter, he stressed its effect in curbing the powers of hierarchical despots and democratic demagogues alike. If, as Weber says, juridical formalism enables the legal system to operate like a "technically rational machine," it thereby "guarantees," he immediately adds, "to individuals and groups within the system a relative maximum of freedom" (*das relative Maximum an Spielraum für seine Bewegungsfreiheit*) ([1921] (1976) 1968, 811 [469]).

Even within the spheres of bureaucratic authority and capitalist economy, moreover, Weber can be shown to have indicated a number of respects in which rationalization promotes situational freedom.

1. In addition to their constraining features, the *formally rational aspects of capitalism and bureaucracy guarantee significant kinds of situational freedom*. A defining feature of the capitalist system is the existence of an open labor market where workers are formally free to sell or withhold their services. Use of the monetary contract, in particular, frees the contracting parties from the all-inclusive obligations which encumbered them in contracts based on status; it thus "represents the archetype of the purposive contract"(1968, 674).[13] Similarly, the formally rational regulations of bureaucracy

13. Appreciation of this Weberian point was for a long time obscured by the translation of this phrase as "coercive contract" rather than "purposive contract," an error based on a misreading of the German text as *Zwangskontrakt* instead of *Zweckkontrakt*, as Guenther Roth has pointed out (Weber 1968, 734, n. 23). The

provide for recruitment to office on the basis of free contractual arrangements, and once in office staff members "are personally free and subject to authority only with respect to their impersonal official obligations" (1968, 220).

2. *The ambiguities inherent in institutionalized rationalization in any sphere enhance situational freedom by opening up options in any situation of action.* Weber's considered position on the matter was that univocal determinations of what is objectively rational within any sphere of action cannot be realized, since "compromise or selection among several bases of rationalization is possible or unavoidable" (1922, 414).[14]

Conflicts of value and related alternative choices representing different axes of rationalization permeate bureaucratic organizations. Weber has often been criticized for failing to appreciate this fact of life; Peter Blau, for example, maintains that Weber's model of bureaucracy sets up "an implicit functional scheme that addresses itself to the problem of how a given element of the organization contributes to its strength and effective functioning and thus fails to examine the conflicts that arise between the elements comprising the system" (1968, 60). On the contrary, I would argue that some of Weber's most revealing insights deal precisely with conflicts among different elements comprising bureaucratic organizations.

(a) One primary area of conflict within bureaucracies is between the obligation to act in accord with the rules in the organization's handbook and the wish to act in accord with the organization's given objectives. Weber could not be more explicit in noting this tension: he depicts the spirit of rational bureaucracy in terms of two general characteristics: formalism, on the one hand; and, on the other hand, a tendency of officials to act "from what is substantively a utilitarian point of view in the interest of the welfare of those under their authority . . . a tendency which is apparently, and in part genuinely, in contradiction to the above [formal rationality]" (1968, 228).

(b) To this tension between formal rationality and substantive rationality is added a tension between both of them and instrumental rationality, when Weber points out that the rationally debatable reasons that stand behind every act of bureaucratic administration concern "*either* subsumption under norms *or* a weighing of ends and

---

misreading was not corrected until the 5th, revised German edition, first published in 1972.

14. "Kompromiss oder Wahl zwischen mehreren solchen Grundlagen der Rationalisierung möglich ist oder unvermeidlich wird."

means" (1968, 979; emphasis mine). The salience of instrumental rationality in Weber's typification of bureaucracy is underscored in passages where Weber speaks of "the feature of bureaucratic administration which makes it specifically rational" as being the possession of "technical knowledge" by officeholders (1968, 225). The formal rationality of orderly and predictable career lines conflicts with the instrumentally rational norm of staffing offices with the technically most qualified candidates (1968, 962).

(c) Different aspects of bureaucratic rationality are congruent with contradictory political value orientations. The formal rationalities of bureaucratic procedure support the values of egalitarian mass democracy, inasmuch as they are responsive to demands for equality before the law and due process and the popular horror of "privilege." Indeed, the modern bureaucratic state has been transformed into an institution for the protection of rights (1968, 983, 908). On the other hand, the requirements of technically qualified officialdom and access to confidential knowledge promote oligarchic tendencies within bureaucratic elites, tendencies which are recurrently opposed by the efforts of democratically oriented constituencies to institute checks and controls—not to mention the controls built in through the limitation of power and the separation of powers which characterize the modern state (1968, 985, 962, 652).

(d) Even along a single axis of rationalization courses of action are by no means always univocally determined. The norm of instrumental rationality, for example, leaves the door open for a variety of technically suitable courses of action, even when a particular end is specified; "as every expert knows, the various technically rational principles come into conflict with one another" ([1922] 1949, 35 [489]); translation altered). Due to ambiguities of this sort, Weber indicates that all bureaucratic officials, though never at liberty to act out arbitrary personal whims, do possess a sphere of "'freely' creative administration," and notes that "even in the field of law-finding there are areas in which the bureaucratic judge is directly held to 'individualizing' procedures by the legislator" (1968, 979).

3. *The constraints imposed by formal rationalization within any one sphere are to some extent offset by the competition among groups within and among different institutional spheres.* Just as the diverse axes of rationalization in any sphere of action possess distinctive inner dynamics, so do the diverse institutional spheres possess distinctive interests and values which compete with one another. Although Weber's language at times sounds as though he

viewed modern society as wholly dominated by bureaucratic officialdom, with its ethos of orderliness, punctuality, reliability, and
adherence to rules, he also makes clear that each of the other major
spheres of modern life has its own protagonists who hearken to
different demons and ethics. The political sphere has acquired "a
peculiarly rational mystique of its own" (1968, 601), wherein the
struggle for power and the promulgation of policy orients action in a
manner quite opposed to the bureaucratic orientation (1968,
1393–1405). A very different alternative is represented by commercial and industrial entrepreneurs, with their rationalized pursuit
of monetary profit in the market; at one point Weber singles out the
capitalist entrepreneur as the type preeminently "able to maintain at
least relative immunity from subjection to the control of rational
bureaucratic knowledge" (1968, 225), just as he repeatedly stresses
that the bureaucratic organizations of private capitalism set up a
countervailing force against domination by the bureaucracy of the
state (1968, 1402). The development of rational science offers a
vocational sphere with its own unique orientation, and still other
options appear in the religious domain where the arms of the
churches remain open to embrace those who find modern science or
politics uncongenial.

A complete Weberian depiction of modern society must therefore
be one which views the power of any sector, including the bureaucratic state, as balanced by the power and claims of various other
sectors, and reveals a condition of situational freedom in which
actors can follow alternative norms and values by selecting from a
plurality of sectors. Still, it might be argued that such a conception
sees the situational freedom of actors as enormously limited once
they have committed themselves to participation in a particular
sector. That is, I believe, how Weber regarded the matter, but there
are two considerations which relax the austerity of this view
somewhat. Weber knew, but did not articulate sociologically (as did
Simmel), two phenomena whose expansion in modern society
greatly enhances the situational freedom of actors: multiple role
playing, and voluntary associations. If, as Weber argued forcefully,
the modern scientist in his properly institutionalized role is constrained not to advance political interests and ideals, outside the
laboratory and the lecture hall he is, as citizen, free to take an active
part in party politics. Moreover, in his later years Weber was
increasingly sensitive to the opportunities afforded by voluntary

associations in opening up new possibilities for action.[15]

Rationalization and Subjective Freedom

Weber's pessimistic utterances regarding the effects of rationalization on freedom had reference specifically to the possibilities for "individually differentiated conduct" under conditions of extensive formally rational regulation of conduct. It is an open question how much of this pessimism represented the idiosyncrasies of his own temperament and personal experience; how much a response to the deeply authoritarian cast of public life in Wilhelmine Germany and of Prussian culture more generally; how much a rhetorical stance designed to prod others to exert themselves in struggle for freedom; and how much a considered analysis of secular tendencies of bureaucratized and industrialized societies. In any case, we have seen that Weber's famous pronouncements regarding the modern threats to freedom have to be qualified by attention to the numerous respects in which his analyses reveal an increased scope for situational freedom due to a variety of rationalizing processes in Western society.

There is, however, another area in which Weber appears quite unambivalent in assessing the effects of rationality on freedom. This is when he considers freedom not in the sense of the absence of situational constraints on action, but in the sense of an actor's subjective disposition to make decisions for himself.

Weber expressed himself on this issue in his two 1905 essays on the logic of the cultural sciences. In those essays Weber sharply criticized the view, associated with Karl Knies and Eduard Meyer, that freedom of the will is a function of the *irrational* aspects of action. Weber, by contrast, defined an actor's decision as "free" when it is "based on his deliberations, without the intrusion of external compulsions or irresistible affects" ([1922] 1975, 191 [132]). Rejecting the notion that incalculability is the hallmark of subjective freedom, Weber argued:

15. Part of Weber's motivation to deliver a number of speeches, including "Science as a Vocation" and "Politics as a Vocation," to the Freistudentische Bund during the last few years of his life was his desire to advance the role of voluntary associations in the reconstruction of postwar Germany (Schluchter 1979a, 116). His interest in this social form was initially kindled by his observations of sects and clubs during his visit to the United States in 1904, and first reported in his 1906 essay, "The Protestant Sects and the Spirit of Capitalism" (1948, 302–22).

> We associate the highest measure of an empirical "feeling of
> freedom" with those actions which we are conscious of
> performing rationally—i.e., in the absence of physical and
> psychic "compulsions," vehement "affects," and "accidental"
> disturbances of the clarity of judgment, in which we pursue a
> clearly conceived "end" through "means" which are the most
> adequate according to our empirically grounded knowledge.
> ([1922] 1949, 124–25 [226]; translation altered)

In thus linking the subjective freedom of autonomous decision
making to the rational capacities of actors, Weber directs our
attention to a dimension of rationality different from that which we
have considered up to this point, namely, to the dimension of
subjective rationality. We must recall Weber's analysis of the four
ways in which social action can be subjectively oriented. It is
evident from that analysis that Weber conceives the four categories
of traditionality, affectivity, value rationality, and means/end rationality as constituting a kind of hierarchy, a hierarchy based on
increasing deliberateness of choice. Rationalization, Weber writes,
can proceed by abandoning ingrained habituation for more deliberate kinds of adaptation; by abandoning emotional values for a
deliberate formulation of ultimate value standards; and by abandoning belief in absolute values for a more skeptical kind of rational
orientation (1968, 30).

With increasing subjective rationality, in other words, Weber
associates an increase in the actor's subjective freedom of choice.
One has little freedom of choice so long as one's actions are
determined by custom or ingrained habituation; somewhat more if
one is free to follow the swings one's emotional moods; still more if
one calculates intentions in order to bring them in line with a
consciously held supreme value; and most of all if one is free to
deliberate about alternative values, means, and their respective
costs and benefits—to take all one's ends as given subjective wants
and arrange them in a scale of consciously assessed relative urgency. In other words, as actors become more conscious of and
deliberate about the means and ends of their actions—as they
become increasingly *zweckrational* in their subjective orientations—
so accordingly do they experience a greater subjective sense of
freedom.

So stated, this is a purely analytic, ahistorical argument, similar in
form (if notably different in substance) to Kant's equating the use of
practical reason with the ideal freedom of human agents. Is it
plausible, now, to link this Weberian formulation regarding subjec-

tive rationality and freedom to his analyses of the historical processes of modern Western rationalization, referred to above as
objectified rationalities in the various institutional spheres? The
question at once directs us to Weber's ideas on the rationalization of
religion and science.

Although instrumental, substantive, and formal types of rationalization can be identified in the areas of religious and scientific
practice, the rationalization of *beliefs* involves the type referred to
above as conceptual rationalization. This in turn, as Weber was well
aware, is a complex development involving a number of elements
which do not always occur together. The principal elements of
conceptual rationalization that Weber refers to include *logic,* the
norms of clarity and consistency; *abstraction,* the norms of comparison and generalization; *verifiability,* the norm of empirically
grounding beliefs; and *reflectivity,* the norm of continuous critical
examination of beliefs. When the general human desire to possess a
meaningful picture of the world was coupled with powerful interests
in intellectual systematization and the elimination of magical ideas,
a conjunction which took place initially in ancient Judaism and again
with renewed force following the Protestant Reformation, the result
was a historically unprecedented development of conceptually rationalized beliefs about the world.

Although the movement toward conceptual rationalization of
world views was initially propelled by the salvation religions,
paradoxically the success of those efforts weakened the position of
their original religious sponsors. Modern science has not only
completed the age-old Judaeo-Christian project of eliminating empirically ungrounded beliefs in magical entities,[16] but also, by
providing more reliable knowledge about the world and demonstrating the inexorable reality of value pluralism, has undermined the
possibility of deriving an intellectually compelling view of the world
from traditional transcendental religious sources.[17]

The ascendance of rationalized science means that the modern
person who abides by the kind of belief systems now institutionalized as legitimate may no longer embrace without question notions

16. This is the true meaning of Weber's concept of *Entzauberung,* which is often
misleadingly translated as "disenchantment." The more accurate, if less euphonious,
translation is "demagicalization."

17. For a stimulating exposition of Weber's account of this paradoxical development, see Schluchter (1979b). It is rarely appreciated that Weber's account is in many
ways parallel to Comte's interpretation of the role of theological philosophy as a
transitional development between animism and positive science.

validated by tradition or prophetic authority. Older cognitive orientations have been undermined at the same time that newer cognitive resources have been provided: increased knowledge about the world which raises awareness of the costs and benefits of utilizing alternative means to pursue diverse goals, and increased clarity about the implications and coherence of diverse values and normative criteria.

It is difficult to separate Weber's descriptive account of this situation from his valuational response to it. Both judgments come together in his formulations on the ethic of responsibility, an orientation in which actors balance considerations of technical adequacy based on the findings of empirical science with considerations of moral appropriateness based on the critical examination of values. I think it must be said that Weber regarded the ethic of responsibility both as an orientation advanced by the achievements of modern science and as the most desirable kind of orientation for what he regarded as the authentic modern personality.[18]

The ethic of responsibility entails the highest degree of subjective rationality, that is, the broader conception of means/end rationality described above. This is a disposition to be constant in employing correctives against unthinking habit, unconscious ideation, emotional biases, fuzzy thinking, and rigid beliefs. By the same token, the ethic of responsibility maximizes the freedom of actors to make their own decisions. Even if one overlooks the many respects in which rationalization enhances situational freedom (as described in the preceding section), it is clear that Weber regarded the rationalization of belief systems as a dynamic process which promotes subjective freedom. As Karl Loewith observed in an exceptional earlier interpretation, "The motive force of Weber's whole attitude was . . . recognition of a rationalized world *and [of] the countertendency to achieve the freedom of self-responsibility*" ([1932] 1970, 120; emphasis mine).

Beyond Weber

Beyond the more adequate comprehension of Weber's stated views on rationality and freedom to be gained through the sort of critical exegesis I have attempted above, the full appropriation and application of his argument at present requires modifications of three major kinds.

18. This interpretation of Weber's ethic of responsibility runs parallel to, and has been reinforced by, that advanced by Schluchter (1979b, 53–59).

1. *Further disambiguation of the concepts of rationality and freedom.* As descriptive concepts, Weber's distinctions among types of rationality possess enduring value. There is now the need to exercise them more systematically as well as relate them to discussions of the concept of rationality by other social scientists and philosophers.

By contrast, Weber's treatment of the idea of freedom is analytically superficial. Work to specify the diverse types or dimensions of freedom by scholars of the last generation such as McKeon (1952; n.d.), Adler (1958–61), and Oppenheim (1961) has enriched the conceptual resources for bringing to the empirical analysis of freedom the kind of sophistication that Weber introduced to the empirical study of rationalization processes.

In Weber's work, the normative treatment of rationality and freedom is not always distinguished clearly from their empirical examination nor is it articulated adequately in its own right. He simply takes as given the modern person's desire for situational freedom: "It is a gross self-deception to believe that without the achievements of the age of the Rights of Man any one of us, including the most conservative, can go on living his life" (1968, 1403). He neither marshals arguments to justify the value of situational freedom nor, in spite of his awareness for the need for authority in organizing human relations, does he provide arguments that justify the erection of limits on situational freedom (as can be found in the thought of sociologists like Simmel, Durkheim, and even Engels) or, apart from a brief discussion of the historical roots of the right to freedom of conscience (1968, 1208–9), that analyze the circumstances under which situational freedom becomes positively valued (see Oppenheim 1961, 211–27). Regarding the value of autonomy, Weber simply asserts as an ultimate value the ideal of maximizing subjective freedom, in flourishes of disdain for "the shallowness of our routinized daily existence" which permits life to run on "as an event in nature" rather than be guided by "a series of ultimate decisions through which the soul—as in Plato—chooses its own fate" (1949, 18), again without elaborating arguments to justify the value of autonomy or, despite his keen awareness of the high costs of living in a condition of anxiety produced by the dissolution of accustomed beliefs, without considering other values which might be competitive with the ideal of maximizing the subject's freedom of choice.

Toward the value of rationality Weber had mixed sentiments. He expresses himself as a great advocate of *ratio* when he speaks of it as the indispensable means for enabling actors to become more responsible in making decisions and as the requirement for leading a nontrivial productive life in modern times. On the other hand, as we have seen, he tends to regard the extension of rationalized routines as suffocating. He failed to incorporate his distinctions regarding rationality into an explicit discussion of the valuable and objectionable features of rationality and of the ways in which rationality may be related to other desired goals.

2. *Further qualification of Weber's conception of bureaucratic rationalization.* Although Weber was clairvoyant in perceiving the centrality of bureaucratic formations in modern society and the inexorability of their continued expansion, his stark image of bureaucracy as an escape-proof shell of bondage must be modified by qualifications implicit in his writings and by considerations of subsequent developments both in modern society and in sociological knowledge. That there are determinate limits to the extent of rationalized regulation of human activities in any sphere of life follows both from his methodological point that human reality is so complicated that it can never be wholly subsumed under any particular axis of rationalized treatment and from his awareness of the inexorable conflict between formal rationality and rationality of other types. Subsequent work on the sociology of bureaucratic organizations, by Peter Blau and others, has illuminated further structural tensions which open up degrees of situational freedom in any bureaucratic setting, even under totalitarian regimes. Moreover, Weber's notion that formally rationalized organization of the bureaucratic sort is the preeminent and all-pervasive mode of organization in modern societies must be corrected by the analyses of Parsons (1968) and others, which indicate the equally crucial role in modern societies played by more self-regulative types of organization—collegial groups, democratic voluntary associations, and markets—not to mention the relatively autonomous character of professional groups and statuses inside bureaucratic structures. Distinctions must also be made between the restriction of the bureaucrat's freedom and the implications of this for clients, which is as likely to be as much a guarantee of rights as it is a restriction of freedom.

Finally, it may be suggested that Weber's view of the oppressiveness of bureaucratic regulation was empirically more descriptive of the situation in the Germany of his time (and, apparently, of the situation in Germany today) than it ever has been in the United States. Weber's generalized conception of bureaucracy has been viewed as biased to some extent by the particular case which he was

closest to. On the basis of observations of a particular historic
situation in which he was enmeshed (Philo and Walton 1973) he was
led to view a sheer increase in formal rationality and domination as
historically indispensable. Even given the organizational imperatives of bureaucratic hierarchy and regulation, such devices as
independent administrative courts and ombudsman offices have
been widely instituted to exert control over the excesses of bureaucratic domination, and recent social research indicates the plausibil-
ity of instituting parallel structures affording greater situational
freedom to salaried employees (see Stein, Kanter, et al. 1979).

3. *Attention to the social-psychological requisites and consequences of subjective rationality.* One of Weber's main oversights
was his failure to consider the implications of the diffusion of an
increasingly *zweckrational* orientation among the inhabitants of
modern societies or, to put it in somewhat different terms, the
difficulty of securing the balance between the self-interested and
moral components that represented his ideal conception of the
means/end rational orientation. Although the phenomenon can be
encompassed easily within his conceptual framework, Weber was
inattentive to certain processes in advanced capitalist societies that
enhance the freedom of self-determination by promoting means/end-
rational orientations, processes identified and analyzed by Toennies
and Simmel, and which represented a focal concern of nineteenth-
century French social thought from de Maistre and Saint-Simon to
Durkheim (see Lukes 1972, 195–99).

At the present time, of course, it is difficult for a sociologist living
in the United States not to be made aware of the cumulative effects
of those long-term secular trends. The institutional spheres where
they are most manifest are those pertaining to socialization, the
areas Weber generally ignored—the spheres of family, education,
and now, psychotherapy. In these areas there has been a marked
trend in some Western societies during the last century toward
emphasis on the cultivation of rational decision making and autonomy. Parental objectives in middle-class American families have
shifted from teaching children the "right way to live" to encouraging them to make up their minds for themselves. In educational
institutions, beginning at the college level but extending now to
some secondary and even primary schools, there has been a growing
emphasis on teaching students how to solve problems and make

independent judgments.[19]

The enormous spread of psychotherapy in recent decades may be seen as additional institutionalized support for the liberation of persons from habitual, emotional, and authoritarian compulsions and the enhancement of their capacities as autonomous rational actors. The attainment of maximum self-responsibility is a primary therapeutic objective for approaches otherwise as disparate as psychoanalytic therapy and *est*. This is true a fortiori for such popular therapeutic modalities as rational therapy, assertion training, and decision therapy.

The general cultural attitudes that legitimate these developments have become apparent in the area where Weber first identified a pattern of enslavement due to rationalization, the economic sphere. Even in Weber's own terms, one might have predicted that, once whatever impetus to methodical rationalization in industry and commerce deriving from the substantive rationalities of ascetic Protestantism had waned, it might not be long before continued rationalization in other spheres and directions would motivate a more balanced pursuit of goals within the economy, creating demands for more humane working conditions in factories and offices, markets for more diversified consumer goods, and a more calculating and critical kind of consumer mentality. To some extent, a central theme of some of the seminal diagnoses of American society of the last generation, from Riesman (1950) to Bell (1976) can be phrased as the antinomy between the objectified formal rationalities of production and the subjective means/end rationalities of consumption.

A number of diagnostic comments on the contemporary United States suggest that its dominant "pathology" is not the hypertrophy of rationalized regulation, as was the case in Weber's Germany (and may be in today's Germany as well), but—more along Durkheimian lines—what appear to be expressions of a relatively unregulated hedonic orientation. These comments refer variously to such phenomena as the weakened position of families as a locus of moral

19. American colleges in the 1960s experienced a quantum jump in the use of pedagogical approaches geared to enhancing student participation in problem finding and problem solving, through problem-oriented texts, teaching by discussion, student research projects, and even curricular structures (and nonstructures) enabling students to construct highly personalized four-year degree programs (see Grant and Riesman 1978).

socialization; widespread cheating and vandalism in schools; low-ered academic standards; permissive attitudes toward the use of chemical substances and sexual experiences of all kinds; the calcu-lated use of incivility and violence in social relations; the expansion of a "consumerist" mentality; the rise of single-interest groups and the decline of responsibility for public concerns; and a greater fickleness regarding personal commitments and cultural styles. However one may evaluate such phenomena, they cannot be said to reflect a condition of repression due to the unchecked processes of formal rationalization, but rather an enormous amount of situational freedom and autonomous decision making promoted by the eroding effects of conceptual and instrumental rationalities on moral author-ity and the bases of moral community.

In the light of these last considerations, the complete Weberian argument seems most wanting in its inattention to the social-psychological context of autonomous decision making. For all his awareness of the nonrational dimensions of action, Weber remained in some deep sense a child of the Enlightenment by holding to an ideal of the human universe as one constituted by heroically rational, free, autonomous monads. In this respect it may be instructive to compare Weber with another pioneering analyst of the nonrational dimensions of human action, his contemporary Sigmund Freud.

8

Freud, Weber, and Modern
Rationales of Conscience

Sigmund Freud and Max Weber belong to that elite of historical personalities whom Benjamin Nelson described as "men of extraordinary range, intellectual and spiritual titans, far removed from the general run of those who win mention in the annals of politics, science, scholarship, or learned pretense" (1965b, 149). They deserve to be understood, he added, not as mere disciplinary specialists, but as makers of ideas, movers of men, and thinkers responding to questions of ultimate significance.[1] Indeed, there is scarcely an aspect of the human condition Freud and Weber did not touch. And yet, despite their extraordinary range, the struggle to create a very distinctive discipline is central to the story of each of their lives. We can learn much about the ambiguous connection between the sciences of man and modern moral sensibilities by reflecting on the broadly similar contours and repercussions of those struggles.

Careers and Crises

We hesitate to compare them, these originative individuals, not least because they founded disciplines often thought of as antitheses: psychoanalysis examines conflict and integration within the individual psyche, and requires investigators to use their own inner responses to subjects as tools of observation; sociology looks at processes of conflict and integration among pluralities of actors, and

1. In its earliest form this chapter was written as a tribute to the memory of the late Benjamin Nelson. The passage just cited appears in an essay in which Nelson compares Weber to Luther, Hegel, and Marx. That he consistently thought of Freud in the same company is clear from many other writings (1954; 1957; 1965a).

typically demands that observers exclude their personal responses
to subjects. And we recall the condescension with which each of
these discipline-builders regarded the other's specialty. For Freud,
after all, sociology was merely "applied psychology" (1921, 71); for
Weber psychoanalysis, though potentially promising, was marred
by inflated pretensions and misguided disciples (Marianne Weber
1975, 375–80), while in any case he thought it was grossly erroneous
to regard any kind of psychology as a foundation for sociology
(1968, 19).

Differences of this order have tended to obscure some striking
similarities between the two disciplines—in particular, their parallels in historical development.[2] Note, for example, that both disciplines took shape in the same years. Although earlier writers had
anticipated their key ideas, both psychoanalysis and sociology
assumed their modern institutionalized form between 1895 and 1915.
During this period, the first professional journals of the two fields
were founded and their first professional associations established.
The half-decade in which Freud published *The Interpretation of
Dreams* and *Three Essays on the Theory of Sexuality* was flanked by
the publication of what are arguably the four decisively germinal
works of modern sociology—Durkheim's *Le Suicide* (1897),
Simmel's *Soziologie* (1908), Cooley's *Social Organization* (1909),
and Weber's essays on the Protestant Ethic (1905, 1906).

The emergence of both fields, moreover, aroused storms of
opposition.[3] In their embattled beginnings, they were nourished by
devoted proponents whose activities have been described in the
suggestive language of collective behavior as the "psychoanalytic
movement" and the "sociological movement." Although the intellectual heartland of both disciplines was continental Europe, they
developed extensively as stable professions only in the more open
society of the United States, just as both were suppressed by the
totalitarian regimes of Bolshevik Russia and Nazi Germany.

Such similarities in the historical setting of these disciplines
suggest that we might fruitfully look for points of comparison

2. This is not to mention the many ways in which the two disciplines have been
viewed or used as providing complementary contributions to the analysis of comparable problems. On the latter topic, see Wallerstein and Smelser (1969) and Levine
(1978).

3. This is not to gainsay Sulloway's strong argument (1979) that the extent to which
Freud's ideas were opposed by his contemporaries, especially in the early years of
the psychoanalytic movement, has been greatly exaggerated by Freud and his
followers.

between their preeminent originative thinkers.[4] Superficial resemblances appear at once. Both Freud and Weber were born in Central Europe just after the middle of the nineteenth century—Freud in Moravia in 1856, Weber in Thuringia in 1864. Both were highly successful university students in conventional fields and served tours of military duty in their twenties. Both lived at their parents' houses through their young adulthood (Freud until twenty-seven, Weber until twenty-nine), as was common at the time for aspiring professionals. At thirty, each achieved his first independent profession status—Freud opening his medical practice in Vienna in 1886, Weber acceding to a chair at Freiburg in 1894. Both men were married within months of their thirtieth birthdays, Freud to Martha Bernays, Weber to Marianne Schnitger. Both marriages were stable though not always happy; both women were devoted wives and outlived their husbands by several years.[5] In the first decade of this century both men made visits to the United States, visits associated with significant developments in their careers. In contrast with these and other biographical parallels, one major difference must be noted: Weber died, suddenly and prematurely, in 1920 at the age of fifty-six, from pneumonia, associated with the influenza pandemic following World War I, while Freud, though losing his daughter Sophie to that same epidemic, survived to the age of eighty-three.

4. Although sociology did not, like psychoanalysis, take shape under the aegis of a central presiding genius, most sociologists today would probably agree that Max Weber was our single most impressive founding father. Although, moreover, in contrast to the talmudic thoroughness with which Freud's writings were continually studied within the psychoanalytic community, Weber's works only began to receive much scholarly attention from sociologists after the middle of this century, today they remain texts with which sociologists of many specialties actively contend and which contain research programs and ideas still judged by many to be at the frontier of the field (see, e.g., Schluchter 1979b, 11–13; Collins 1980). Weber's *current* stature within sociology can thus be taken to qualify him to stand alongside Freud as the preeminent founding genius of his discipline (a fortiori of that conception of it which he baptized as "interpretive sociology"). Even so, it should be noted that this honor must be shared with Emile Durkheim and Georg Simmel, a point which Nelson alluded to in the 1965a paper mentioned above.

5. The contrasting roles played by these women in the two marriages should be noted. Martha Freud was the more conventional housewife and mother. She gave birth to and raised six children. She shared little of Freud's professional interest. Marianne Weber remained childless, but was much more of an intellectual companion to her husband. She cohosted his famous intellectual salons, and it is to her editing of Weber's posthumous publications and to her biography of him that we owe much of the recovery of Weber's life work.

Freud and Weber resembled each other temperamentally as well—startlingly so. Of serious, often stern demeanor, they were yet men of lively humor; masters of irony, both in self-deriding wit and in polemic; possessed of a demanding sense of honor, and prickly in pride; distant in personal relations, and marginal to the institutional establishments of their time; harsh in judging others, yet capable of empathy and help for an enormous diversity of other human types; impatient with sentimentality of any sort; scornful of modern apologists for religion, yet powerfully attracted to the interpretation of religion as a historical phenomenon; animated by a lust for understanding and a capacity for intellectual work of gigantic proportions, and devoted above all to an ethic of intellectual integrity.

Of all the parallels between the lives of Freud and Weber perhaps the most dramatic is the fact that in the very same year, 1897, both men entered a period of emotional turmoil triggered by the recent deaths of their fathers, periods which biographers of each have identified as turning points in the development of their mature intellectual orientations. The death of Freud's father made him "feel quite uprooted," and intensified a malaise, extending from 1894 through 1900, in which he suffered moods of depression, moments of intellectual paralysis, and various somatic disturbances (Jones 1953, 324–25; Sulloway 1979, 215). Freud's response to this turbulence included his rigorous self-analysis, in the course of which he uncovered early erotic feelings toward his mother and hostile wishes against his father, discoveries that provided insights and confirmations for his prodigious work on the interpretation of dreams and on the Oedipus complex.

Weber's experience was more traumatic. In June 1897, on or just after his parents' wedding anniversary, Weber had an angry confrontation with his father, in which he "ordered his father out of his house to permit his mother and himself the undisturbed enjoyment of one another's company. It was the first time that Weber had ever revealed to his father the full depths of his bitterness" (Mitzman 1970, 152). Seven weeks later, without the two men meeting again, his father died. The aftermath for the young Weber was a spell of nervous exhaustion that began five years of intense suffering, including chronic insomnia, depression, and intermittent paralysis of his mental function (far worse than Freud's). Describing the onset of this affliction, Marianne Weber wrote that "an evil thing from the unconscious underground of life stretched out its claws toward him," but she records Weber's own view that the illness was "perhaps only a long-gathering cloud, whose final discharge would almost be like a liberation from a mysteriously threatening, hostile power," a liberation which "might prepare the way for a greater *harmony* of his vital powers in the future" (1975, 234, 236). When Weber recovered, he embarked on one of the most momentous periods of intellectual creativity ever achieved, and in directions— Mitzman has shown—that reflect the working through of materials reflecting a long suppressed closeness to the values of his mother.

Discipline Shifts

Although further details of the dynamics of these acute episodes of what Ellenberger (1970) has termed "creative illness" may be of interest for other purposes, what I want to stress here is that those periods marked watersheds in the transition from one kind of disciplinary orientation to another. Freud, in his thirties, considered himself a neurologist and neuroanatomist. He analyzed human phenomena in terms of neuronal connections, and utilized the impersonal imagery of mechanical equilibria, electric circuits, and circulatory systems. He sought, as he wrote in 1895 in the words of his unpublished *Project for a Scientific Psychology,* "to represent psychical processes as quantitatively determined states of specifiable material particles" (p. 295).

By his late forties, Freud had adopted a new professional self-image. Abandoning the biophysical approach, he viewed himself now as a revolutionary in the field of psychology. Although, as Sulloway has shown in his masterly intellectual biography (1979), Freud retained a strong though transformed identification with biology, his discipline building, based on his earlier discovery that the somatic symptoms of hysterical patients had a psychological meaning, was couched in terms of the interpretations of meanings and motives. The new discipline of psychoanalysis did not, he argued, deny the importance of biological or constitutional factors; but its distinctive mission and expertise was to disclose the hidden and forgotten motives underlying human behavior. Freud would go on to insist that "psychoanalysis is not a specialized branch of medicine," but only a "part of psychology" (1927a, 252).

Weber's professional orientation also changed in mid-career. Trained in legal and economic history, Weber started his career with appointments in economics at the universities of Freiburg and Heidelberg. His scholarly writings analyzed historical phenomena in terms of such impersonal categories as forms of property, size of rural estates, forms of trading association, and conflict between economic classes. Following the period of his breakdown, Weber turned away from a career as professor of economics. Like Freud, Weber came to prefer to work outside the constraints of a university environment. What is more, he could no longer stand being tied down to the discipline of economics. And in the first major scholarly production following his recovery, Weber shifted his analytic interest to emphasize the ideas and motives that organize different kinds of economic activity, an emphasis reflecting insights he had gained during the 1890s: the significance of subjectively held ideals in inducing farm workers to emigrate from the estates of East Prussia, and the role of religious ideas in developing the spirit of modern capitalism.

In his late forties, moreover, Weber began to identify himself with the discipline of sociology, a field he had previously referred to with a certain disdain.[6] He did not, however, embrace the prevailing sociologies of the day, but rather a new version, which he designated *verstehende Soziologie*—a sociology oriented to understanding the subjective meanings and motives of individuals. Although Weber never neglected the importance of such variables as geographic settings, demographic factors, property arrangements, and technological levels,[7] he came to argue for his kind of sociology that what was "decisive for its status as a science" was its capacity to provide interpretations of meaningful action, a task which "it alone can do" (1968, 24, 17).

6. Weber's shift to sociology was prompted by a number of considerations, including his interest in promoting the *empirical* examination of certain subjects, notably law and the state, which had largely been studied from a normative perspective; his wish to undertake the *comparative* examination of questions that previously were studied chiefly in a particularized, historical manner; and his hope (to some extent shattered by his experience with the German Sociological Association) to find colleagues similarly disposed to investigate social phenomena in a "value-free" scientific manner. Weber's disdain for much of what was produced in his adopted field never faded. "Most of what goes under the name of sociology is humbug *[Schwindel]*," he declared in his farewell address at Heidelberg in 1919. It was to rescue sociology from its collectivistic and organicist concepts, he once remarked, that he had come to label himself a sociologist, and this concern underlay his repeated stress, in programmatic statements, on its mandate to interpret the actions of individuals.

7. Indeed, in his later writings on religious evolution, social classes, and the organization of medieval cities Weber achieved exemplary syntheses of materialist explanations with subjective interpretations, even though at some moments he "regressed" into rather one-sided accounts (Alexander 1983).

Thus Freud and Weber began their intellectual careers in disciplines that disposed them to analyze human phenomena in impersonal terms through the language of material causation. As they became increasingly sensitive to the significance of subjective meanings and motives in accounting for action, they became dualists, holding and never relinquishing the view that both material conditions and purposive ideas are important determinants of conduct. Yet, despite the continuing prominence of biological notions in Freud's thought and Weber's lifelong preoccupation with institutional structures and economic imperatives, each man moved beyond his earlier disciplinary commitments to create a new discipline whose mission he held to be a distinctive capacity to provide ways of understanding the vicissitudes of human intentionality.

Beyond a shift in disciplinary self-image, Freud and Weber developed in two other ways that were remarkably similar, following their periods of depression and emotional crisis. One was their emergence as critics of modern civilization. In the first decade of this century, both issued generalized critiques of modern conditions as a source of pernicious constraints on human freedom. Weber began in 1905 with scattered shots against the stifling effects of mechanized industrial production and capitalist commerce, and went on to attack the no less repressive "animated machine" of state bureaucracy.[8] Freud, with his 1908 paper on "civilized" sexual morality and modern nervous illness, prefigured his later critique of the powerfully repressive price of modern civilization.

Neither man was disposed to mobilize constituencies to take arms against the repressive forces which they diagnosed so cuttingly. Instead, each found a way to sublimate in his professional work his desire to enhance freedom under the conditions of modern life. Thus, another parallel change in their orientations was the disposition to stress the emancipatory potential of the new disciplines they were shaping. The aesthetic, therapeutic, and political functions of the new sciences seemed less important than the capacity to help people become more aware of the unconscious premises of their thoughts and deeds and thereby reach heightened levels of self-conscious free choice. Freud was consistently cautious about the therapeutic potential of psychoanalysis, a caution that increased with age, but he never lost faith that the interpretation of dreams was the road to the unconscious, and that the arduous work of

8. For more extended discussion of Weber's views on the repressiveness of modern economic and political institutions, see Beetham (1974), as well as chapter 7 above.

psychoanalytic collaboration was justified because it helped the analysand "to acquire the extra piece of mental freedom which distinguishes conscious mental activity . . . from unconscious" (1915, 170).

Weber rejected as illusions the older justifications of scientific endeavor—science as the way to "true being," "true art," "true nature," "true God," or "true happiness" (1948, 140–43)—as well as the attempts of his contemporaries to make social science a vehicle for political action. Rather, he saw sociology valuable chiefly as a means to enhance subjective freedom. It does this by disclosing the empirical and normative implications of alternative values and goals, thereby enabling actors to transcend the "in-articulate half-consciousness or actual unconsciousness" of the meanings of their action which characterizes the "shallowness of our routinized daily existence," so that activities are not "permitted to run on as an event in nature but are instead to be consciously guided." This reflected his conviction that when we are conscious of performing actions rationally—in the absence of physical and psy-chic compulsions, vehement affects, disturbed judgment, and encrusted custom—we then experience the "highest measure of an empirical feeling of freedom" (1968, 21; 1949, 18, 124–25).

Scholars or Prophets?

Protracted emotional crises drove Freud and Weber toward the creation of the new disciplines of psychoanalysis and interpretive sociology—disciplines whose programs were to investigate human motives and whose declared missions were to help combat the repressive features of modern society by fortifying actors with additional reserves of mental freedom. But what were those emo-tional crises?

Whatever else was involved—and, of course, much was—it is clear that Freud and Weber alike experienced a deep conflict between the commitment to the professional norms of scientific work and an urge to play some kind of prophetic role. Much as they sought to abide by—indeed, to institute—rigorous procedures for the analysis of human phenomena, they struggled no less to find a way to shape the conscience of their times. In adulthood, both expressed discomfort with the pedantic requirements of a career in science. Something of the romantic tenor of Freud's boyhood dreams to become a great military or political leader never left him. "I am not really a man of science, not an observer, not an experimenter, and not a thinker," Freud confessed at the age of forty-four. "I am nothing but by temperament a *conquistador* . . . with the curiosity, the boldness, and the tenacity that belong to that type of being" (Jones 1953, 348). Weber's political aspirations are well known, and they nagged him all his life.[9] It seemed that as a young man he had little calling indeed for what he would later describe as the true life of a scientist, one who eschews the quest for active experience, who can readily put on blinders, one disposed to make tens of thousands of quite trivial computations in his head for months at a time. "Nothing is more abominable to me than the arrogance of the 'intellectual' and learned professions," he declared in his mid-twenties (Mitzman 1970, 66).

With the doors to political activism closed to them—Freud because of his Jewish background and his expedient adjustment to a career in medical practice, Weber because of his disdain for the quality of German politicians and the ineffectualness of the Wilhelmine parliament—each seems to have transformed his ambition to be a leader of men into a wish to become some kind of moral prophet. Although they shared a deep antagonism to organized religion and were convinced that for educated moderns to resort to religion betrayed a weakness of character and intellect, Freud and Weber had the strongest admiration for the religiously inspired leader Oliver Cromwell and, like Cromwell, maintained strong identifications with prophetic figures from the Old Testament. At fifteen, Weber (not a Jew) had studied Hebrew in order to read the Old Testament in the original. Both men devoted their last major substantive investigation to the study of ancient Judaism, producing interpretations that were revolutionary, in different ways, for emphasizing the world-historical impact of the moralizing work of the biblical Jews. As is well known, Freud attributed his capacity to tolerate a position of heroic nonconformity to having a character specifically Jewish. It was Moses (albeit Egyptianized) whom he credited with laying the basis for that character, and Freud more than once intimated that he likened himself to the figure of Moses (1939, 107–11; Fromm 1959, 76–80). Weber similarly seems to have maintained a strong identification with the haranguing prophets of Judea, and with Jeremiah in particular (Marianne Weber 1975, 593–94; Weber 1948, 26–27).

9. "All his life Weber was passionate in following political events, relating to them, and speaking of them. . . . Max Weber did not become a leading statesman; he remained a political writer. But although he did not come to engage in political action, he lived as in a state of perpetual readiness to do so" (Jaspers 1946, 7, 9).

If Freud and Weber did not hold Nietzsche's view that the Jews had introduced a debilitating moral force into European culture, they did have a keen post-Nietzschean sense that their time was one in which the old gods were dead or dying, that people were searching for new ones, and that a heroic response was in order. Both felt some impulse to provide prophetic answers for their contemporaries, and both aroused in their followers and readers some expectation that they had the capacity to provide those answers. On the other hand, both felt constrained to tell themselves and others time and again that the wish for new prophets represented an immature desire and that in any case they held no warrant from their strictly observed professional code to minister to such a wish.

Close observers of the two men have left us comparable accounts of what seems to have been a prophetic disposition, riven by conflict. Max Graf, participant in the Wednesday evening meetings of the first psychoanalytic society, described the atmosphere of those sessions as that of a religious meeting and portrayed Freud as a kind of religious prophet, albeit the prophet of a new scientific methodology (1942, 471; see also Sulloway 1979, 480–81). Philip Rieff's intimate review of the Freudian canon concludes:

> Freud did not have a religious temperament. He looked forward to no salvations. . . . Freud is a prophet nonetheless. . . . He could not avoid drawing morals from his diagnoses and influencing attitudes by his interpretations. In psychoanalysis, Freud found a way of being the philosopher that he desired to be. (1978, x, 3)

Erich Fromm has made the point less circumspectly: "Freud's wish to have founded a new philosophical-scientific religion was repressed and thus unconscious" (1959, 93).

Heinrich Rickert, Weber's lifelong friend and colleague, observed that Weber struggled with a passion to pull others along with him like a mighty preacher, and that his charismatic effect as lecturer stemmed from conveying to his listeners a sense that he was suppressing an appeal that was much more powerful than his words let on (1926, 236). Karl Jaspers, Weber's student and friend, hailed Weber as "the true philosopher of the time in which he lived," but went on to note that

> Weber did not teach a philosophy; he was a philosophy. . . . As his life was a unique philosophic expression . . . so his scholarly work is a unique, fully actualized expression of his

mode of concrete philosophizing. . . . Sociology is only an arm of Weber's deeper philosophical nature, a nature that he keeps concealed and that becomes visible only indirectly. (1946, 42, 8, 41)

What these descriptions suggest is that both men worked out the following compromise formation: they devised disciplines through which they could pack into the interstices of their professional work the elements of a new moral annunciation.

What was the content of that annunciation? I suggest that it consisted, in both cases, of the following five elements.

First, psychoanalysis and interpretive sociology were, in effect, each deemed by their creators to be the prime vehicle of moral enlightenment for civilized persons living in the age of modern science. They were thus to replace the authoritative agencies of church, state, and social custom.

Second, these disciplines were not to replace old beliefs with new doctrines. Both men insisted that the practitioners of their disciplines were not to be purveyors of value judgments, and they both railed against those who tried to construct and impose *Weltanschauungen* on patients or students.

Third, the moral contribution of these disciplines was seen, rather, as a matter of enhancing the rational capacities of autonomous actors. It was to free them from being bound by the inner compulsions of unconscious drives and the external compulsions of group opinion.

Fourth, this entailed the patient and dispassionate examination of all relevant facts in one's situation and of one's own unconscious assumptions about them. The effect of the passions in creating and sustaining illusions was to be counteracted through the efforts of professionals trained in the neutral analysis of human wishes: the mirroring responses and interpretations of the psychoanalyst, the value-neutral empathic understanding and explanatory hypotheses of the interpretive sociologist.

Fifth, this purely formal and technical approach to moral education presumed a commitment to certain values. Freud and Weber joined an apparently neutral procedural formula to a gospel of intellectual integrity, courage, subjective freedom, and self-responsibility. Intellectual integrity is required if investigators are to provide truthful and adequate interpretations. Courage is required if investigators and their clients are to assimilate what are inevitably painful facts about human realities. Subjective freedom from un-

conscious compulsions of varying sorts is the proximate goal which
justifies those demanding exertions, and personal responsibility is
the ultimate objective for which enhanced subjective freedom is
needed. Time and again, forthrightly or by implication, Freud and
Weber emerged as advocates of this complex of values.

This was no ethic for the fainthearted. It promised no garden of
pleasures or universal happiness. Psychoanalysis in Freud's mature
view was a long and arduous process, making great demands on
analyst and analysand alike. It could provide "the inestimable
service of making the patient's hidden . . . impulses immediate and
manifest," but this could at best result in transforming a person's
neurotic symptoms into "common unhappiness" (1912, 108; 1895b,
305). In similarly sober terms, Weber announced:

> We are not striving for a world in which more men will have
> greater happiness. No one who sees the prospects of things
> anticipates that more happiness lies ahead in the foreseeable
> future. We strive rather to promote the distribution of those
> traits of personal self-responsibility . . . which our culture has
> taught us to hold dear. (Nelson 1965b, 158)

Their ethic called above all for the abandonment of tenacious
illusions about the world, illusions which reflect the persistence of
childish needs for dependence and consolation.[10] Freud and Weber
alike hoped that "'the trained relentlessness of vision' for the world
as it is" which their teachings instilled would help those who
followed them to gain "greater strength to endure it and be equal to
its everyday manifestations" (Marianne Weber 1975, 684).

A Vulnerable Morality

In the last few decades critics of Freud and Weber have called
attention to some of the problematic repercussions of these moral

10. Freud protested "against every romance and against the enthusiasms that
accompany each stage of life—the id illusions of dependence, love, happiness, union;
the super-ego illusions of the good society, progress, brotherhood, fatherhood, finally
even of health; the ego illusion of reason, energetic, independent, and purposeful in
a purposeless and meaningless universe" (Rieff 1978, xii).

"Everyone who finds himself encumbered or inconvenienced by what I am
tempted to call the 'Social Reality Principle' will want to polemicize against Weber.
Weber is both 'stumbling block' and 'scandal' to all who ardently quest for the total
and the instant regeneration of self, society and culture; all utopians and ideologists—
whether of the left, right or center—who are confirmed in their irrefutable assurances
by every turn of history" (Nelson 1965a, 193).

teachings. Weber has been faulted for abandoning any principled defense of liberal constitutionalism, thus making it easier for erstwhile followers like Robert Michels and Carl Schmitt to go on to embrace Fascism and Nazism. Freud has been accused of propounding ideas used by some of his followers to advance a cult of unbridled hedonism and an ideal of shamelessness. Such charges typically neglect to point out that totalitarianism and hedonism are positions far from what either man personally found tolerable, that those positions have been roundly attacked by most of their followers, and that no author can be held responsible for the misuse of his ideas by others. Even so, it remains important to ask whether there is anything in their teachings that does lend itself to being cast in such questionable directions. In particular, is there any basis to the repeatedly leveled charge that the teachings of Freud and Weber support a kind of nihilism—a position that rules out any firm, rationally defensible moral commitments?[11]

It must indeed be acknowledged that a purely formal ethic of maximizing subjective freedom is compatible with courses of action that most of us find morally repugnant. Recent efforts to promote the teaching of this sort of ethics in American schools, it can be argued, only accentuate already pervasive trends toward moral cynicism and flabbiness. That people can freely elect to oppress groups whom they detest, to devote their lives to sadistic pleasures, or to support the idea of nuclear warfare—all of these options in the name of freedom, of course—is a fact of our times.

Freud and Weber get into the embarrassing position of seeming to tolerate such positions because they did not distinguish sharply enough between their professional ethics as disciplined investigators and the moral orientations appropriate for human beings and citizens. As we have seen, their urge to provide a prophetic charter for modern man was reined in by a strong sense of professional propriety as well as by an aversion to efforts to promulgate illusionary moral codes for modern publics. By subordinating their moral prophecies to what could be justified for the circumscribed professional work of psychoanalysts and interpretive sociologists they undercut the possibility of grounding what might have been a more adequate ethical position.

11. For discussions of the charge that nihilism is implied by their teachings, see, for Freud, LaPiere (1959, 53) and Rieff (1978, 321); for Weber, Strauss (1953, 36–78) and Factor and Turner (1979).

The two men responded to this dilemma in different ways. Freud continually expressed his commitment to certain substantive values, but he tended to present them as givens and did not attempt to ground them through philosophical argument. On the one hand, he took the value of psychological health as a scientific premise. He believed that the functional capacities for productive work and genital love were self-evidently preeminent human ideals. As a corollary of this belief, he advocated a greater degree of instinctual (erotic) satisfaction in order to reduce the extent of guilt, aggression, and neurotic suffering which he linked with excessive suppression of Eros in the modern world. On the other hand, Freud took for granted the enduring value of the monumental achievements and demanding standards of European high culture. He thought it self-evident that people would continue to cherish those achievements: "New generations . . . who have simply experienced the benefits of culture early in life . . . will feel culture to be their own possession, and will be ready to make the sacrifice in labor and instinctual renunciation necessary for its preservation" (1927b, 8).

Weber, by contrast, evinced greater philosophic clarity in these matters than Freud, but at the cost of appearing to abandon support of a moral community where any values whatsoever were assumed as fundamental. Weber heaped scorn on those followers of Freud who considered mental hygiene to be the touchstone of morality. He lampooned the values of the psychiatric profession—with their ideal of "the wholly banal, healthy *nerve-proud person (Nervenprotz),*" oriented to "discredit some 'norms' by proving that their observance is not 'beneficial' to the dear nerves" (Marianne Weber 1975, 377). He expressed still greater impatience with any effort to smuggle in any value judgments under the guise of science. "*No* branch of scholarship and no scientific knowledge, be they ever so important—and I certainly number the Freudian discoveries among the scientifically important ones if they stand the test in the long run—provide a *Weltanschauung,*" he noted (Marianne Weber 1975, 380).

If Weber did not share Freud's commitment to the value of mental hygiene, he did share his enthusiasm for the monuments and high cultural standards of European civilization. Here, too, however, he insisted that to assert such values meant to take a relatively arbitrary personal stand, one that could not be advanced as though speaking in the name of professional scholarship. He remained clear and consistent in proclaiming that "the intrusion of normative statements into scholarly questions is the work of the Devil"; in the work of scholarship, he sermonized, "there is no place for an essay that wants to be a sermon" (1924, 417; Marianne Weber 1975, 380).

The positions of both men are vulnerable. Freud is vulnerable to the Weberian objection that his implicit values and world view appear as arbitrary injections, inadmissible rhetoric insofar as they were promulgated in the name of a specialized science of psychic phenomena. Weber is vulnerable to the objections of those who argue, as did Freud, that certain constraints must be acknowledged as moral givens, which is to say that life in society is unthinkable without some balance between gratifications and renunciations. Freud argued publicly, as Weber did only privately or implicitly, that renunciation of some degree of egoism, aggression, and sexuality is indispensable for civilized life.

To acknowledge these weaknesses is not to argue that an ethic of strenuous self-understanding and self-determination cannot be justified. It is to elicit, rather, certain expanded implications of that ethic which Freud and Weber did not articulate.

To begin with, to elevate subjective freedom as the ultimate value is psychologically unrealistic. To maximize the pursuit of self-analysis and to glorify, above all else, the freedom to choose can numb the capacity for action. Intense and total self-consciousness invites an overload of stimuli and options, which disorient and paralyze the will. The flow of conduct requires a number of sturdy constraints.

Freud and Weber could afford to neglect such considerations because they took for granted the existence of many such constraints. Weber assumed that most action would continue to be shaped by the pressures of custom and institutional regulation. Freud assumed that the agents of society would continue to instill moral directives, and that in any case individual psyches were structured in part by certain reaches of "primal repression," antecedent to all socialized morality. In our own time, however, confusion flourishes in part because positions associated with Freud and Weber—however incorrectly—seem to provide no authority or legitimacy for such sources of control. Our culture encourages that profusion of unlimited strivings which Durkheim classically described in his portrait of anomie, which Simmel represented as the oppression by a vast world of cultural commodities (1971, xlii), and which Rieff more recently has scored as "the absolute dominion of desires, the mass production of endless 'needs' as the object of late modern culture . . . a prescription for filling our common lives with panic and emptiness" (1978, 371).

What this suggests, then, is that an ethic of self-awareness and self-determination must be buttressed by a more realistic social psychology, one that hearkens to some older and perhaps wiser traditions running from Durkheim back to the Greek philosophers. This entails an emphasis on the capacity for the control of impulse and the curtailment of egoistic strivings, on the formation of habits of character in early childhood and their maintenance throughout life by just and effective laws and institutions. For Freudian psychology, this must mean, in particular, a willingness to view families as well as isolated individuals as units of analysis and treatment. For Weberian sociology, it must mean a willingness to focus on the agencies of moral socialization—an area of sociological concern rather neglected in the Weberian corpus.

To attend to the social psychology of good character formation is not to abandon the quest for personal autonomy; it is, I am arguing, the only realistic way to make genuine autonomy possible. But the attainment of autonomy does not mean, I must add, that persons are thereby supposed to be free to carry out any actions they choose. At this point another line of revision must be inserted, one deriving from the tradition of moral philosophy.

This tradition asserts that the free use of reason necessarily imposes substantial restraints upon what one considers acceptable lines of conduct. For Freud, the psychic agent of moral inhibition, the superego, was essentially an irrational formation. It was a body of injunctions and ideals expressive of authority, originally located in the parents, and animated by aggressive impulses turned against the self. The work of psychoanalysis was to use the voice of reason to reduce the constricting effect of all noxious unconscious activities, including the unconscious sense of guilt. For Weber, reason could be associated with the creation of strict normative codes, an alliance that produced what he called value-rational types of action. But Weber regarded such orientations as doctrinaire, closing off degrees of rationality and freedom made possible by a more fully developed rational orientation, which he called *Zweckrationalität*—best translated as means/end rationality. This kind of rationality Weber held to be morally relevant to the highest degree, inasmuch as it requires actors to take into account the costs and consequences of their practical goals, and to scrutinize the logic of their moral premises for clarity and consistency. Nonetheless, beyond this, Weber assumed that actors have complete freedom, and that there is no way to establish consensus or impel assent to moral notions through the use of rational argument.

This Weberian assumption has been thrown into question by recent developments in moral philosophy. Approaching the matter in a variety of ways, several philosophers have sought to revive the project of demonstrating that substantive moral implications follow from a formal ethic of intellectual integrity—for example, by adhering to what R. M. Hare (1965) depicts as the notions of universalizability and prescriptiveness entailed in the very usage of the term "ought," what Alan Donagan (1977) has formulated as the principle of respect for all rational creatures, or what Alan Gewirth (1978) has codified as the "principle of generic consistency." Although such efforts remain open to debate, it is noteworthy that the idea of founding a substantive morality on a properly understood notion of consistency or rationality is far from dead in professional philosophy, and continues to appeal to some of the most thoughtful of contemporary moral philosophers. Moreover, not all philosophers who reject the project of deriving a universal ethic from the dictates of formal logic thereby gainsay a role for reason in ethics. Other contemporary work in this area seeks to recast the type of role that is suitable for reason to play. Alasdair MacIntyre (1981), for example, repudiates contemporary universalizing efforts by analytic philosophers as vain attempts to revive the Enlightenment chimera of producing a universal secular morality, because they falsely assume that human beings possess an individuality prior to and outside of all social roles. Even so, MacIntyre advocates a strenuous role for reason in ethics both for the sake of clarifying the virtues proper to diverse social roles and for pursuing fruitful communal deliberation about appropriate ends.

Weber is correct, I believe, in maintaining that a commitment to reason is something that cannot itself be rationally induced; yet his own position provides the basis for the more expanded orientation I am suggesting here. If the work of psychoanalysis or of interpretive sociology is to go on at all, it presumes the nonrational grounding of an interest in rational habits of mind among professionals and clients alike and it presumes as well the willingness to be bound by the "dictates of reason" wherever they lead.[12]

12. To say this is not to invalidate Weber's claim regarding the irreconcilability of certain ultimate values. The issue is complex and requires extended discussion. Let me simply clarify the kind of position I am adopting here by suggesting a basic distinction—between a rationally determinate moral domain, involving types of action which are universally prescribed, and a morally pluralistic domain, involving types of action where individuals seek to actualize themselves by pursuing culturally variable ideals or types of roles that entail the cultivation of different virtues.

Modern Rationales of Conscience

That Freud and Weber, men of extraordinary originality, with such diverse disciplinary backgrounds and such contrasting new disciplinary commitments, should nevertheless have undergone such comparable intellectual and spiritual journeys at the same historical period suggests that something may be gained by reviewing those journeys in broader cultural context.

Central Europe at the end of the last century can be seen as a crucible in which two revolutionary cultural forces unleashed in the sixteenth and the seventeenth centuries were brought together under extraordinary circumstances. Following Benjamin Nelson's ideas for the interpretation of this process, we can say that the medieval "court of conscience," a central tribunal which claimed the right and had the will to oversee the acts and opinions of all Christians, was successfully challenged by two discrete developments. The first was the Protestant Reformation, which opposed the idea of a human court of conscience with the notion of individual responsibility in the realms of religion, morality, and politics. The second was the scientific and philosophical revolution, which established new canons for valid knowledge and objective certainty. These developments sundered those logics of decision whose close interdependence is signified by the duality of reference of the Latin *conscientia* (and French *conscience*): the moral conscience, on the one hand, and philosophical and scientific knowledge, on the other. Those two revolutions, constitutive of the makings of early modern cultures, thus involved, in Nelson's terms, fundamental "reshapings of the rationales of conscience." As Nelson observed, "from the late nineteenth century forward, first mainly in Germany . . . then in the United States and elsewhere, the by-products and the off-shoots of these *makings* were fused at great heats" (1968, 166).

Freud and Weber were in the vanguard of those who struggled to rejoin those two dimensions of modern *conscience,* scientific rationality and ethical autonomy. They sought, in effect, to link the tradition that proceeded from Galileo, Descartes, and Hobbes through Ricardo, Helmholtz, and Darwin with a tradition that proceeded from Luther, Calvin, and Kant through Fichte, Kierkegaard, and Nietzsche. They began with superb training and performance in the impersonal modes of scientific rationality, so highly developed in German and Austrian universities in the latter half of the nineteenth century. Their indomitable individuality led them to struggle against the suppression of subjectivity that this entailed. Finding in their work in the early 1890s that the subjective orientations of actors seemed highly significant for explaining some of the phenomena which their professional disciplines could not otherwise fully account for, they proceeded, through a process involving intense inner turmoil, to fashion disciplines that focused on the internal motivations of individual actors, and whose value, furthermore, they could justify as leading to a historically unprecedented level of moral autonomy. The result was a rationale of conscience which maintained, first, the cognitive supremacy of modern scientific modes of observation and analysis, and yet, second, an ethic based on maximizing the autonomy of actors through enhanced rational understanding.

To achieve that synthesis, it should be noted, scientific rationality and moral autonomy had to be qualified in certain ways. The scientific values they most prized and encouraged were not the impersonal norms of parsimony, logical closure, operational reliability, and axiomatization, but the trained capacity to accept personally distasteful and painful realities. The notion of subjective freedom they most prized and encouraged was not that given to sentimental enthusiasms, utopian fantasies, and impulsive spontaneity, but one nourished by openness to information, intellectual integrity, thoughtfulness, and a sense of responsibility.

Of powerful appeal in their time and ours, the modern rationale of conscience forged by Freud and Weber has two serious shortcomings, as I have suggested. Writing at a time when old-style patriarchal authority and Victorian prudery seemed insufferable (Weinstein and Platt 1969) and when newer modes of industrial and political organization seemed irremediably coercive, Freud and Weber tended to exaggerate the extent of repressiveness in modern culture (see chapter 7; also Rieff 1978, 338). They neglected the other side of the critique of modern culture which thinkers like Durkheim and Simmel found no less problematic, the dissolution of standards and of stable points for moral orientation. Sticking, moreover, to a strict construction of their mission as disciplinary specialists, they neglected to examine and to advocate both the social requisites of moral autonomy[13] and the possibilities for creating rational grounds of constraint on arbitrary freedom.

13. For an exception to this general neglect, one might cite the emphasis in some of Weber's political writings on the significance of parliament as a school for developing the moral autonomy of political leaders.

   To sustain a rationale of conscience that is adequate for our time
therefore requires, I believe, that those who have internalized the
ideals of Freud and Weber must perform the work of transmuting
those ideals. It requires that a policy of analysis, terminable and
interminable, and an ethic of honesty and self-conscious choice be
supplemented by a forthright endorsement of the constraints that
can be built into socialized character and engendered by the
expanded use of reason in ethics.

9

On Subjective and Objective
Rationality in Simmel . . .
and Weber . . . and Parsons

Current discussions of rationality are bedeviled by the fact that the concept of rationality is elusively ambiguous. This is not to say that conceptual ambiguity as such is an unusual or even a merely obstructive feature of social theory and philosophy. Many of our central notions are essentially contested concepts—concepts so linked to substantive debates, normative issues, and historical contexts that their meaning can never be fixed with a single definition. Their very multivocality offers a continuing invitation for proponents of diverse perspectives to engage in fruitful conversations and to embark on fresh inquiries. What is extraordinary in this case is the extent to which proponents of a particular meaning of rationality remain unaware of how other major thinkers and disciplines use the concept, thereby losing sight of hard-won distinctions and their attendant insights, and making broad statements about rationality *tout court* that are simply unsupportable.

What complicates the matter is that rationality figures as a central construct in a number of disciplines whose practitioners typically communicate rather little across disciplinary boundaries. Economics, philosophy, political science, and psychology are the pre-eminent disciplines in question, but the sociological tradition must also be credited with a record of productive work on the topic of rationality. The very establishment of sociology as a discipline was coterminous with efforts to portray the evolution of human society as a manifestation of the increasing rationality of human actors. Comte in France and Toennies in Germany connected their influential analyses of the emergence of urban-industrial societies with assumptions about the constitutive role of rational orientations in the modern world. Nearly every major sociological theorist since then has dealt originatively with modern rationality in one form or other. And it may well be that the sociological tradition contains uniquely valuable resources for disambiguating the notion.

About four decades ago, the most widely influential sociological formulation on rationality was that of Karl Mannheim. In *Man and Society in an Age of Reconstruction* Mannheim addressed the challenge posed by the collapse of the Enlightenment belief in the progress of Reason in history. Although his work did not sustain much of a following in subsequent decades, his formulations remain pertinent for any effort to deal with current confusions about rationality. Not only does Mannheim begin his analysis of rationality by noting that "few words are used in so many contradictory ways"; he goes on to clarify the matter by introducing a fundamental distinction between two radically distinct senses of the term, which he designates "substantial rationality" and "functional rationality" (1940, 51ff.).

I make this reference to Mannheim's famous distinction not because I find it an adequate summation of the literature he cites or consider it the most useful point of departure for productive research programs in this area, but because his distinction embodies a dichotomy of illustrious pedigree in the history of social theory and one that is, moreover, of enduring significance despite its virtual eclipse in our contemporary literature. This is the distinction between subjective and objective modalities of rationality. In Mannheim's usage, the subjective modality is represented by his category of substantial rationality. This he defines as "an act of thought which reveals intelligent insight into the inter-relations of events in a given situation" (1940, 53). His category of functional rationality, on the other hand, signifies the organization of a series of actions in such a way that they have reference to the attainment of a definite goal and exhibit a consequent calculability when viewed from the standpoint of an outside observer. Because the functional type of rationality has reference not to the cognitive orientations of a thinking subject but to properties of actions estimable by an independent party, I designate it a kind of objective rationality.

Comparable distinctions between subjective and objective rationality appear in the work of a number of social theorists in the century before Mannheim, although these theorists define the two modalities of rationality in ways that differ among themselves as well as from Mannheim. Comte distinguished the intellectual faculties of individuals from the organization of knowledge in rational systems of compelling force. Hegel distinguished Subjective Mind, the active self-consciousness of human subjects and its expression in art, religion, and philosophy, from Objective Mind, the embodiment of increasingly perfected systems of morality in the state and its laws. Toennies distinguished the rational will (*Willkür* or *Kürwille*) as one major mode of subjective voluntarism from the objective embodiment of that rationality in the constitutional forms and judicial agencies of *Gesellschaft*. Pareto featured a distinction between what he called subjective logicality, signifying the conscious intentions of actors, and objective logicality, signifying the independently assessable (instrumental) appropriateness of their conduct.

The foregoing should suffice to make us wonder whether contemporary work on rationality might not benefit from a determined effort to recover a distinction between subjective and objective rationalities. My intention here is to develop that possibility by drawing on resources provided by three of the preeminent sociologists of rationality: Georg Simmel, Max Weber, and Talcott Parsons. In so doing, I want to use a mode of analysis that both respects the diverse contexts in which authors employ essentially ambiguous notions and also seeks ways to relate complementary treatments of those concepts in a productive manner. Although Simmel, Weber, and Parsons conceive their analyses in radically different frameworks and direct them to quite disparate ends, their formulations can be translated into one another's terms with results no one of them would have himself ended with.

Simmel on Subjective Culture

Simmel stood in the forefront of those who strove to advance, at a time of triumphant positivism, what Andrew Arato (1974) has called the "neo-idealist defense of subjectivity." In the domain of epistemology, Simmel sought to balance the claims of knowledge that is valid insofar as it corresponds to the properties of objects with an insistence on the irreducible subjective dimension in the constitution of all cognitive domains—history, philosophy, science, whatever. In the investigation of sociological phenomena he sought to balance the claims of social relationships objectified in institutional structures with a continuous focus on the phenomenology of personal experience and the assertions of subjective individuality. Both of these themes are taken up in Simmel's first masterwork, the *Philosophie des Geldes*. Indeed, in that work and in a number of kindred pieces—especially "The Metropolis and Mental Life,"

"The Intersection of Social Circles," and "The Tragedy of Culture"—Simmel portrayed the tensions between subjectivity and objectivity as historical modalities with a richness and depth that has scarcely been matched before or since.

In the *Philosophy of Money,* as Mannheim himself observed, Simmel "attempts to determine the sociological consequences of the rationalization of life brought about by the use of money" (1940, 52). In the course of assessing those consequences Simmel comes to make three rather different points. The first is that the establishment of a money economy produces an otherwise unattainable degree of separation between subjective experience and objective structures. By making it possible to compensate individuals for their services while keeping their personalities outside the transaction, money provides the most effective means of differentiating between the subjective center and the objective achievements of a person. By rendering the ownership and exchange of personal possessions wholly independent of personal status, a money economy brings to complete realization "the division of labor between subjectivity and the norms of the object" (Simmel 1978, 334, 337).

What is more, the very impersonality of a money economy—and its ecological matrix, the modern metropolis—favors the capacities of subjects to develop their appropriate individualities. Modern relational forms liberate individuals from ties to groups based on birth and propinquity and facilitate their participation in groups that issue from "conscious reflection and intelligent planning" (1955, 137). The prolixity of voluntary associations enables persons to construct distinctive sets of group affiliations that in turn configure them with distinctive social personalities. The indeterminacy and the universality of money as a pure instrumentality provide unparalleled opportunities for individuals to assert their wills and cultivate their unique selves.

The second point to be noted is Simmel's argument that the impersonal calculations inherent in a money economy have the effect of promoting the purely cognitive dispositions of actors at the expense of their emotional or sentimental dispositions. Preoccupation with the calculation of instrumental series transforms more and more of life into means, making the practical world one which places a premium on intelligence and progressively eliminates the emotional reactions and decisions involved in the articulation of purposes. The consequence, Simmel concludes, is that "the conceivable elements of action coalesce, both objectively and subjectively, into calculable, rational relations'' ([1908] 1978, 431 [483]; translation modified).

On the other hand, finally, Simmel discusses respects in which the rational order of modern money economies has the effect of weakening the mental capacities of subjects. Money economies and their attendant division of labor facilitate the enormous "development, elaboration, and intellectualization of objects"—a profuse development of "objective culture" that in the course of the nineteenth century went far toward surpassing the capacities of individuals to absorb it. In this part of his argument, Simmel stresses that the "intellectual potential of modern life has been transferred from the form of the individual . . . to the form of objects" (1978, 483). The hypertrophy of objective culture, both in the production process and in the consumption of its resultant products, results in a diminished level of cultivation of individual minds, as well as a sense of being oppressed by and alienated from those objectivations of mind.

In sum: Simmel argues that the objective rationalizations of the modern order are associated not only with an enormous development of the sphere of subjectivity, but beyond that with both an increase and a diminution of the capacities for rationality possessed by human subjects. His discussions are limited, here as elsewhere, by the absence of any extended effort to clarify and relate the concepts involved. Moreover, true to his penchant for finding formal analogies among phenomena in different life spheres, Simmel illuminates the similarities among different manifestations of rationalism—formal law, symbolic logic, and the money economy—without considering their equally significant differences. But his work opens up the complexities of the problem of modern rationality in ways that have yet to be fully appreciated.

Weber on Forms of Rationality

It is well known that Max Weber carefully studied the *Philosophy of Money* shortly before embarking on his massive investigations of rationalization processes in the modern West and elsewhere. Although it remains difficult to document the full extent of Simmel's influence on Weber's subsequent work, it is notable that a number of characteristic Weberian themes—including the compulsively calculating spirit fostered by modern capitalism, the modern separation of scientists from their means of production, and the ways in which formally rationalized law both equalizes its subjects and enables the well-situated to gain yet more advantage over the disadvantaged—

were incisively broached in the monograph by Simmel. Whatever their historical connection on this problem, when comparing the two authors it becomes clear that it was precisely in the areas of Simmel's greatest weakness—his failure to articulate a differentiated conceptual scheme and to identify the different forms of rationalization in various spheres—that Weber produced his most enduring contributions.

In chapter 7 I argued that there are grounds for attributing to Weber the distinction between subjective and objective manifestations of rationality. The most serious reason is that in at least two passages in his methodological essays Weber articulates that distinction. In those passages, subjective rationality is taken to refer to action that is conscious and deliberate (contrasted with action springing from motives that are unconscious or disavowed) and/or action that is oriented to means that are regarded as correct for a given end. Objectively rational action, by contrast, is taken to refer to action that uses technically correct means in accord with scientific knowledge and/or has been subjected to some process of external systematization. Weber goes on to insist that a progressive subjective rationalization (*fortschreitende subjektive Rationalisierung*) of conduct is not necessarily the same as an advance in the direction of objectively rational conduct; and that what appear to be objectively rational human adaptations have in numerous historical instances come into being through the working of completely irrational motives.

Building on Weber's terse statements in the passages just cited, and linking them with his well-known late classification of the four main types of social action, we can say that subjective rationality refers to a set of dispositions to act in certain ways, dispositions that have in common the properties of being (1) conscious and deliberate (i.e., not traditional or habitual), and (2) not suffused by impulse and emotion (i.e., not *affektuell*). We can find in Weber's work indications of four different dispositions of that sort. There is a disposition to act on the basis of decisions that involve calculating the costs and benefits of alternative goals and of alternative means of attaining them; this is means/end-rational orientation. There is a disposition to act on the basis of commitment to a particular set of values no matter what the costs; that is value-rational orientation. There is a disposition to secure social order by enacting regulative norms, a tendency that Weber describes in one passage as "one of the factors motivating social action" (1968, 333). And there is a disposition to strive for a meaningful order, to achieve some kind of cognitive mastery of the world.

Each of these four kinds of subjective rationality has its counterpart in some corresponding type of objectified rationality, as I also argued above:

1. Instrumental rationality—the attainment of given ends through precise calculation of adequate means
2. Substantive rationality—the subordination of courses of action to explicit values
3. Formal rationality—the methodical ordering of activities through the establishment of fixed rules and routines
4. Conceptual rationality—the intellectual mastery of reality through precise and abstract concepts

Thus conjoined, the ideas of Simmel and Weber together provide good resources for disambiguating rationality. Simmel's strong use of the distinction between subjectivity and objectivity fortifies the insertion of that distinction into the Weberian framework on rationality; Simmel's rather weak conceptualization of rationality becomes transformed by the adaptation of Weber's rich distinctions. Yet there remain major questions about the constructs thus generated for which the theoretical resources provided by Simmel and Weber do not suffice. We still want to know what are the generic characteristics of subjective and objective rationality, and whether their fourfold typology represents an accidental compilation of historical types or whether it can be grounded systematically with reference to a general theory of human needs and purposes. The work of Talcott Parsons suggests answers to those questions.

Parsons on Systemic Functions

If Simmel's emphasis on the tension between subjectivity and objectivity appears only in muted form in Weber, it scarcely appears at all in the entire corpus of Parsons' work. Nor does one find there much sensitivity to the array of contrasting kinds of rationalization that Weber so laboriously uncovered. Yet the distinctions Parsons drew in order to identify the various components of action systems remain valuable tools for analyzing all sorts of phenomena. One can readily employ them to locate the different forms of rationality derived from Simmel and Weber in a more systematic frame.

Fundamental to all stages of Parsons' work is a distinction between the motivational orientations of actors—what in *The Social*

System were called need-dispositions—and the institutionalized
norms that operate to regulate the expression of those dispositions
in all minimally stable interaction systems. Of course, as Parsons
(following Durkheim and Freud) stressed, the external norms become to some extent internalized in the personalities of actors; they
become part of what Parsons came to refer to as the "internal
environment of personality" (1981, 192)—the entire set of
motivationally connected symbolic entities. Yet the distinction
remains crucial, and provides a basis for refining the rudimentary
dichotomy between subjective and objective rationality through the
more differentiated structure of Parsonian theory. In these terms,
we may say, provisionally, that rationality is manifest subjectively
when the dispositions of actors are such that they operate consciously and in an affectively neutral manner.[1] Imputations of
objective rationality, on the other hand, can be made when the
actions of persons or collectivities conform with institutionalized
norms of rationality. Parsons' way of putting the matter thus makes
clear what is still muddled in Weber: that a sociological distinction
between subjective and objective kinds of rationality does not
discriminate between grounds of judgment—personally biased versus impersonally valid—but rather between kinds of phenomena—
whether the properties of rationality are being predicated of personal dispositions or of institutionalized norms.

Parsons himself treated rationality chiefly in its objective manifestation as just defined. He located rational action at the level of the
social system, defining rationality as "a mode of action institutionalized in social systems . . . [and as] characterized by conformity
with cognitive norms and values where such conformity is relevant"
(Parsons and Platt 1973, 80). It remains to be seen whether it is
possible to incorporate the array of Weberian forms of rationality
within this perspective.

I would like now to suggest that the four forms of rationality
identified as constitutive of Weber's analytic schema closely parallel
the four functions of action systems elaborated by Parsons. What all
four modes of objectified rationality represent are ways of ordering
actions, symbols, or relationships in such a manner that one
particular function is optimally attained. Instrumental rationality
clearly corresponds to the adaptive function. It concerns the organization of resources so as to enhance the ability of individual or

1. 'Affective neutrality' is a salient concept in Parsons' thought after 1950 and a fair
counterpart to Weber's notion of action that is not *affektuell*.

collective actors to optimize their attainment of goals generally. Substantive rationality, by contrast, concerns the organization of resources in ways that maximize the attainment of a particular value. Substantive rationality may therefore be regarded as corresponding to the goal-attainment function. Formal rationality is treated by Weber—in the spheres of economic action, law, and religion alike—as the establishment of rules and procedures that consistently regulate conduct in a calculable manner. So, too, the integrative function is served by the institution of procedures that subordinate diverse inclinations to a common, expectable set of rules. Finally, what I have called conceptual rationality signifies that mode of ordering oriented to the production of a clear and coherent set of meanings about the world or some part of it. This type of rationality clearly corresponds to the pattern-maintenance function.

By understanding the four types of rationality as ways of ordering reality which serve purposes corresponding to the four principal functions of action systems, one can situate the different historical spheres of rationalization more precisely and coherently than Weber was able to. The primary discriminations here must be between rationalization at the level of the cultural system and at the level of the social system.

With respect to cultural systems, instrumental rationality signifies the production of symbolic resources that optimize the attainment of cognitive, aesthetic, moral, or constitutive functions. Substantive rationality concerns the extent to which symbolic work is ordered to the attainment of some well-articulated purpose. Formal rationality concerns the extent to which the attainment of those purposes is regulated by well-established procedures and standards. And conceptual rationality concerns the extent to which the meaning of those purposes has been grounded in a coherent and systematic outlook.

At the level of social systems, instrumental rationality signifies the organization of roles in ways that optimize the attainment of ends; substantive rationality, the organization of roles toward maximizing the attainment of a given goal; formal rationality, the subordination of roles under systematized procedural norms; and conceptual rationality, the organization of roles to maximize the extent to which they embody a coherent conception of the world.

These distinctions, with reference to the economic sphere, may be illustrated by a more fully differentiated typology of modes of economic rationality than could be presented in chapter 7 (figure 6).

Figure 6

Rationality in Economic Symbolization: The Cultural System	
Instrumental rationality	Application of the calculus in economic theory
Substantive rationality	Organization of economic investigations toward a specified goal, such as producing a general theory of economic behavior or figuring how to reduce unemployment
Formal rationality	Regulation of the work of economists by such standards as clarity, consistency, coherence, or falsifiability
Conceptual rationality	Grounding of economists' work in a general view of social science, such as the ideal of a general axiomatized theory of human behavior or that of removing popular distortions as a part of evolutionary adaptation
Rationality in Economic Organization: The Social System	
Instrumental rationality	Use of efficient production or marketing techniques
Substantive rationality	Increasing the GNP growth rate or allocating resources by a standard of fairness
Formal rationality	Capital accounting
Conceptual rationality	Grounding economic activity under some coherent ideology, such as the notion of economic action in a vocation or of producing nonalienated labor in an egalitarian society

Using Parsons' distinction between the cultural and social levels of action, then, I have reworded his formula that rationality is a mode of action institutionalized in social systems to read: *objective* rationality is a mode of action institutionalized in social *and* cultural systems. How, then, may we adapt his concepts to characterize the phenomena of subjective rationality?

The obvious place to consider subjective rationality in Parsonian terms is at the level of the personality system. To do this, however, is to encounter the difficulty that the elements of personality, while fully amenable to interpretation as subjective phenomena, can scarcely be represented as rational orientations. According to the Freudian scheme, which Parsons largely follows, the id refers to symbolic representations of physiologically grounded needs and drives; the superego, to the introjection of aggressive energies against the self; the ego-ideal, to the introjection of emotionally cathected objects; and the ego, to the executive implementation of goals through the mobilization of psychic resources. In Weberian terms, the action orientations within the personality system are either affectual or, when fixed as bound and repetitive structures, traditional (defined as actions to which people have become habitually accustomed).

It is true that Freud—and later psychoanalytic theorists even more—have represented the ego as having certain rational potentialities. They do this by assigning to the ego the functions of apprehending external reality and adjudicating among conflicting inputs. Yet the psychoanalytic conception of these rational functions relegates them to a residual category, such that they do not become the focus of systematic analysis or receive a central place in any explanatory schema. The tradition of work pioneered by Jean Piaget nonetheless makes clear that the cognitive functions fully deserve such attention. Through the more differentiated framework of Parsonian theory produced by Lidz and Lidz (1976), those rational functions can now be conceived as proper to a category of action system that is distinguished from the personality system, one which they designate as the behavioral system.

Lidz and Lidz define the behavioral system as the locus of various kinds of intelligence whose development they conceive, following Piaget, to be inherent in human maturation and essential for the operation of all action systems. They thus continue to understand the personality system as the organization of individual motives while taking the behavioral system to refer to the organization of schemas and intelligent operations used to coordinate behavior. Since the distinction between the two systems is said to "parallel the classic distinctions between thought and feeling, reason and emotion, intelligence and affectivity" (203), one can use it to reformulate the Simmel-Weberian distinction between subjectively rational and subjectively affective orientations and thereby anchor that dichotomy in a more encompassing body of theory.

Beyond that, one can replace the still fairly crude Weberian distinction between *Zweckrational* and *Wertrational* orientations with a more differentiated, theoretically grounded typology of subjectively rational dispositions. For Lidz and Lidz proceed to delineate four broad categories of intelligence well articulated in the Piagetian tradition and fully consistent with the systemic functions of Parsonian theory. These are (1) the capacity to produce adaptive representations of the actor's external and internal environment; (2) the ability to coordinate diverse wishes and resources into organized projects for action; (3) the capacity to adapt to the normative expectations of the actor's outer and inner environments and synthesize a system of norms to regulate one's conduct; and (4) the ability to establish generalized patterns of meaning by using formal categories that provide a common logical order throughout an individual's behavioral system.

In addition to grounding the subjective/objective distinction and related forms of rationality in a coherent general theory, the Parsonian adduction helps to clarify something that was touched on earlier: the asymmetry between subjective and objective rationality. The subjective dimension has now been depicted as made up of two parallel systems, one that is perfectibly rational and one that is irreducibly affective. This construction vividly represents the point that whereas social systems and cultural systems are susceptible to an indefinitely extended process of objective rationalization at the expense of traditional and other nonrational features, the subjective domain will always be constituted by affective and habitual components as well as by intelligence. This amounts to still another way of putting what was a concluding point in the last two chapters.

Rationality Disambiguated

Conceptual disambiguation can proceed by assigning a different term to each of the several usages of a concept or else by employing the generic concept with appropriate qualifiers. Both approaches appear in the following list of what have emerged as twelve distinct properties that one might signify when describing a phenomenon as rational.

A. Objective Rationality
1. Conceptual symbolic — intellectual coherence
2. Formal symbolic — normative consistency
3. Substantive symbolic — symbolic effectiveness
4. Instrumental symbolic — technical adequacy
5. Conceptual organizational — ideological consistency
6. Formal organizational — procedural regularity
7. Substantive organizational — organizational effectiveness
8. Instrumental organizational — technological efficiency

B. Subjective Rationality
1. Logical — logico-deductive intelligence
2. Self-regulative — normative intelligence
3. Purposive — instrumental intelligence
4. Representational — cognitive realism

Although this list does not pretend to exhaust all current meanings of rationality, it may be helpful in sorting out some of the confusion surrounding that term. Presented as a blandly uniform enumeration, it conceals the divergent currents of thought brought together to produce it. The list could not have been derived from the work of any one of the authors in this synthesis. Both in their substantive agendas and their intellectual styles, the authors were headed in three clearly different directions.

Simmel viewed the master process of modern life as one of objectification, of the transformation of all of life's content into impersonal objects. Against that process he struggled to articulate and protect the claims of an increasingly vulnerable subject—as a champion of the "neo-idealist defense of subjectivity." Keenly attuned to the process of what analysts before and after him referred to as rationalization, he nevertheless conceptualized that process chiefly in terms of various kinds of opposition between subject and object. Such distinctions as he drew concerned the various ways in which human subjectivity expressed itself and found itself threatened. His penchant for analogical thinking, moreover, inclined him to see similarities among the various manifestations of modern rationalism rather than to seek ways of discriminating among them.

Although Max Weber found himself gripped quite as strongly as Simmel by the predicament of selfhood under the onslaught of modern objectification, he framed that dilemma as an outcome of the extreme rationalization of modern Western economic, political, and legal institutions. For Weber the decisive propulsion into modernity occurred through the overcoming of traditional norms governing economic life and traditional patterns of political authority. Aware as he was that impulses toward rationalization have occurred in other periods and cultures, Weber became determined to track down just what distinguished the modern Western kind of rationalization and what enabled it to supplant traditionalism so decisively.

This was the substantive interest that led Weber to focus on the theme of rationality and to discriminate among types of rationality. That effort was advanced by his basic intellectual style: Weber was as strong on making distinctions as any social scientist has ever been. His chief objection to Simmel's style concerned the latter's disposition to use the analogical mode of thought. So where Simmel would enjoy showing the similarities among various kinds of rationalism, Weber would take pains to differentiate them.

The work of Parsons features neither the tension between self and object nor that between different forms of rationality. This, too, was a matter of intellectual style. It was characteristic of Parsons' mode of theorizing to integrate materials from a wide diversity of spheres within a common theoretical framework, and to highlight ways in which partially autonomous systems of action interpenetrate at different levels and through different media of interchange. This he accomplished at the expense of focusing on constitutive tensions among different spheres and systems levels.

Beyond that, Parsons represented the master process of modernization as one of structural and functional differentiation. Although historical differentiation can involve a fair amount of conflict and confrontation, as Spencer and Durkheim knew, it is easy to present it in a rather more bland manner than objectification (with its antagonism to subjectivity) or rationalization (with its antagonism to traditionalism). In representing the modernization process as one of differentiation, Parsons evaded both the tensions of subjectivity-objectivity found in Simmel (whom he chose to neglect) and the tensions among diverse forms of rationalization found in Weber (whom he knew very well). By bringing their ideas back into play, together with the illuminating categories of Parsonian theory, we have secured a valuable key with which to unpack the meanings of rationality.

The Ambiguous Relation of Modernization to Subjectivity

The distinction between subjective and objective modes of rationality, recovered from Mannheim and more fully articulated through the foregoing synthesis of arguments from Simmel, Weber, and Parsons, may be useful in disambiguating a notion that social scientists of many persuasions find they cannot live without but with which they do not seem to live very satisfactorily. But that synthesis also helps us to understand better one of the central empirical ambiguities of modern life: the relation of modernization to subjectivity. The ambiguities of that relation have rarely been articulated so well as by that triad of propositions on subjectivity and objectivity that emerge from Simmel's work:

1. The conditions of modern society are such as to produce an unprecedented amount of separation between objective structures and the domain of personal subjectivity, and therewith the basis for the fullest realization of each sphere.

2. The effects of a money economy and of demographic concentrations in urban centers are such as to require enormous amounts of calculation in social organization, with the result that the rational faculties in subjective life are fostered at the expense of the affective.

3. The efficient production of commodities and cultural works made possible by the money economy, urban concentrations, and division of labor threatens the integrity of modern selves by overwhelming modern subjects with products from whose creation they are alienated and whose consumption they can no longer intelligently manage.

Conceptual tools provided by Weber and Parsons enable us now to clarify and deepen these insights.

Common to the Weberian and Parsonian accounts of modernization is the notion of a progressive specialization of different spheres of action. For Weber, this was conceived as a process of rationalization of the diverse spheres of life such that they come to follow their own internal norms (*innere Eigengesetzlichkeiten*). For Parsons, the comparable language is that of the adaptive differentiation of separate structures serving different functions. For the most part, these separations are visualized along a horizontal line: the different spheres or institutions separate and coexist side by side. In Parsons' framework, however, separations on a vertical axis are also envisaged: the increasing differentiation between the cultural and the social system levels of organization.[2] What remains to be specified is that this differentiation among levels must also affect the lower system levels as well. The enormous complexity entailed by the modern differentiation of numerous cultural and social subsystems requires that the personality and behavioral systems of actors be comparably differentiated internally, such that individuals can function in a plurality of specialized subsystems simultaneously. That the behavioral systems and the personality systems of individual subjects come to constitute increasingly autonomous boundary-maintaining systems is not just a Parsonian reformulation but an analytic extension of Simmel's thesis about the modern separation between objectivity and subjectivity.

Simmel's discourse on the cultural effects of a money economy found its counterpart in Weber's saying that what in precapitalist

2. For exemplary analyses of modernization predicated on the identification of cultural and social systems as independently variable, see Geertz (1959) and Bell (1976).

societies was a relatively secondary institutional sector—the economy—had become, under capitalism, the most fateful force in our
modern life. Treating the matter more in logical than in
psychocultural terms, Simmel argued that the widespread use of
money, that instrumentality par excellence, diverts energies to the
calculation of means at the expense of the ends of action. The
subjective adaptation to this system is one in which "intellectual
energy" is produced to an extraordinary degree, "in contrast to
those energies generally denoted as emotions or sentiments . . .
[and] which attach themselves to the turning points of life, to the
final purposes," rather than to the calculation of means (1978, 429,
431).

The institutionalized concern with means is what Weber meant by
instrumental rationality. Simmel likens this manifestation of rationality to the rationalism of modern law, in that both forms are
impersonal, universalizing, indifferent to individual qualities and to
interests that can be morally of the most perverse sort. Although the
rationalism of both spheres is aptly analogized by Simmel, Weber's
distinctions make it possible to note the different characters and
consequences of formal rationality in the law and instrumental
rationality in the economic sphere. Common to both instrumental
and formal rationalities, however, is a disregard for the substantive
ends of action as constituted by emotionally driven commitments.
We may thus refine Simmel's point by saying that insofar as modern
institutions sanction instrumental or formal rationalities, with their
varying patterns and objective consequences, the subjective consequences are likely to include the enhancement of ratiocinative
powers at the expense of emotional powers—which can take the
form, in more current terms, either of a repression of affect or its
dissociation from rational functioning.

Attuned, as ever, to the existence of countertendencies and
opposing currents, Simmel counterposed to his depiction of the
effects of objective rationalization on the cultivation of selfhood and
individual intelligence an analysis of the ways in which modern
social forms threaten the self and overwhelm individual intelligence.
His basic thesis, which he referred to succinctly as the "tragedy of
culture," was that the objectification of mind in modern cultural
products has outdistanced the capacities of subjective minds to
appropriate them, and thus "our freedom is crippled if we deal with
objects that our ego cannot assimilate" (1978, 460). Where Parsonian theory projects a modern social order which individuals are
socialized to sustain and in which they are kept from deviance by

mechanisms of social control, Simmel's theory, in Parsonian terms, would assert that the differentiation of behavioral and personality systems from social and cultural systems entails not only the possibilities of enhanced autonomous development of each, and constructive mutual interpenetrations, but significant areas of conflict that are constitutive of that order and in principle not superable.

If one were to venture a diagnostic statement based on the foregoing analyses, it might be that the most fundamental tension and imbalance in modern life is not between rationality and nonrationality, but between objectivity and subjectivity. The work of Simmel, Weber, and Parsons, along with others, together provides a portrait of the modern order as essentially constituted by relatively autonomous, rationalized, interpenetrating institutional spheres, a portrait that is persuasive, profound, and penetrating. What Simmel's work uniquely contributes—a contribution that is substantially enhanced when complementary constructs from Weber and Parsons are incorporated into it—is a delineation of the effects of this order on subjective experience.

Simmel proceeds from the assumption that "for every cultural community the relationship in which its objectified mind, and the evolution of that mind, stands to its subjective minds is a matter of the utmost importance" (1978, 476, translation modified; 1907, 529). Once that concern is acknowledged, the implications of Simmel's analysis must continue to haunt all diagnoses of our time. The conclusion must be that there are profound subjective deficiencies in this order—deficiencies that may be ineradicable but whose redress is clearly indicated: the diversion of resources into the enhancement of actors' capacities both for intelligent understanding and for affective expression. That the analyses by Simmel, Weber, and Parsons of the processes of objectification, rationalization, and differentiation also disclose conditions that could promote historically unprecedented levels of subjective development gives one reason to believe that the call for such resources is not a mere anachronism.

Epilogue:
Two Cheers for Ambiguity in Science

Whatever the shade of meaning one affixes to the notion of science[1] there can be no doubt that the four positive functions of univocality identified in chapter 2 adhere to any plausible conception of the scientific enterprise. (1) The point of any secular effort to surpass commonsense understandings is to achieve some determinate cognitive mastery of our various environments. (2) This in turn requires a disciplined expression of our ideas through formulations that can be taken literally. (3) The presumption that such ideas remain continuously open to scrutiny from a community of scientific enquirers enjoins us to communicate them openly in a nondeceptive manner. (4) To be useful the ideas must be clearly predicable of bounded classes of phenomena located in specifiable times, places, and circumstances. Durkheim was surely right to insist on this assumption and thereby to justify his demand for univocal terms and propositions.

Because of the ineluctable ambiguity of all natural language, however, the ideal of a thoroughgoing univocality remains unattainable. The physicist Fritjof Capra has made this point as follows:

> Mathematical models and their verbal counterparts . . . are rigorous and consistent as far as their internal structure is concerned, but their symbols are not directly related to our experience. The verbal models, on the other hand, use concepts

1. The last half-century of debate in the history and philosophy of science fully demonstrates that the notion of science is itself an essentially contested concept. From Hempel to Popper to Kuhn to Toulmin to Lakatos to Feyerabend we have witnessed a succession of inconclusive efforts to establish a diacritical marker for scientificity.

which can be understood intuitively, but are always inaccurate and ambiguous. (1984, 20)

The question is whether this fact is merely to be regretted as a consequence of confessed inevitable shortcomings of human language or whether it is also to be seen as pointing toward that goal of enhanced understanding which is the general objective of scientific endeavor.

The burden of these essays has been to suggest that there indeed are benefits to be gained from the ambiguities of scientific discourse. Of the four previously identified functions served by ambiguity, two remain outside the boundaries of scientific work. The function of attaining enlightenment through the intuition of indeterminacy belongs to mysticism, or perhaps to philosophy and poetry, not to the disciplined activity of science. And the protection of one's meanings and intentions through ambiguously opaque utterance, while perhaps useful as a protective ploy in scientific competition, cannot be sanctioned as appropriate conduct for a scientific enquirer.

Through its two other functions, however—the evocative representation of complex meanings and the bonding of a community through diffuse symbols—ambiguity has long served and will continue to serve the general objectives of scientific activity. It is useful for scientific formulations to express an abundance of meanings, for these can ignite a cluster of insights that in turn lead to novel explorations. Gillian Beer has expressed this point with unmatched eloquence for the scientific work of Charles Darwin:

> Darwinian theory will not resolve to a single significance nor
> yield a single pattern. It is essentially multivalent. It renounces
> a Descartian clarity, or univocality. Darwin's methods of
> argument and the generative metaphors of *The Origin* lead . . .
> into profusion and extension. The unused, or uncontrolled,
> elements in metaphors such as 'the struggle for existence' take
> on a life of their own. They surpass their status in the text and
> generate further ideas and ideologies. They include 'more than
> the maker of them at the time knew.' (1983, 9)

And if ambiguous formulations can provide semantic benefits for biology, the social sciences should claim more abundant gains of this sort since, as noted earlier, social scientists study phenomena that are themselves vehicles of ambiguous experience and utterance.

Equally relevant for science is the bonding into a vital transgenerational community of a body of diverse enquirers holding somewhat different views of what are essentially contested concepts or simply concepts whose meaning alters as they become enmeshed in varying contexts. We have witnessed benefits gained as well as costs incurred when a Merton transforms Durkheim's anomie into new agendas and contexts or when a Park inspires imaginative work on marginal men by recasting the figure of Simmel's stranger. We have witnessed the progressive enrichment of a long tradition of work on the notions of rationality and freedom, from Kant and Hegel through Toennies, Simmel, and Weber, by scholars energized through some sense of dealing with a common topic even though the actual construction of its meaning has differed from one author to the next or even within the career of a single author.

Conversely, we have witnessed the losses suffered when a sequence of extraordinary scholars felt compelled to disavow a brilliant thinker like Simmel because of their inability to tolerate the ambiguous relation of his work to theirs. And we have witnessed the constriction of discourse attendant on the efforts of Freud and of Weber to compress the possibilities of practical reason into the mold of a discipline conceived as a vocation for theoretic rationality.

Even so, the appreciation of ambiguity has its limits: it must be linked to a willingness and an ability to press toward disambiguation at appropriate moments. These essays have attempted to show the benefits to be gained by taking such a step after the process of semantic accretion and confusion has run its course for a while. It has seemed beneficial to disentangle the numerous meanings of anomie and to differentiate and codify the various kinds of strangers. And I hope it has been profitable to recover the matrix of discriminable forms of rationality that Weber laboriously worked out but barely articulated.

Withal, however, I have stopped short of a sustained effort to disambiguate the essentially contested concept of ambiguity. I have discriminated distinct functions of ambiguity but not its diverse manifestations. That may be a project for readers who have been convinced of the interesting problems connected with ambiguity. One could go on, for example, to discriminate the type of phenomena of which ambiguity has been predicated: ambiguous matters, divided, for example, among (1) media—language; nonverbal symbols; (2) subjects—attitudes and affects; goals and preferences; and (3) objects—normative expectations; future events. Ambiguous phenomena could also be distinguished according to the characteristics predicated by ambiguity. The forms of ambiguity have included (1) polysemy, (2) vagueness, (3) inconsistency, and (4) instability.

But the ambition of this book has been to affirm a process and an attitude toward the intellectual life, not to devise an encompassing scheme. Its heart has been a wish to replace the credo of Hobbes and Condorcet with a doctrine formulable as a kind of prayer: Lord, give me the capaciousness and wit to tolerate and enjoy ambiguity when it is appropriate, the clarity of mind and firmness of will to be unambiguous when it's not, and the wisdom to know what time it is.

Appendix

Weber's Summary Formulation Regarding the Forms Of Rationality

At this point it should be noted once again: "rationalism" can mean very different things. It means one thing if we think of the kind of rationalization the systematic thinker performs on the image of the world: an increasing theoretical mastery of reality be means of increasingly precise abstract concepts.

(1) *conceptual rationality*

Rationalism means another thing if we think of the methodical attainment of a particular given practical end by means of an increasingly precise calculation of adequate means.

(2) *instrumental rationality*

These types of rationalism are very different, in spite of the fact that ultimately they belong inseparably together. Further distinctions can be made within the intellectual comprehension of reality: for instance, the differences between English physics and Continental physics have been traced back to distinctions of this sort.

That rationalization of the conduct of life which concerns us here can assume unusually varied forms. In the sense of the absence of all metaphysics and almost all residues of religious anchorage, Confucianism is rationalist to such a far-going extent that it stands at the extreme boundary of what one might possibly call a "religious" ethic. At the same time, Confucianism is more rationalist and sober, in the sense of the absence and the rejection of all non-utilitarian yardsticks, than any other ethical system, with the possible exception of J. Bentham's. Yet Confucianism remains extraordinarily different from Bentham's as well as from all other Occidental types of practical rationalism in spite of its innumerable actual and apparent analogies with them.

(conceptual)

(instrumental)

221

"Rational" in the sense of belief in a valid "canon" was the supreme artistic ideal of the Renaissance. The Renaissance view of life was also rational in the sense of rejecting traditionalistic bonds and of having faith in the power of naturalis ratio, despite its strains of Platonizing mysticism. *(3) substantive rationality (conceptual)*

In yet another wholly different sense of the term, "rational" means "ordered according to plan" [*Planmässigkeit*]. The following are rational in this sense: methods of mortificatory or magical asceticism, or methods of contemplation in their most consistent forms, as in yoga or in the manipulations of prayer machines in later Buddhism. *(4) formal rationality*

In general, all kinds of practical ethics that were systematically and unambiguously oriented to fixed goals of salvation were "rational" both in this latter sense of being formally methodical and in the former sense of distinguishing between the normatively "valid" and the empirically given. *(formal) (substantive)*

Source: Weber 1920: 265–66; 1948, 293–94 (translation modified and marginal glosses added by the author)

Acknowledgments

Most of the chapters in this book are revised versions of previously published essays or unpublished conference papers. Chapter 3 was published in *Journal of Social Issues* 24 (1968): 129–41. Chapter 5 appeared originally as "Simmel at a Distance: On the History and Systematics of the Sociology of the Stranger" in *Sociological Focus* 10 (1977): 15–29. Chapter 7 appeared originally as "Rationality and Freedom: Weber and Beyond" in *Sociological Inquiry* 51 (1981): 5–25. Chapter 8 was published in *Psychoanalysis: The Vital Issues*, Volume 1: *Psychoanalysis as an Intellectual Discipline*, edited by John E. Gedo and George H. Pollock (New York: International Universities Press, 1984). I am grateful to the original publishers for permission to reprint these essays.

Chapter 2 is a wholly transformed and greatly expanded version of a paper presented at the World Congress of Sociology in Washington, D.C., in 1962. Chapter 9 is a revision of a paper presented at the World Congress of Sociology in Mexico City in 1982. A German translation of an earlier version of chapter 6 appears in *Georg Simmel und die Moderne*, edited by Heinz-Jürgen Dahme and Otthein Rammstedt (Frankfurt: Suhrkamp, 1984).

I am deeply grateful to hundreds of colleagues and students who provided help at various stages in the production of these essays and to the Center for Advanced Study in the Behavioral Sciences for providing a congenial ambience for working on several of them.

References

Abel, Theodore. 1929. *Systematic Sociology in Germany*. New York: Columbia University Press.
———. 1959. "The Contribution of Georg Simmel: A Reappraisal." *American Sociological Review* 24: 473–79.
Adler, Mortimer J. 1958, 1961. *The Idea of Freedom*. 2 vols. Garden City, N.Y.: Doubleday.
Adorno, T. W., Frenkel-Brunswick, E., Levinson, D. J., and Sanford, R. N. 1950. *The Authoritatian Personality*. New York: Harper.
Albrow, Martin. 1970. *Bureaucracy*. New York: Praeger.
Alexander, Jeffrey C. 1983. *The Classical Attempt at Synthesis: Max Weber*. Berkeley and Los Angeles: University of California Press.
Almond, Gabriel. 1960. "A Functional Approach to Comparative Politics." *The Politics of the Developing Areas*. Princeton, N.J.: Princeton University Press.
Arato, Andrew. 1974. "The Neo-Idealist Defense of Subjectivity." *Telos* 21: 108–61.
Arato, Andrew, and Breines, Paul. 1979. *The Young Lukács and the Origins of Western Marxism*. New York: Seabury Press.
Baker, Keith Michael. 1975. *Condorcet: From Natural Philosophy to Social Mathematics*. Chicago: University of Chicago Press.
Baker, Paul J. 1973. "The Life Histories of W. I. Thomas and Robert E. Park." *American Journal of Sociology* 79: 243–60.
Barry, Brian. 1982. "A Grammar of Equality." *New Republic,* May 12: 36–39.
Basch, Michael F. 1983. "The Perception of Reality and the

Disavowal of Meaning." *Annual of Psychoanalysis* 11: 125–54.

Becker, Howard. 1950. *Man in Reciprocity*. New York: Praeger.

Beckingham, C. F., and Huntingford, G. W. B. 1961. *The Prester John of the Indies*, vol. 2. Cambridge: Cambridge University Press.

Beer, Gillian. 1983. *Darwin's Plots*. London: Routledge and Kegan Paul.

Beetham, David. 1974. *Max Weber and the Theory of Modern Politics*. London: Allen and Unwin.

Bell, Daniel. 1976. *The Cultural Contradictions of Capitalism*. New York: Basic Books.

Bellah, Robert N., ed. 1973. *Emile Durkheim on Morality and Society*. Chicago: University of Chicago Press.

Bendix, Reinhard. 1965. "Max Weber's Sociology Today." *International Social Science Journal* 17 (January): 9–22.

Berque, Jacques. 1961. "Expression et signification dans la vie arabe." *L'homme* 1 (2): 50–67.

Blau, Peter. 1968. "The Study of Formal Organization." In *American Sociology*, ed. Talcott Parsons, 54–65. New York: Basic Books.

Bonacich, Edna. 1973. "A Theory of Middleman Minorities." *American Sociological Review* 38 (October): 583–94.

Boskoff, Alvin. 1969. *Theory in American Sociology*. New York: Thomas Y. Crowell.

Bottomore, Tom, and Frisby, David. 1978. "Introduction to the Translation." In Georg Simmel, *The Philosophy of Money*, 1–49. London: Routledge and Kegan Paul.

Bouglé, C. 1910. Review of G. Simmel, *Soziologie*. *L'année sociologique* 11: 17–20.

Bradburn, Norman, and Caplovitz, David. 1965. *Reports on Happiness: A Pilot Study of Behavior Related to Mental Health*. Chicago: Aldine.

Bruun, H. H. 1972. *Science, Values and Politics in Max Weber's Methodology*. Copenhagen: Munksgaard.

Byrne, Noel. 1977. "The Anomie-Anomia Nexus: A Reexamination." Paper presented at the 72d Annual Meeting of the American Sociological Association.

Cahnman, Werner. 1978. Review of Arthur Mitzman, *The Iron Cage*. *Journal of the History of the Behavioral Sciences* 14 (April): 189–91.

Camic, Charles. 1979. "The Utilitarians Revisited." *American Journal of Sociology* 85: 516–50.

Capra, Fritjof. 1984. *The Tao of Physics*. Rev. ed. New York: Bantam Books.

Cassirer, Ernst. 1951. *The Philosophy of the Enlightenment*, trans. F. Koelln and J. Pettegrove. Princeton, N.J.: Princeton University Press.

Chao, Yuen Ren. 1959. "Ambiguity in Chinese." In *Studia Serica Bernhard Karlgren Dedicata*, ed. S. Egerod and E. Glahn, 1–13. Copenhagen: Munksgaard.

Chojnacki, S. 1964. "Brief Introduction to Ethiopian Painting." *Journal of Ethiopian Studies* 2.

Cohen, Michael D., and March, James G. 1974. *Leadership and Ambiguity*. New York: McGraw-Hill.

Collins, Randall. 1980. "Weber's Last Theory of Capitalism: A Systematization." *American Sociological Review* 45 (December): 925–42.

Condorcet, Marie J. A. M. de. [1795] 1955. *Sketch for a Historical Picture of the Progress of the Human Mind*, trans. June Barraclough. London: Weidenfeld and Nicolson.

Cooley, Charles Horton. 1909. *Social Organization*. New York: Scribner's.

Coser, Lewis A. 1964. "The Political Functions of Eunuchism." *American Sociological Review* 29 (December): 880–85.

———. 1972. "The Alien as a Servant of Power: Court Jews and Christian Renegades." *American Sociological Review* 37 (October): 574–81.

———. 1977. *Masters of Sociological Thought*. 2d ed. New York: Harcourt Brace Jovanovich.

Coser, Rose Laub. 1979. *Training in Ambiguity*. New York: Free Press.

Daniels, Arlene Kaplan. 1967. "The Low-Caste Stranger in Social Research." In *Ethics, Politics, and Social Research*, ed. Gideon Sjoberg, 267–96. Cambridge, Mass.: Schenkman.

Davids, Anthony. 1966. "Psychodynamic and Sociocultural Factors Related to Intolerance of Ambiguity." In *The Study of Lives: Essays on Personality in Honor of Henry A. Murray*, ed. Robert W. White, 160–77. New York: Atherton Press.

Dewey, Richard. 1979. "Comment on F. W. Riggs." *American Sociologist* 14: 190–92.

Donagan, Alan. 1977. *The Theory of Morality*. Chicago: University of Chicago Press.

Duncan, Hugh D. 1959. "Simmel's Image of Society." In *Georg Simmel, 1858–1918*, ed. Kurt H. Wolff, 100–118. Columbus: Ohio

228									References

State University Press.

Durkheim, Emile. 1895. "L'enseignement philosophique et l'agrégation de philosophie." *Revue philosophique* 39: 121–47.

_____. 1902. Review of G. Simmel, *Philosophie des Geldes*. *L'année sociologique* 5: 140–45. Previously published in *Notes critiques* 2 (1901): 65–69.

_____. 1903a. Review of G. Simmel, "Über räumliche Projectionen socialer Formen." *L'année sociologique* 7: 646–47.

_____. 1903b. Review of G. Simmel, "The number of members as determining the sociological form of the Group." *L'année sociologique* 7: 647–49.

_____. 1915. *The Elementary Forms of the Religious Life*, trans. J. Swain. New York: Free Press.

_____. [1902, 2d ed.] 1933. *The Division of Labor in Society*, trans. George Simpson. New York: MacMillan.

_____. [1895] 1938. *The Rules of Sociological Method*, trans. Sarah Solovay and John Mueller, ed. George Catlin. Chicago: University of Chicago Press.

_____. [1897] 1951. *Suicide*, trans. George Simpson. New York: Free Press.

_____. [1900] 1960. "Sociology and Its Scientific Field." In *Emile Durkheim, 1858–1917*, ed. Kurt H. Wolff, 354–75. Columbus: Ohio State University Press.

_____. [1914] 1960. "The Dualism of Human Nature and Its Social Conditions." In *Emile Durkheim, 1858–1917*, ed. Kurt H. Wolff, 325–40. Columbus: Ohio State University Press.

_____. [1925] 1973. *Moral Education*, trans. Everett K. Wilson and Herman Schnurer, ed. E. K. Wilson. New York: Free Press.

_____. [1902] 1975. "Note sur l'influence allemande dans la sociologie francaise." In Emile Durkheim, *Textes,* I, ed. Victor Karady, 400. Paris: Minuits.

_____. [1903] 1975. "Sociologie et sciences sociales." In Emile Durkheim, *Textes,* I, ed. Victor Karady, 121–59. Paris: Minuits.

_____. [1899] 1978. "Note on Social Morphology." In Emile Durkheim, *On Institutional Analysis,* ed. Mark Traugott, 88–90. Chicago: University of Chicago Press.

_____. [1909] 1978. "Sociology and the Social Sciences." In Emile Durkheim, *On Institutional Analysis,* ed. Mark Traugott, 71–87. Chicago: University of Chicago Press.

Echewa, T. Obinkaram. 1982. "A Nigerian Looks at America." *Newsweek,* July 5: 13.

Edelmann, Murray. 1964. *The Symbolic Uses of Politics*. Urbana:

University of Illinois Press.

Ellenberger, Henri F. 1970. *The Discovery of the Unconscious*. New York: Basic Books.

Empson, William. 1947. *Seven Types of Ambiguity*. 2d ed. London: Chatto and Windus.

Eulau, Heinz. 1977. "The Hoover Elite Studies Revisited." *Social Science History* 1: 392–400.

Factor, Regis, and Turner, Stephen. 1979. "The Limits of Reason and Some Limitations of Weber's Morality." *Human Studies* 2: 301–34.

Fallers, Lloyd A. 1967. *Immigrants and Associations*. The Hague: Mouton.

Frenkel-Brunswik, Else. 1949. "Intolerance of Ambiguity as an Emotional and Perceptual Personality Variable." *Journal of Personality* 18: 108–43.

Freud, Sigmund. 1895a. *Project for a Scientific Psychology*. In *The Standard Edition of the Complete Psychological Works of Sigmund Freud*, ed. James Strachey. London: Hogarth Press and the Institute of Psychoanalysis, 1953–74. Vol. 1.

———. 1895b. *Studies on Hysteria*. In *Standard Edition*, 2.

———. 1908. "'Civilized' Sexual Morality and Modern Nervous Illness." In *Standard Edition*, 9.

———. 1912. "The Dynamics of the Transference." In *Standard Edition*, 12.

———. 1915. "Observations on Transference-Love." In *Standard Edition*, 12.

———. 1921. *Group Psychology and the Analysis of the Ego*. In *Standard Edition*, 18.

———. 1927a. "Postscript" to *The Question of Lay Analysis*. In *Standard Edition*, 20.

———. 1927b. *The Future of an Illusion*. In *Standard Edition*, 21.

———. 1939. *Moses and Monotheism*. In *Standard Edition*, 23.

———. 1949. *Group Psychology and the Analysis of the Ego*, trans. J. Strachey. New York: Liveright.

Frisby, David. 1981. *Sociological Impressionism*. London: Heinemann.

Fromm, Erich. 1959. *Sigmund Freud's Mission*. New York: Harper.

Gallie, W. B. 1964. "Essentially Contested Concepts." In *Philosophy and the Historical Understanding*, 157–91. London: Hatteau and Windus.

Galston, William A. 1975. *Kant and the Problem of History*. Chicago: University of Chicago Press.

Gassen, Kurt, and Landmann, Michael. 1958. *Buch des Dankes an Georg Simmel*. Berlin: Duncker und Humblot.

Geertz, Clifford. 1959. "Ritual and Social Change." *American Anthropologist* 61: 991–1012.

———. 1960. *The Religion of Java*. Glencoe, Ill.: Free Press.

———. 1962. "Social Change and Economic Modernization in Two Indonesian Towns." In *On the Theory of Social Change,* ed. E. E. Hagen, 385–407. Homewood, Ill.: Dorsey Press.

Gewirth, Alan. 1978. *Reason and Morality*. Chicago: University of Chicago Press.

Gieryn, Thomas F. 1982. "Durkheim's Sociology of Scientific Knowledge." *Journal of the History of the Behavioral Sciences* 18: 107–29.

Graf, Max. 1942. "Reminiscences of Professor Sigmund Freud." *Psychoanalytic Quarterly* 11: 465–76.

Granet, Marcel. 1958. *Chinese Civilization*. New York: World.

Grant, Gerald, and Riesman, David. 1978. *The Perpetual Dream: Reform and Experiment in the American College*. Chicago: University of Chicago Press.

Greifer, Julian. 1945. "Attitudes to the Stranger: A Study of the Attitudes of Primitive Society and Early Hebrew Culture." *American Sociological Review* 10 (December): 739–45.

Grusky, Oscar. 1960. "Administrative Succession in Formal Organizations." *Social Forces* 39 (December): 105–15.

Hare, R. M. 1965. *Freedom and Reason*. New York: Oxford University Press.

Harris, Marvin. 1968. *The Rise of Anthropological Theory: A History of Theories of Culture*. New York: Thomas Y. Crowell.

Hauter, Charles. 1958. "Erinnerung an Simmel." In *Buch des Dankes an Georg Simmel,* ed. Kurt Gassen and Michael Landmann, 251–57. Berlin: Duncker und Humblot.

Hobbes, Thomas. [1651] 1978. *De Cive*. In *Man and Citizen,* ed. Bernard Gert, 87–386. Gloucester, Mass.: Peter Smith.

Hubner-Funk, Sibylle. 1976. "Ästhetizismus und Soziologie bei Georg Simmel." In *Ästhetik und Soziologie um die Jahrhundertwende: Georg Simmel,* ed. Hannes Bohringer and Karlfried Grunder, 44–58. Frankfurt: Vittorio Klostermann.

Hughes, Everett C. 1949. "Social Change and Status Protest: An Essay on the Marginal Man." *Phylon* 10 (First Quarter): 58–65.

Inkeles, Alex. 1964. *What is Sociology?* Englewood Cliffs, N.J.: Prentice-Hall.

Jaensch, E. R. 1938. *Der Gegentypus*. Leipzig: Barth.

Jaspers, Karl. 1946. *Max Weber: Politiker, Forscher, Philosoph.* Bremen: J. Storm Verlag.

Jaworski, Gary Dean. 1983. "Simmel and the Année." *Journal of the History of Sociology* 5: 28–41.

Johnson, Barbara A., and Turner, Jonathan H. 1977. "Anomie Theory Revisited Again: Clarifying Key Concepts and Propositions." Paper presented at the 72d Annual Meeting of the American Sociological Association.

Jones, Ernest. 1953. *The Life and Work of Sigmund Freud,* vol. 1. New York: Basic Books.

Kadushin, Charles. 1962. "Social Distance between Client and Professional." *American Journal of Sociology* 67 (March): 517–31.

Kalberg, Stephen. 1980. "Max Weber's Types of Rationality." *American Journal of Sociology* 85 (March): 1145–79.

Kant, Immanuel. [1784] 1963. "Idea for a Universal History from a Cosmopolitan Point of View." In *Kant on History,* ed. Lewis White Beck, 11–26. Indianapolis: Bobbs-Merrill.

Kaplan, Abraham, and Kris, Ernst. 1948. "Esthetic Ambiguity." *Philosophy and Phenomenological Research* 8: 415–35.

Kline, Morris. 1953. *Mathematics in Western Culture.* New York: Oxford University Press.

Kooij, J. G. 1971. *Ambiguity in Natural Language.* Amsterdam: North-Holland.

Kruskal, William. 1981. "Statistics in Society: Problems Unsolved and Unformulated." *Journal of the American Statistical Association* 76: 505–15.

Kytle, Jackson. 1977. "The Anomie-Anomia Paradigm: Further Specifications." Paper presented at the 72d Annual Meeting of the American Sociological Association.

LaCapra, Dominick. 1972. *Emile Durkheim: Sociologist and Philosopher.* Ithaca, N.Y.: Cornell University Press.

Laitin, David D. 1977. *Politics, Language, and Thought.* Chicago: University of Chicago Press.

LaPiere, Richard. 1959. *The Freudian Ethic.* New York: Duell, Sloan, and Pierce.

Lasch, Christopher. 1979. *The Culture of Narcissism.* New York: Norton.

Lauman, Edward O. 1966. *Prestige and Association in an Urban Community.* Indianapolis: Bobbs-Merrill.

Levi, Edward H. 1948. *An Introduction to Legal Reasoning.* Chicago: University of Chicago Press.

Levine, Donald N. 1959. "The Structure of Simmel's Social Thought." In *Georg Simmel, 1858–1918,* ed. Kurt H. Wolff, 9–32. Columbus: Ohio State University Press.

———. 1965. *Wax and Gold: Tradition and Innovation in Ethiopian Culture.* Chicago: University of Chicago Press.

———. 1974. *Greater Ethiopia: The Evolution of a Multiethnic Society.* Chicago: University of Chicago Press.

———. 1978. "Psychoanalysis and Sociology." *Ethos* 6: 175–85.

———. [1957] 1980. *Simmel and Parsons: Two Approaches to the Study of Society.* New York: Arno Press.

———. 1981. "Sociology's Quest for the Classics: The Case of Simmel." In *The Future of the Sociological Classics,* ed. Buford Rhea, 60–80. London: Allen and Unwin.

———. 1985. "On the Heritage of Sociology." In *The Challenge of Social Control: Citizenship and Institution Building in Modern Society,* ed. Gerald Suttles and Mayer Zald, 13–19. Norwood, N.J.: Ablex Publishing Company.

Levine, Donald N., Carter, E. B., and Gorman, E. M. 1976. "Simmel's Influence on American Sociology." In *Ästhetik und Soziologie um die Jahrhundertwende: Georg Simmel,* ed. Hannes Bohringer and Karlfried Grunder, 175–228. Frankfurt: Vittorio Klostermann.

Lewis, Sir Aubrey, M.D. 1970. "The Ambiguous Word 'Anxiety.'" In *International Journal of Psychiatry* 9: 62–79.

Lidz, Charles W., and Lidz, Victor Meyer. 1976. "Piaget's Psychology of Intelligence and the Theory of Action." In *Explorations in General Theory in Social Science,* ed. J. Loubser, R. Baum, A. Effrat, and V. Lidz, 195–239. New York: Free Press.

Linton, Ralph. 1936. *The Study of Man.* New York: Appleton Century.

Locke, John. [1690] 1975. *An Essay Concerning Human Understanding,* ed. Peter Nidditch. Oxford: Clarendon Press.

Loevinger, Jane, and Wessler, Ruth. 1970. *Measuring Ego Development.* San Francisco: Jossey-Bass.

Loewith, Karl. [1932] 1970. "Weber's Interpretation of the Bourgeois-Capitalistic World in Terms of the Guiding Principle of 'Rationalization'." In *Max Weber,* ed. Dennis Wrong. Originally (in slightly different version): "Max Weber und Karl Marx," *Archiv für Sozialwissenschaft und Sozialpolitik* 67.

Lofland, Lyn. 1973. *A World of Strangers.* New York: Basic Books.

Lukács, Georg. 1933. "Mein Weg zu Marx." In Lukács 1967, 323–29.

_____. 1958. "Georg Simmel (Nachruf)." In *Buch des Dankes an Georg Simmel,* ed. Kurt Gassen and Michael Landmann, 171–76. Berlin: Duncker und Humblot.

_____. [1954] 1962. *Die Zerstörung der Vernunft.* Neuwied and Berlin: Luchterhand.

_____. 1967. *Schriften zur Ideologie und Politik,* ed. Peter Lutz. Neuwied and Berlin: Luchterhand.

_____. 1970. *Magyar irodalom, magyar kúltura* ("Hungarian Literature, Hungarian Culture"). Selected Studies. Budapest: Gondolat. Excerpts translated in F. Tökei, 1972, "Lukács and Hungarian Culture," *New Hungarian Quarterly* 13: 108–122.

_____. [1923] 1971. *History and Class Consciousness,* trans. Rodney Livingstone. Cambridge, Mass.: MIT Press.

_____. 1975. *Conversations with Lukács,* ed. Theo Pinkus. Cambridge, Mass.: MIT Press.

Lukes, Steven. 1972. *Emile Durkheim: His Life and Work.* New York: Harper and Row.

McFarland, David, and Brown, Daniel J. 1973. "Social Distance as a Metric: A Systematic Introduction to the Smallest Space Analysis." In *Bonds of Pluralism,* ed. Edward O. Laumann, 213–53. New York: Wiley.

MacIntyre, Alasdair. 1981. *After Virtue: A Study in Moral Theory.* Notre Dame, Ind.: University of Notre Dame Press.

McKeon, Richard. 1952. *Freedom and History.* New York: Noonday Press.

_____. 1964. "The Flight from Certainty and the Quest for Precision." *Review of Metaphysics* 18: 234–53.

_____. n.d. "Philosophic Semantics and Philosophic Inquiry." Unpublished paper.

McLemore, S. Dale. 1970. "Simmel's 'Stranger': A Critique of the Concept." *Pacific Sociological Review* 13 (Spring): 86–94.

Mannheim, Karl. 1940. *Man and Society in an Age of Reconstruction.* New York: Harcourt Brace and World.

Manuel, Frank E. 1965. *The Prophets of Paris.* New York: Harper and Row.

Marcuse, Herbert. 1941. *Reason and Revolution.* New York: Oxford University Press.

Marks, Stephen. 1974. "Durkheim's Theory of Anomie." *American Journal of Sociology* 80: 329–63.

Martin, David. 1969. *The Religious and the Secular: Studies in Secularization.* London: Routledge and Kegan Paul.

Matthews, Fred H. 1977. *Quest for an American Sociology: Robert*

E. Park and the Chicago School. Montreal and London: McGill-Queen's University Press.

Mayhew, Leon. 1968. "Ascription in Modern Society." *Sociological Inquiry* 38: 105–20.

Merton, Robert K. 1938. "Social Structure and Anomie." *American Sociological Review* 3: 672–82.

———. 1949. *Social Theory and Social Structure.* 1st ed. Glencoe, Ill: Free Press.

———. 1957. *Social Theory and Social Structure.* 2d ed. Glencoe, Ill.: Free Press.

———. 1964. "Anomie, Anomia, and Social Interaction: Contexts of Deviant Behavior." In *Anomie and Deviant Behavior,* ed. Marshall Clinard, 213–42. Glencoe, Ill.: Free Press.

———. 1968. *Social Theory and Social Structure.* 3d ed. New York: Free Press.

———. 1976. *Sociological Ambivalence and Other Essays.* New York: Free Press.

Michels, Robert. 1925. "Materialien zu einer Soziologie des Fremden." *Jahrbuch für Soziologie* 1: 296–319.

Mitzman, Arthur. 1970. *The Iron Cage: An Historical Interpretation of Max Weber.* New York: Knopf.

Moges, Alemayhu. 1956. *Sewāsew Ge'ez.* Addis Ababa: Tasfā Press.

Moraitis, George. 1981. "The Psychoanalytic Study of the Editing Process and Its Application to the Interpretation of an Historical Document." *Annual of Psychoanalysis* 9: 237–63.

Mowrer, Ernest. 1942. *Disorganization: Personal and Social.* Philadelphia: Lippincott.

Nakamura, H. 1960. *The Ways of Thinking of Eastern Peoples.* Japanese National Commission for UNESCO.

Nash, Dennison. 1963. "The Ethnologist as Stranger." *Southwestern Journal of Anthropology* 19 (Summer): 149–67.

Nash, Dennison, and Wolfe, Alvin W. 1957. "The Stranger in Laboratory Culture." *American Sociological Review* 22 (August): 400–405.

Nelson, Benjamin. 1954. "The Future of Illusions." *Psychoanalysis* 2: 16–37.

———. 1957. *Freud and the Twentieth Century.* New York: Meridian.

———. 1965a. Comments. In *Max Weber und die Soziologie heute,* ed. Otto Stammer, 192–201. Tübingen: Mohr.

———. 1965b. "Dialogs across the Centuries: Weber, Marx, Hegel,

Luther." In *The Origins of Modern Consciousness,* ed. John Weiss, 149–65. Detroit: Wayne State University Press.

———. 1968. "Scholastic *Rationales* of 'Conscience,' Early Modern Crises of Credibility, and the Scientific-Technocultural Revolutions of the 17th and 20th Centuries." *Journal for the Scientific Study of Religion* 7: 157–77.

Nye, D. A., and Ashworth, C. E. 1971. "Emile Durkheim: Was He a Nominalist or a Realist?" *British Journal of Sociology* 22: 133–48.

Oakes, Guy. 1980. "Introduction." In Georg Simmel, *Essays on Interpretation in Social Sciences,* 3–94. Totowa, N.J.: Rowman and Littlefield.

O'Brien, George Dennis. 1975. *Hegel on Reason and History.* Chicago: University of Chicago Press.

Oppenheim, Felix E. 1961. *Dimensions of Freedom.* New York: St. Martin's Press.

Packard, Vance. 1972. *A Nation of Strangers.* New York: MacKay.

Page, Benjamin I. 1978. "The Art of Ambiguity." In *Choices and Echoes in Presidential Elections,* 152–91. Chicago: University of Chicago Press.

Pankhurst, R. K. P. 1965. "The Beginnings of Modern Medicine in Ethiopia." *Ethiopia Observer* 9: 114–60.

Pareto, Vilfredo. 1963. *The Mind and Society: A Treatise on General Sociology,* trans. A. Bongiorno and A. Livingston, ed. A. Livingston. New York: Dover.

Park, Robert E. 1928. "Human Migration and the Marginal Man." *American Journal of Sociology* 33 (May): 881–93.

———. 1950. *Race and Culture.* Glencoe, Ill.: Free Press.

Park, Robert E., and Burgess, Ernest W. 1921. *Introduction to the Science of Sociology.* Chicago: University of Chicago Press.

Parsons, Talcott. 1932. "Economics and Sociology: Marshall in Relation to the Thought of His Time." *Quarterly Journal of Economics* 46 (February): 316–47.

———. 1934. "Some Reflections on 'The Nature and Significance of Economics.'" *Quarterly Journal of Economics* 48: 511–45.

———. 1935a. "The Place of Ultimate Values in Sociological Theory." *International Journal of Ethics* 45 (April): 282–316.

———. 1935b. "Sociological Elements in Economic Thought, I." *Quarterly Journal of Economics* 49 (May): 414–53.

———. 1935c. "Sociological Elements in Economic Thought, II." *Quarterly Journal of Economics* 49 (August): 646–67.

———. 1951. *The Social System.* New York: Free Press.

_____. 1966. *Societies: Evolutionary and Comparative Perspectives.* Englewood Cliffs, N.J.: Prentice-Hall.

_____. [1937] 1968a. *The Structure of Social Action.* New York: Free Press.

_____. 1968b. "Components and Types of Formal Organizations." In *Comparative Administration Theory,* ed. Preston P. Le Breton, 3–19. Seattle: University of Washington Press.

_____. 1979. "Letter to Jeffrey Alexander, 19 January 1979." Unpublished.

_____. 1981. "Revisiting the Classics throughout a Long Career." In *The Future of the Sociological Classics,* ed. Buford Rhea, 183–94. London: Allen and Unwin.

Parsons, Talcott, and Platt, Gerald. 1973. *The American University.* Cambridge, Mass.: Harvard University Press.

Phelps, General John Wolcott. 1873. *Secret Societies, Ancient and Modern.* Chicago.

Philo, Greg, and Walton, Paul. 1973. "Max Weber on Self-Interest and Domination." *Social Theory and Practice* 2 (Spring): 335–46.

Pope, Whitney. 1976. *Durkheim's 'Suicide': A Classic Analyzed.* Chicago: University of Chicago Press.

Redfield, Robert. 1947. "The Folk Society." *American Journal of Sociology* 52: 293–308.

_____. 1956. *Peasant Society and Culture.* Chicago: University of Chicago Press.

Rickert, Heinrich. 1926. "Max Weber und seine Stellung zur Wissenschaft." *Logos* 15: 222–37.

Rieff, Philip. 1978. *Freud: The Mind of a Moralist.* 3d ed. Chicago: University of Chicago Press.

Riesman, David, et al. 1950. *The Lonely Crowd.* New Haven: Yale University Press.

Riggs, Fred W. 1979. "The Importance of Concepts: Some Considerations on How They Might be Designated Less Ambiguously." *American Sociologist* 14: 172–84.

Rose, Peter I. 1967. "Strangers in Their Midst: Small-Town Jews and Their Neighbors." In *The Study of Society,* ed. Peter I. Rose, 463–79. New York: Random House.

Rudolph, Susanne H., and Rudolph, Lloyd I. 1967. *The Modernity of Tradition: Political Development in India.* Chicago: University of Chicago Press.

Runciman, W. G., ed. 1978. *Max Weber: Selections in Translation.* New York: Cambridge University Press.

Scalapino, Robert. 1965. "Ideology and Modernization: The Japanese Case." In *Ideology and Discontent,* ed. David Apter, 93–127. New York: Free Press.

Schacht, Richard. 1970. *Alienation.* Garden City: Doubleday Anchor Books.

Schluchter, Wolfgang. [1971] 1979a. "Value-Neutrality and the Ethic of Responsibility." In Guenther Roth and Wolfgang Schluchter, *Max Weber's Vision of History,* 65–116. Berkeley: University of California Press.

———. [1976] 1979b. "The Paradox of Rationalization: On the Relation of Ethics and the World." In Guenther Roth and Wolfgang Schluchter, *Max Weber's Vision of History,* 11–64. Berkeley: University of California Press.

Schutz, Alfred. 1945. "The Homecomer." *American Journal of Sociology* 50 (March): 269–76.

Shils, Edward A. 1956. *The Torment of Secrecy.* Glencoe, Ill.: Free Press.

Simmel, Georg. 1890. "Über soziale Differenzierung." *Staats- und Sozialwissenschaftliche Forschungen* 10: 1–147.

———. 1896. "Zur Methodik der Sozialwissenschaft." *Jahrbuch für Gesetzgebung, Verwaltung und Volkswirtschaft* 20: 227–37.

———. 1897. "Comment les formes sociales se maintiennent." *L'année sociologique* 1: 71–109.

———. 1898. "Die Selbsterhaltung der sozialen Gruppe. Soziologische Studie." *Jahrbuch für Gesetzgebung, Verwaltung und Volkswirtschaft* 22: 589–640.

———. 1907. *Philosophie des Geldes.* 2d ed. Leipzig: Duncker und Humblot.

———. 1908. *Soziologie.* Munich and Leipzig: Duncker und Humblot.

———. 1919. "Aus Georg Simmels nachgelassenem Tagebuch." *Logos* 8: 121–51.

———. 1920/1921. "Zur Philosophie des Schauspielers. Aus dem Nachlass herausgegeben." *Logos* 9: 339–62.

———. 1955. *Conflict and the Web of Group Affiliations,* trans. Kurt H. Wolff and Reinhard Bendix. Glencoe, Ill.: Free Press.

———. 1971. *On Individuality and Social Forms,* ed. Donald N. Levine. Chicago: University of Chicago Press.

———. [1907, 2d ed.] 1978. *Philosophy of Money,* trans. Tom Bottomore and David Frisby. London: Routledge and Kegan Paul.

———. [1918] 1980. "On the Nature of Human Understanding." In *Essays on Interpretation in Social Science,* trans. and ed. Guy

Oakes, 97–126. Totowa, N.J.: Rowman and Littlefield.

Singer, Milton. 1960. "Changing Craft Traditions in India." In *Labor Commitment and Social Change in Developing Areas*, ed. W. Moore and A. Feldman, 258–76. New York: Social Science Research Council.

Siu, Paul C. P. 1952. "The Sojourner." *American Journal of Sociology* 58 (July): 34–44.

Skinner, Elliott P. 1963. "Strangers in West African Societies." *Africa* 33 (October): 307–20.

_____. 1979. "Conclusions." In *Strangers in African Societies*, ed. W. A. Schack and E. P. Skinner, 279–88. Berkeley: University of California Press.

Stammer, Otto, ed. 1971. *Max Weber and Sociology Today*, trans. Kathleen Morris. Oxford: Blackwell.

Stein, Barry, et al. 1979. "Can Industrial Workers Reform Their Work?" Paper presented at the 74th Annual Meeting of the American Sociological Association.

Stonequist, Everett. 1937. *The Marginal Man*. New York: Scribner's.

Strauss, Leo. 1953. *Natural Right and History*. Chicago: University of Chicago Press.

Sulloway, Frank J. 1979. *Freud, Biologist of the Mind*. New York: Basic Books.

Tenbruck, F. H. 1959. "Formal Sociology." In *Georg Simmel, 1858–1918*, ed. Kurt Wolff, 61–99. Columbus: Ohio State University Press.

Tilly, Charles. 1981. *As Sociology Meets History*. Studies in Social Discontinuity. New York: Academic Press.

Tiryakian, Edward A. 1973. "Perspectives on the Stranger." In *The Rediscovery of Ethnicity*, ed. Sallie TeSelle, 45–58. New York: Harper and Row.

Toennies, Ferdinand. 1926. *Soziologie: Studien und Kritiken*, vol. 2. Jena: Gustav Fischer.

_____. [1887] 1957. *Community and Society*, trans. Charles P. Loomis. New York: Harper and Row.

_____. 1971. *On Sociology: Pure, Applied, and Empirical*, ed. Werner J. Cahnman and Rudolf Heberle. Chicago: University of Chicago Press.

_____. 1974. *On Social Ideas and Ideologies*, ed. E. G. Jacoby. New York: Harper and Row.

Toynbee, Arnold. 1935. *A Study of History*, vol. 2. New York: Oxford University Press.

Wallerstein, R. S., and Smelser, N. J. 1969. "Psychoanalysis and Sociology." *International Journal of Psychoanalysis* 50: 693–710. Reprinted in *Psychotherapy and Psychoanalysis: Theory, Practice, Research,* ed. Robert S. Wallerstein. 1975. New York: International Universities Press.

Weaver, Richard. 1958. "Individuality and Modernity." In *Essays on Individuality,* ed. Felix Morley, 63–81. Philadelphia: University of Pennsylvania Press.

Weber, Marianne. 1975. *Max Weber: A Biography,* trans. Harry Zohn. New York: Wiley.

Weber, Max. 1905. "Die protestantische Ethik und der 'Geist' des Kapitalismus." *Archiv für Sozialwissenschaft und Sozialpolitik* 20: 1–54. Revised ed. and translation, (1920) 1958b.

———. 1906. "The Protestant Sects and the Spirit of Capitalism." In Weber (1948), 302–22.

———. 1913. "Über einige Kategorien der verstehenden Soziologie." *Logos* 4: 253–94. In Weber (1922), 403–50. English translation, 1981.

———. 1920. *Gesammelte Aufsätze zur Religionssoziologie,* vol 1. Tübingen: Mohr.

———. 1922. *Gesammelte Aufsätze zur Wissenschaftslehre.* Tübingen: Mohr.

———. 1923. *Gesammelte Aufsätze zur Religionssoziologie,* vol. 2. Tübingen: Mohr.

———. 1924. *Gesammelte Aufsätze zur Soziologie und Sozialpolitik.* Tübingen: Mohr.

———. 1948. *From Max Weber: Essays in Sociology,* trans. H. H. Gerth and C. Wright Mills. London: Routledge and Kegan Paul.

———. 1949. *The Methodology of the Social Sciences,* trans. Edward Shils and Henry A. Finch. Glencoe, Ill.: Free Press.

———. [1906] 1958a. "Zur Lage der bürgerliche Demokratie in Russland." Excerpted in *Gesammelte Politische Schriften,* ed. Johannes Winckelmann. Tübingen: Mohr.

———. [1920] 1958b. *The Protestant Ethic and the Spirit of Capitalism,* trans. Talcott Parsons. New York: Scribner's.

———. 1958c. *The Religion of India,* trans. H. H. Gerth and Don Martindale. Glencoe, Ill.: Free Press.

———. 1968. *Economy and Society,* ed. Guenther Roth and Claus Wittich. New York: Bedminster. Translation of edited version of *Wirtschaft und Gesellschaft,* 4th ed.

———. 1972. "Georg Simmel as Sociologist," with an introduction by Donald N. Levine. *Social Research* 39: 155–63.

_____. [1922] 1975. *Roscher and Knies: The Logical Problems of Historical Economics,* ed. Guy Oakes. New York: Free Press.

_____. [1921] 1976. *Wirtschaft und Gesellschaft,* 5th ed., ed. Johannes Winckelmann. Tübingen: Mohr.

_____. [1913] 1981. "Some Categories of Interpretive Sociology," trans. Edith E. Graber. *Sociological Quarterly* 22: 151–80.

Weinstein, Fred J., and Platt, Gerald. 1969. *The Wish to Be Free.* Berkeley: University of California Press.

Westie, Frank R. 1953. "A Technique for the Measurement of Race Attitudes." *American Sociological Review* 18 (February): 73–78.

Wiese, Leopold von. 1910. "Neuere soziologische Literatur-Kritische Literaturübersichten." *Archiv für Sozialwissenschaft und Sozialpolitik* 31: 900.

_____. 1959. "Die Deutsche Gesellschaft für Soziologie: Personliche Eindrücke in den Ersten Fünfzig Jahren." *Kölner Zeitschrift zur Soziologie* 11: 11–20.

Williams, Robin M., Jr. 1964. *Strangers Next Door: Ethnic Relations in American Communities.* Englewood Cliffs, N.J.: Prentice-Hall.

Wood, Margaret Mary. 1934. *The Stranger: A Study in Social Relationships.* New York: Columbia University Press.

Zajonc, Robert. 1952. "Aggressive Attitudes of the 'Stranger' as a Function of Conformity Pressures." *Human Relations* 5 (May): 205–16.

Index

Abel, Theodore, 125, 133
Addison, Joseph, 3
Adler, Mortimer, 17, 174
Albrow, Martin, 16 n. 3
Aleqa Gabra Hanna, 34
Alexander, Jeffrey, 184 n. 7
Alienation: ambiguity of, 16, 73; Simmel on, 105–8, 109, 150 n. 3, 193; Lukács on, 105–6, 107, 109
Almond, Gabriel, 41
Ambiguity: and American culture, 28, 31–34, 36–39, 44; and Durkheim, 10, 61–63, 65–72, 217; as essentially contested concept, 15–17, 219; experiential definition of, 8; of freedom, 65–66, 142–50, 165; forms of, 8, 37, 219; functions of, 29–37, 40, 217–19; historical attitudes toward in West, 1–8, 24, 37–38; in the law, 33, 41–42; linguistic, 20–31; literary, definition of, 8; and modernization, 37, 39–43; of modern subjectivity, 212–15; of natural languages, ix, 20–21; in organizations, 11; pathos of, 14; and politics, 4–5, 41–43; of rationality, 142, 143–78; science and, 2–8, 217–20; Simmel on, 132–41; of

social distance, 81–82; in statistical research, 14; strategies for dealing with, 17–18, 88, 210; tolerance of, 12–13, 53, 124, 131, 138–40; in traditional cultures, 22–24, 26; Weber on, 7, 152–53. *See also* Amhara culture; essentially contested concepts
American culture: and ambiguity, 28, 31–32, 36–39, 44; social-psychological features of, 176–78
Amhara culture: and language ambiguity, x, 13, 25–28, 29, 31, 38; 44; consistency/inconsistency in, 51–54; diversity in, 46–48; persistence of patterns in, 48–49; sources of change, 49–51; strangers in, 86; uniformity in, 45
Anomie: Durkheim on, 61–66, 193; Merton on, 56–61, 63–65, 219; scale (Leo Srole), 51
Arabian language and culture, 23, 86
Arato, Andrew, 106–7, 201
Aristotle: on human action, 1; on language ambiguity, 20
Ashworth, C. E., 55, 72
Atomic naturalism, 113, 126, 129, 130

241

242   Index

Hume, David, 3, 126

Jaensch, Erik, 11–12
Japanese language, 22, 38
Jaspers, Karl, 187 n. 9, 188–89
Java, 23
Jaworski, Gary Dean, 94 n. 2
Johnson, Barbara, 57
Johnson, Samuel, 3
Judaism, 187–88

Kadushin, Charles, 80
Kalberg, Steven, 158 n. 11, 159
Kant, Immanuel: on history, 144–
    45; influence on Simmel, 111,
    135–36; on morality, 143–44; on
    rationality and freedom, 143–45,
    155; and Weber, 150 n. 4
Kaplan, Abraham, 28, 231
Kline, Morris, 4
Knies, Karl, 95–97, 170
Kooij, J. G., 28
Kracauer, Siegfried, 132–33
Kruskal, William, 14–15
Kytle, Jackson, 57

LaCapra, Dominick, 55, 56
Laitin, David, 23–24, 36
Landmann, Michael, 135, 136
LaPiere, Richard, 191 n. 11
Laumann, Edward O., 80
Law: and ambiguity, 2, 33, 41–42;
    rationalization of, 158, 160, 165–
    66, 203, 214
Lebna, Dengel, 50
Leibniz, G. W. von, 2
Lenin, Nikolai, 109, 126
Levi, Edward H., 42
Lewis, Aubrey, 16
Lidz, Charles, 209–10
Lidz, Victor, 123, 209–10
Lincoln, Abraham, 34
Linton, Ralph, 46–47
Locke, John, 3, 24, 126
Loevinger, Jane, 12
Loewith, Karl, 173

Lofland, Lyn, 87
Lukács, Georg: and Communist
    Party, 108, 109; *History and
    Class Consciousness*, 108–10;
    The Destruction of Reason (*Die
    Zerstörung der Vernunft*), 110,
    and Marxism, 107, 108, 109, 128–
    29; *Philosophy of Art*, 106, 106
    n. 10; praxis, 107; radical evolu-
    tionism, 128; reification and
    alienation, 105–6, 107, 109; on
    religious atheism, 110–11; and
    Simmel: 103–12, 128–29, 134,
    139; critique of Simmel on ratio-
    nality, 110–11; obituary essay on
    Simmel, 107, 108; on Weber, 103
    n. 8, 112
Lukes, Steven, 55, 56 n. 1, 66 n.
    13, 90, 94 n. 2

McFarland, David, 80–81
MacIntyre, Alasdair, 195
McKeon, Richard: on freedom,
    174; on historical semantics, 18;
    on limits of univocality, ix, 43
McLemore, S. Dale, 77
Mannheim, Karl, 200, 202, 212
Manuel, Frank, 4
March, James, 11
Marginal man: Merton on, 83 n. 2;
    Park on, 75; Park's followers on,
    76–77
Marks, Stephen, 65
Marshall, Alfred, 119, 121; Par-
    sons' critique of, 121, 126, 130
Martin, David, 16
Marx, Karl: Lukács and, 126, 128–
    29; on modernization, 39–40; and
    Weber, 151 n. 6
Matthews, Fred, 113, 117
Mayhew, Leon, 39 n. 5
Mead, George Herbert, 126
Merton, Robert K: on anomie, 56–
    61, 63–65, 219; on marginal man,
    83 n. 2; on Puritanism and sci-
    ence, 37; on sociological ambiva-

246

Index

Rationality: ambiguity of concept,
142, 143–78, 199; conceptual,
157–58, 172–73, 208, 221–22; economic, 160, 208; Enlightenment
philosophers on, 142–43, 163; as
essentially contested concept,
199; formal (methodical), 158,
159, 208, 214, 221–22; forms of,
157–60, 205–8; and foundations
of sociology, 199–200; and freedom, 142–78; French philosophes
on, 143; Freud on, 186–90, 194,
209; functional, 200, Hegel on,
145–46, 153, 201; instrumental,
157–59, 167, 168, 208, 221, 222;
Kant on, 143–45; Mannheim on,
200; Montesquieu on, 143; objective, 148, 152, 153, 157–59, 160–
62, 172, 201, 205–8; Pareto on,
172, 201; Parsons on, 206–8;
Simmel on, 148–50, 153, 201–3;
subjective, 153–72, 176–78, 212–
15; subjective vs. objective, 200–
201, 201–3, 203–5, 205–12; substantial, 200; substantive, 158,
159, 207, 208, 221–22; Toennies
on, 146–48, 152, 201; Weber on,
96–98, 150–72, 152 n. 8, 203–5,
208, 214, 221–22; *Zweckrationalität*, 171, 194, 209. *See also* Rationalization; Weber
Rationalization: ambiguities in Weber's account of, 167–68, 175–76;
bureaucratic (organization), 163,
164, 165, 166–68, 175–76; economic, 160, 208, and freedom,
163–70; of law, 158, 160, 165–66,
203, 214; of religion, 160; of science, 172, 196; Simmel on, 213–
15; types, in Weber, 161–62, 204,
205, 208, 213, 221–22
Ratzel, Friedrich, 91
Reading of classics, 56, 132; psychology of, 137–38; Simmel's
manner of, 132
Redfield, Robert, 46, 51

Repressiveness of modern society,
40–41, 163–64, 177–78, 185, 197
Rickert, Heinrich, 95, 127, 188
Rieff, Philip, 188, 190 n. 10, 193
Riesman, David, 51, 177, 177 n. 19
Rilke, Rainer Marie, 21
Rose, Peter I., 76
Roth, Guenther, 166 n. 13
Rousseau, Jean-Jacques, 67, 126

Saint-Simon, Claude Henri, comte
de, 126, 176
Santayana, Georgia, 132
Savigny, Friedrich von, 126
Schact, Richard, 16, 17
Schleiermacher, Friedrich, 126
Schluchter, Wolfgang, 170 n. 15,
172 n. 17, 173 n. 18, 181 n. 4
Schutz, Alfred, 85
Science: ambiguity of term, 217;
flight from ambiguity in, 2–8;
role of ambiguity in, 217–19; and
mysticism contrasted, 30–31, 37,
218; rationalization of 172, 196
Shils, Edward A., 33
Sieyès, abbé Emmanuel-Joseph, 5
Simmel, Georg: aestheticism of,
104, 133; and ambivalence, 9;
ambiguity of, 132–41, 219; on
alienation, 105–7, 109, 150 n. 3,
193; C. Bouglé on, 89–90, 94 n.
1; culture, modern, 197; culture,
subjective, 201–3; culture, tragedy of, 105–6, 111, 202; and
Dilthey, 98; and Durkheim, 89–
94, 126–27, 139; forms and contents of association, 90–93, 99–
103, 127; as a founder of modern
sociology, 181 n. 4; on freedom,
148–50; and Hegel, 136; historical understanding, 97–98; on history, 103; Hübner-Funk on, 134;
intuitive approach to understanding, 132, 132 n. 9; on intellectual
appropriation, 136, 138; individualism (sociological nominalism),

Vernunft: in Hegel, 145, 146; in
    Kant, 143, 145, 155
Verstehen, 97, 127–28, 132 n. 19
Voltaire, François-Marie Arouet
    de, 143

Washington, Booker T., 114
Washington, George, 28, 34
"Wax and gold," 25–28, 29, 38
Weaver, Richard, 40
Weber, Marianne (née Schnitger),
    181, 181 n. 5, 182, 187, 190
Weber, Max: on ambiguity, 7, 152–
    53; on ambiguities in rationaliza-
    tion, 167–68, 175–76; biography,
    180–84, 186–90; on bureaucracy,
    167–68; critique of modern civili-
    zation, 185; *Economy and Socie-
    ty,* 101, 102, 105, 154; ethic of re-
    sponsibility, 173; ethic of self-un-
    derstanding and self-determina-
    tion, 189–90, 193–95; forms of
    human association, 102; on free-
    dom, 162–178, 174–75; German
    hermeneutic-historical tradition,
    127–28; and Hegel, 150 n. 4; on
    history, 103; instrumental ratio-
    nality, 157–59, 167–68; Jaspers
    on, 187 n. 9, 188–89; and Judaic
    tradition, 187–88; Kalberg on,
    158 n. 11; "Knies and the Prob-
    lem of Irrationality," 96–98; and
    Lukács, 106, 110–11, 112; mean-
    ings of actors, 102, 149 n. 2;
    meanings, subjective and objec-
    tive, 101; methodology of social
    science, 7, 95–103; monistic and
    dualistic causation, 195; as
    "moral prophet," 187–90; and
    morality, 191–92; objective ratio-
    nality, 153–72; and Parsons, 118,
    119–20, 175; Puritan mentality,
    31; Protestant ethic and the spirit
    of capitalism, 150 n. 4, 152, 170
    n. 15, 180; on psychoanalysis,
    180; as providing support for ni-
    hilism, 190–95; rational and em-
    pathic understanding, 155; ratio-

nality, 96–98, 152–72; rationality,
conceptual, 157–58, 172–73, 208,
221–22; rationality, definition of,
152 n. 8; rationality, formal (methodical), 158, 208, 214, 221–22;
rationality, instrumental, 157–59,
167, 168, 208, 214, 221–22; rationality, objective, 153–72, 203–5;
rationality, subjective, 153–72,
176–78, 203–5; rationality, substantive, 158, 208, 221–22; rationality and freedom, 96–98, 150–
52, 186; rationalization, 150, 152
n. 8 (def); rationalization and
freedom, 163–73; rationalization
in various institutional spheres,
163–64, 166–70, 174–75; organizational rationalization (bureaucracy), 163–68, 175–76; types of
rationalization, 161–62, 204, 205,
213; and Simmel, 94–103, 128,
139–40, 150 n. 4; social action,
types, 102, 155–56; sociology,
emancipatory potential of, 185–
86; 189–90; sociology, as a
founder of, 181 n. 4, 181 n. 6, sociology, domain of, 100–103; sociology as vehicle for moral enlightenment, 189–90; "spheres of
life," 156; subjective, role in action of, 85, 101–3; and Toennies,
150 n. 4; ultimate points of view,
156–57, 195; understanding, rational and empathic, 155, 189;
univocality in social science, 7,
152–53; value-neutrality, 101, 184
n. 6, 189, 192; *Verstehen,* 97;
verstehende Soziologie, 103, 150
n. 4, 184; *Zweckrationalität,* 156,
156 n. 9, 160, 171, 176, 194, 209
Wessler, Ruth, 12
Wiese, Leopold von, 133
Williams, Robin M., Jr., 87
Windelband, Wilhelm, 95, 113
Wolfe, Alvin W., 78, 79
Wood, Mary Margaret, 77, 85, 87

Zajonc, Robert, 78–79